Personal Politics in the Postwar World

Personal Politics in the Postwar World

Western Diplomacy Behind the Scenes

Susanna Erlandsson

BLOOMSBURY ACADEMIC
LONDON • NEW YORK • OXFORD • NEW DELHI • SYDNEY

BLOOMSBURY ACADEMIC
Bloomsbury Publishing Plc
50 Bedford Square, London, WC1B 3DP, UK
1385 Broadway, New York, NY 10018, USA
29 Earlsfort Terrace, Dublin 2, Ireland

BLOOMSBURY, BLOOMSBURY ACADEMIC and the Diana logo
are trademarks of Bloomsbury Publishing Plc

First published in Great Britain 2022
This paperback edition published 2023

Copyright © Susanna Erlandsson, 2022

Susanna Erlandsson has asserted her right under the Copyright, Designs
and Patents Act, 1988, to be identified as Author of this work.

For legal purposes the Acknowledgements on pp. xiii–xiv constitute an
extension of this copyright page.

Cover image © Conde Nast via Getty Images

All rights reserved. No part of this publication may be reproduced or transmitted
in any form or by any means, electronic or mechanical, including photocopying,
recording, or any information storage or retrieval system, without prior permission
in writing from the publishers.

Bloomsbury Publishing Plc does not have any control over, or responsibility for,
any third-party websites referred to or in this book. All internet addresses given in
this book were correct at the time of going to press. The author and publisher
regret any inconvenience caused if addresses have changed or sites have ceased
to exist, but can accept no responsibility for any such changes.

A catalogue record for this book is available from the British Library.

Library of Congress Cataloging-in-Publication Data

Names: Erlandsson, Susanna, author.
Title: Personal politics in the postwar world : Western diplomacy behind
the scenes / Susanna Erlandsson.
Description: London ; New York : Bloomsbury Academic, 2022. | Includes
bibliographical references and index.
Identifiers: LCCN 2021032687 (print) | LCCN 2021032688 (ebook) | ISBN
9781350150744 (hardback) | ISBN 9781350150751 (pdf) |
ISBN 9781350150768 (ebook)
Subjects: LCSH: Netherlands–Foreign relations–1948- |
Netherlands–Foreign relations–1898–1948. | Kleffens, Eelco van. |
Kleffens, Margaret van. | Diplomacy–Social aspects. | International
relations–Social aspects. | World War, 1939–1945–Diplomatic history. |
Diplomats–Netherlands–Biography.
Classification: LCC DJ288 .E75 2022 (print) | LCC DJ288 (ebook) | DDC
327.492009/04–dc23/eng/20211012
LC record available at https://lccn.loc.gov/2021032687
LC ebook record available at https://lccn.loc.gov/2021032688

ISBN:	HB:	978-1-3501-5074-4
	PB:	978-1-3502-8917-8
	ePDF:	978-1-3501-5075-1
	eBook:	978-1-3501-5076-8

Typeset by RefineCatch Limited, Bungay, Suffolk

To find out more about our authors and books visit www.bloomsbury.com
and sign up for our newsletters.

For all the people behind the scenes

Contents

List of Illustrations	ix
Preface	xi
Acknowledgements	xiii
Introduction The personal politics of daily diplomacy	1
Diplomacy as a gendered institution	3
The micro study as method: background and materials	6
Conceptualizing trust as a bridge between personal and political	11
Setting the scene	15
Part One The Diplomatic Couple	17
1 The persistent notion of the incorporated wife	20
2 In love and diplomacy	27
3 Carte blanche? Diplomatic secrecy and marital trust	35
4 The diplomatic couple as template	44
Concluding remarks on the diplomatic couple	52
Part Two The Diplomatic Home	55
5 Homemaking for diplomats	58
6 Domestic staff	65
7 The home as a diplomatic arena	75
Concluding remarks on the diplomatic home	89
Part Three Dinner Diplomacy	93
8 Dinner diplomacy as an everyday practice	97
9 Diplomatic food	114
Concluding remarks on dinner diplomacy	125

Part Four Diplomatic Aptitude	129
10. Diplomatic appearances	131
11. Diplomatic discourse	149
Concluding remarks on diplomatic aptitude	171
Conclusion Behind the scenes of building the postwar world	175
Everyday power structures in Western diplomacy	175
Political impact of personal relationships	179
Diplomacy as a likeminded institution	189
Bibliography	197
Index	209

Illustrations

1.1 Eelco and Margaret van Kleffens with their dog Jansen, New York City, September 1946. Courtesy of the Netherlands National Archives, The Hague, with permission of the Van Kleffens family. — 9
1.2 Women at work for the Netherlands Emergency Committee, London 1941. Anefo/HIE. Courtesy of the Netherlands National Archives, The Hague. — 22
1.3 Margaret van Kleffens with Vijaya Lakshmi Pandit at the United Nations General Assembly of 30 September 1954. Bettman/Getty Images. — 51
1.4 Margaret van Kleffens (left) at work for the Dutch Red Cross at North Row in London during the war. Anefo/HIE. Courtesy of the Netherlands National Archives, The Hague. — 53
2.1 Drawing room of the Dutch embassy/residence in Washington, DC, May 1948. Courtesy of the Netherlands National Archives, The Hague, with permission of the Van Kleffens family. — 55
2.2 Household staff plus Jansen the poodle, 'minus chauffeur Mac, and the laundress (Gonzalez)' on the steps of the Dutch Washington embassy/residence in 1950. Courtesy of the Netherlands National Archives, The Hague, with permission of the Van Kleffens family. — 66
2.3 Margaret van Kleffens with her nephew Clive Wilson during the war, probably 1941. Courtesy of Clive Wilson. — 83
2.4 Margaret van Kleffens with Jansen's predecessor, the Cairn terrier Vicky (short for Victory), in the summer of 1943. Courtesy of Clive Wilson. — 84
2.5 Aileen Emilie 'Dicky' Wilson, née Horstmann. Raymond Wilson. Courtesy of their grandson Edward Wilson. — 88
2.6 Margaret and Eelco van Kleffens giving the press an image of domestic idyll by playing a game of Scrabble, 1954. Orlando/Three Lions/Getty Images. — 91
3.1 Swedish minister Erik Sjöborg and the Van Kleffenses eat 'beschuit met muisjes' in London, 28 January 1943. Sport & General. Courtesy of Rijksmuseum, Amsterdam, Netherlands. — 119

4.1	Anglo-Netherlands Society luncheon, London 24 July 1944. Courtesy of the Netherlands National Archives, The Hague, with permission of the Van Kleffens family.	138
4.2	Spread from Margaret van Kleffens's diary 4 and 5 May 1948. Courtesy of the Netherlands National Archives, The Hague, with permission of the Van Kleffens family.	142
4.3	Delegation East Indonesia received by Queen Wilhelmina at Huis ten Bosch palace, 17 September 1947. Anefo. Courtesy of the Netherlands National Archives, The Hague.	146
4.4	Eelco van Kleffens seated next to actress Sylvia Regis de Oliveira, whose father had been a Brazilian ambassador, at a dinner party given by Elsa Maxwell in 1945. Peter Stackpole/LIFE/Getty Images.	163

Preface

When I first stumbled across the diaries of Margaret van Kleffens, I had no idea what a treasure I had found. Like so many other historians of international history, I had been focusing on public records and discussions among the official representatives of countries to seek explanations for foreign policy behaviour. My dissertation, a comparison of Dutch and Swedish security ideas and strategies in the 1940s, did not have a single reference to gender and did not mention any women besides the Dutch queen. Studying foreign policy and the relations between states in the 1940s, there were simply no women to write about. Or so I thought.

Having noted with some surprise that the personal archive of the Dutch foreign minister contained 31 diaries belonging to his wife, I returned my focus to letters and notes that revealed his reasoning about Dutch security. Access to the diaries was restricted until 2020 anyway, and I had my dissertation to finish. But their existence kept nagging at me; they were always at the back of my mind so, once I had finished my dissertation, I asked permission to look at the diaries. They were written in English and, in one of them, I found a copy of a letter from Eelco van Kleffens to Dr Grayson L Kirk of Columbia University in the United States about microfilming another volume of his wife's diaries, referring to them as 'this chronicle of contemporaneous history and daily life'.[1] Her husband had recognized the value of preserving her experiences and notes for posterity and had made sure they would be accessible not only to a Dutch but also to an American audience. Yet I couldn't remember ever seeing anything written about Margaret van Kleffens beyond her childlessness and poor health.

That was the beginning of a project that has kept growing. When I started to look into the matter more systematically and read up on diplomatic wives, it was as if I had crossed the border to a different reference system. The impetus of the project changed as my initial curiosity was replaced by concern. The empirical evidence I was studying left no doubt that gendered norms were central to the functioning of diplomacy. I found it disconcerting that someone like me,

---

[1] Diary of Margaret van Kleffens (MvK diary) 20 December 1950–29 June 1952, inv. nr 402, Archive of E.N. van Kleffens access number 2.05.86, National Archives in The Hague, the Netherlands (NL-HaNA).

specializing in diplomatic history, could have spent years in the field without coming across any research on gender and diplomacy.

As I started to pay better attention, I noted that books on gender or women and diplomacy are seldom found on the library shelves for diplomacy or foreign policy. Library classification systems simply don't have gender or women as a subcategory to international relations. Therefore, books with 'women' or 'gender' in the title or as main key words are often categorized under sociology or social questions, which do have gender relations or women's history as subcategories. Books that are solely about men and diplomacy are not categorized under gender or men's history but under diplomatic history (unless they have a very explicit gender perspective). You get the impression that books about women and diplomacy are primarily about women, while books on men and diplomacy are primarily about diplomacy. Therefore, if you are primarily interested in diplomacy, chances are you will overlook the books on women.[2]

This book is a conscious attempt to break through a divide which, in my view, hampers our understanding of diplomatic history. It is driven by a sincere wish to understand how international relations work in practice. I think it will be of interest both to people whose focus is gender and diplomacy and to those who are intrigued by the individual historical actors of more traditional diplomatic history. Judging by the hundreds if not thousands of biographical works (not to mention films) written on Winston Churchill, Adolf Hitler, Franklin Delano Roosevelt, Joseph Stalin, and a number of other twentieth-century men in prominent positions, it seems evident that many people are prepared to accept that the personal charisma and relationships of a few highly placed men may have changed the course of history. This book brings the significance of the relationships of less well-known people to the fore, arguing that if we truly want to understand the political impact of personal relations, we need to understand the systemic nature of personal politics.

Susanna Erlandsson
August 2021

---

[2] This is just one of the reasons for a division of the field that I discuss at greater length in Swedish in Susanna Erlandsson, 'Kvinnor och Genusperspektiv i ett Splittrat Forskningsfält: Modern Diplomatihistoria', *Historisk Tidskrift* 141: 3 (2021): 553–63.

Acknowledgements

My work on this book has received the support of a lot of people and organizations behind the scenes. The research project was made possible by a grant from the Swedish Research Council (Vetenskapsrådet project nr 2017-00264). A smaller grant from the foundation Helge Ax:son Johnsons Stiftelse bought me the extra time I needed to go through new, relevant material that turned up at a late stage of the project.

Dividing my time between Uppsala University, the University of Amsterdam and the London School of Economics and Political Science has given me the benefit of three fantastic research environments for my daily work. In Uppsala, I had the luxury of having two interns help me with some of the transcriptions. Thank you, Rachel Bott and Alexander Mullan! At all three universities I have had access to the best of libraries, supporting staff and colleagues. The opportunity to present and discuss my research in different contexts has been invaluable. Besides presentations at universities and conferences, two workshops of the network Gender and Diplomacy allowed me to test my ideas on an interdisciplinary group. I am forever grateful to all of you who took the time to read and comment and who gave me valuable tips on literature and source material. Needless to say, any remaining flaws are mine.

No historical research would be possible without archivists and librarians. I have relied on many of them in archives and libraries in different countries and always found them prepared to go out of their way to help. An illustrative story is how one day towards the end of my research period, I received an e-mail from Diederick Kortlang, a Dutch archive collection manager. He had learned about my research on the internet and thought I might be interested in a box of letters that he had found in the depot of the Netherlands National Archives. The box contained the correspondence between Eelco and Margaret van Kleffens that was previously believed to have been lost. I think all historians who read this can imagine my excitement. Thank you Diederick and so many others who go above and beyond the call of duty.

A special thank you goes to Monique van Kessel of the Netherlands Institute for War Documentation (NIOD) who helped me decipher diary notes made in shorthand. Thank you also to Matthew Jones at LSE who pointed me in the direction of the Avon papers and wrote a letter of introduction for me and to the Avon Trustees for granting me permission to consult said papers.

I want to especially thank the families of Eelco and Margaret van Kleffens for their readiness to facilitate my research. Eelco van Kleffens (grandson of the brother of the Eelco van Kleffens featured in this book) not only gave me permission to study Margaret van Kleffens's diaries but helped me get an exemption from the rule that restricted access material could only be read on location. That I was allowed to make scans of the voluminous material – with an excellent scanner available for free at the National Archives in The Hague, I might add – made it possible for me to continue my work from home. My heartfelt thanks to Clive Wilson, the nephew of Margaret van Kleffens, who engaged the whole family in answering my many questions, crucial to my grasp of the context. He and his wife Catherine generously welcomed me in their home to look at his mother's letters, only weeks before COVID-19 restrictions made such a visit unthinkable. Thank you, also to the rest of the Wilson/Horstmann family.

When it comes to the actual writing of the book, it was great to have an editor who was enthusiastic about the project from the start and always quick to answer my questions. Thank you Maddie Holder at Bloomsbury Academic. I am immensely grateful to the anonymous peer reviewers who reviewed first the book proposal and later the whole manuscript. Your comments were incredibly helpful. Thank you also to Abigail Lane for assisting with the production process, always checking up on me, to Paula Devine for copy-editing the manuscript so efficiently, and to Merv Honeywood for smooth assistance at the proofreading stage.

In practical terms, my writing depended on the behind-the-scenes work of many others, from yoga instructor Lillith Turk and physical therapist Anna-Karin Olsson, who kept me fit to write in spite of cervicobrachial syndrome, to my husband who made me eat and laugh regularly. I rely daily on family and friends, on colleagues who have become friends, and on friends who have become family. Thank you all.

Finally, I think I have always known that a salary is no good indicator of the importance of someone's work, even if it took some time before I thought about it in relation to historical analysis. My mother, Birgitta Margareta Erlandsson, née Bordin, a trained nurse, was a housewife for most of my youth and is one of the hardest-working people I know. I dedicate this book to her and to all the other paid or unpaid people who tirelessly work behind the scenes.

Introduction

The personal politics of daily diplomacy

[A]s a woman Mrs. Molotov will understand this: surely she can persuade Mr. Molotov to give us his help.[1]

Foreign Office dispatch to Clementine Churchill 1945

E. rang up this evening to say that we got off as lightly as he could have hoped, over the Ind. situation, thanks to a veto by my French friend Parodi in our favour[.][2]

Diary of Margaret van Kleffens, 1947

Thank you so much for your letter ... enclosing the paper about the possible future moves in negotiations for a European Free Trade Area. ... My wife and I enjoyed ourselves very much yesterday evening and were glad to see you well again.[3]

Letter from Paul Gore-Booth to Eelco van Kleffens 1958

In May 1945, the British Foreign Office enlisted the help of the Prime Minister's wife to try to convince the political leadership of the Soviet Union to release the Soviet wives of British ex-soldiers by way of a tête-à-tête with Polina Molotov, wife of the Soviet Minister of Foreign Affairs. The dispatch reveals that the UK ambassador had raised the issue 'countless times' to no avail; earlier attempts

---

[1] 3 May 1945 dispatch to Mrs Churchill, written at the request of the Embassy of the United Kingdom in the USSR. FO 181/1082, The National Archives of the United Kingdom (UKNA).
[2] Diary of Margaret van Kleffens (MvK diary) 25 August 1947, inv nr 397, Archive of EN van Kleffens 2.05.86, Nationaal Archief The Hague, Netherlands (NL-HaNA). Alexandre Parodi was the French delegate to the UN Security Council.
[3] 19 November 1958, PH Gore-Booth, Deputy Under-Secretary (Economic Affairs) of the UK Foreign Office, to EN van Kleffens, Dutch representative to the High Authority of the European Coal and Steel Community, FO 371/134515, UKNA.

included a 'personal message' from Secretary of State for Foreign Affairs Anthony Eden to Vyacheslav Molotov in 1943. 'Our next hope is Mrs. Churchill', the Chancery had said.[4] Two years later, Margaret van Kleffens, wife of the Dutch ambassador and recent representative to the United Nations Security Council (UNSC), Eelco van Kleffens, referred to the UNSC representative from France as 'my French friend' when he acted in a way which was politically advantageous to the Netherlands. Other diary entries reveal that she and Alexandre Parodi had a long history of flirting.[5] About a decade later, a UK Foreign Office Deputy Under-Secretary ended an official letter to a Dutch Representative to the European Coal and Steel Community (ECSC) by thanking him for a dinner party that he and his wife had attended the previous evening and commenting on the health of the latter.

These are all examples of the fundamental entanglement of personal and political relations in diplomacy in the early postwar period. The first reveals the strategic and gendered use of a personal plea by a non-official to achieve a political goal. The second implies at least a perceived link between political behaviour and personal liking. The third shows how officials mixed political with personal, even seemingly private, messages. None of the above quotes refers to behaviour that was unusual, as this book will show. On the contrary; the mixing of personal and professional relationships was fundamental to diplomatic practices. The nominally apolitical status of wives regularly came in handy for diplomatic ends. Modest flirting between men and women was a perfectly normal part of diplomatic socializing, as was an overlap between social guest lists and political preferences. References to personal relations and (semi-) private gatherings in official letters were frequent, as anyone going through any significant amount of correspondence in Foreign Ministry archives can see.

There are countless studies of the origins of the Cold War, European integration, decolonization and other developments that have come to characterize postwar international history. While these studies often recognize the importance of diplomacy, few incorporate any analyses of the roles played by the personal relationships of diplomats and their entourages.[6] Though anecdotal stories abound, those are primarily based on what diplomats, in retrospect, have

---

[4] 3 May 1945 Dispatch; 10 March 1945 Letter from Chancery. FO 181/1082, UKNA.
[5] MvK diary 19/20 April 1947, inv nr 396; MvK diary 18 November 1952, inv nr 403, 2.05.86, NL-HaNA.
[6] Important exceptions include Frank Costigliola and Barbara Keys who have highlighted the influence of personal relations and emotions in shaping foreign policy: Frank Costigliola, *Roosevelt's Lost Alliances: How Personal Politics Helped Start the Cold War* (Princeton, NJ: Princeton University Press, 2012); Frank Costigliola, 'Pamela Churchill, Wartime London, and the Making of the Special Relationship', *Diplomatic History* 36, no 4 (2012): 753–62; Barbara Keys, 'Henry Kissinger: The Emotional Statesman', *Diplomatic History* 35, no 4 (2011): 587–609 Their focus is on leading personalities rather than on the daily relationships of more average diplomats.

chosen to accentuate; they tend to focus on the extraordinary, leaving us with little systematic knowledge about how diplomats' personal relationships and networks functioned on a day-to-day basis. Even diplomats' biographers and scholars who emphasize individual diplomatic undertakings and personal networks tend to overlook the political significance of wives, households and other matters that they seem, *a priori*, to assume are apolitical.[7]

To understand how Western diplomacy shaped postwar international relations, I argue that we need to pay attention not only to formal treaties and organizations but to the classed, gendered and racialized practices that governed it. To do that, it is necessary to zoom in on everyday diplomatic work. In order to achieve a sufficiently detailed level of analysis, this book features a micro study as a tool to unravel the mechanisms of daily Western diplomacy in the 1940s and 1950s. Asking when and how personal relations intermeshed with political ones, it foregrounds people and practices who have usually not made their way into history books, finding clues in activities often dismissed as irrelevant to high politics. This book is about diplomacy in the full sense of the concept, including those parts that scholars have constantly omitted, leaving us with an incomplete understanding of how postwar diplomacy worked. Focusing on the political culture of mid-twentieth century diplomacy, it offers a new perspective on how this shaped the postwar world in practice.

Diplomacy as a gendered institution

Feminist scholars often point out that few institutions besides the military have remained as persistently male-dominated as diplomacy. The diplomatic service co-produced policies and masculinities, and even though in many countries female diplomats have entered the service in increasing numbers from the mid-twentieth century onwards, women's rise to high-ranking positions has been exceedingly slow and arduous. Indeed, at the beginning of the third decade of the twenty-first century, diplomatic gender equality still seems far off. Historical marginalization of women would appear the cause, opposition to female diplomats ingrained in an inherently masculine diplomatic culture.[8]

---

[7] For example, Albertine Bloemendal, *Reframing the Diplomat: Ernst van Der Beugel and the Cold War Atlantic Community* (Leiden: Brill, 2018).
[8] Karin Aggestam and Ann Towns, 'The Gender Turn in Diplomacy: A New Research Agenda', *International Feminist Journal of Politics* 21, no 1 (2019): 9–28; Jennifer A Cassidy and Sara Althari, 'Introduction. Analysing the Dynamics of Modern Diplomacy through a Gender Lens', in *Gender and Diplomacy*, ed. Jennifer A Cassidy (Abingdon and New York: Routledge, 2017), 1–31.

The reality, however, is more complex. The image of women's historical exclusion from diplomacy is more to do with a historiographical than a historical absence of women. For the better part of the twentieth century, most countries in practice were represented not only by an appointed diplomat who was almost invariably male, but also by his wife. Diplomacy was a fundamentally gendered institution, not only in the ways it excluded women, but in how it included them. With the rise of New Diplomatic History, historians have called for a holistic approach to diplomacy, with attention to diplomatic processes as well as political results, and non-official as well as official diplomatic actors.[9] As they have pointed out, diplomatic history has traditionally paid attention only to some sides of diplomacy, focusing chiefly on the political contents of diplomatic negotiations. Such a narrow approach to diplomacy hides the fact that throughout history, women have played important diplomatic roles, including as hostesses, networkers, and 'she-intelligencers'.[10] Attention for the roles of twentieth-century wives of diplomats is a rather recent phenomenon in diplomatic history and IR, but the research grows steadily. Scholars like Arlie Hochschild, Hillary Callan, Cynthia Enloe, Molly Wood, Nevra Biltekin and Kenneth Weisbrode have pointed to the importance of diplomats' wives in the twentieth century, not only to further their husbands' masculinities and diplomatic careers, but also to the Diplomatic Service as they performed vital daily diplomatic work.[11]

[9] Karen Gram-Skjoldager, 'Never Talk to Strangers? On Historians, Political Scientists and the Study of Diplomacy in the European Community/European Union', *Diplomacy & Statecraft* 22, no 4 (2011): 699; Giacomo Giudici, 'From New Diplomatic History to New Political History: The Rise of the Holistic Approach', *European History Quarterly* 48, no 2 (2018): 314–15; Giles Scott-Smith and Kenneth Weisbrode, 'Editorial', *Diplomatica* 1, no 1 (2019): 1–4. See, for more examples, the website of the New Diplomatic History network. Available at: www.newdiplomatichistory.org.

[10] The term 'she-intelligencer' comes from Nadine Akkerman, *Invisible Agents: Women and Espionage in Seventeenth-Century Britain* (Oxford: Oxford University Press, 2018), 4–6; Corina Bastian et al, eds, *Das Geschlecht der Diplomatie: Geschlechterrollen in den Außenbeziehungen vom Spätmittelalter bis zum 20. Jahrhundert* (Köln/Weimar/Wien: Böhlau, 2014); Glenda Sluga and Carolyn James, eds, *Women, Diplomacy and International Politics since 1500* (Abingdon and New York: Routledge, 2016); My Hellsing, 'Tillit inom Hovpolitiken. Exempel från den Franska Beskickningen i Stockholm 1783–1789', in *Tillit och Diplomati. En Diskussionsbok om Personliga Relationer och Diplomatiska Processer 1670–1990*, ed. Susanna Erlandsson and Sari Nauman, Opuscula Historica Upsaliensia 56 (Uppsala: Opuscula Historica Upsaliensia, 2019).

[11] Arlie Hochschild, 'The Role of the Ambassador's Wife: An Exploratory Study', *Journal of Marriage and Family* 31, no 1 (1969): 73–87; Hilary Callan, 'The Premiss of Dedication', in *Perceiving Women*, ed. Shirley Ardener (London; New York: Dent, 1975), 87–104; Cynthia Enloe, *Bananas, Beaches and Bases: Making Feminist Sense of International Politics*, 2nd edn, completely revised and updated. (Berkeley, CA: University of California Press, 2014); Molly M Wood, 'Diplomatic Wives: The Politics of Domesticity and the "Social Game" in the U.S. Foreign Service, 1905–1941', *Journal of Women's History* 17, no 2 (2005): 142–65; Molly M Wood, '"Commanding Beauty" and "Gentle Charm": American Women and Gender in the Early Twentieth-Century Foreign Service', *Diplomatic History* 31, no 3 (2007): 505–30; Nevra Biltekin, 'The Diplomatic Partnership: Gender, Materiality and Performance in the Case of Sweden c. 1960s–1980s', *Genesis* XI, no 1–2 (2012): 253–65; Nevra Biltekin, 'The Performance of Diplomacy: The Residence, Gender, and Diplomatic Wives in Late Twentieth-Century Sweden', in *Women, Diplomacy and International Politics since 1500*, ed. Glenda Sluga and Carolyn James

This book takes off in the understanding that the gendering of diplomacy is as much to do with the important roles of women in diplomacy as with the dominance of men. Scholars examining different countries (Norway, the United Kingdom, Sweden and the Netherlands in the works cited here) have pointed to the fact that far into the twentieth century, Foreign Services evaluated not only diplomats, but also their wives.[12] In spite of this evidence of their perceived political importance, research on diplomats' wives has yet to make a mark on mainstream scholarship on diplomatic relations. It is as if, contrary to diplomatic actors themselves, diplomatic scholars focusing on male diplomats assume that the tasks performed by diplomats' wives were nothing to do with the tasks performed by their husbands, and so continue to neglect the part played by women, treating research on diplomats' wives as a separate and peripheral part of diplomatic history. This book will show that male and female diplomatic tasks were certainly not equal or the same. They were, however, deeply intertwined and mutually constitutive. Daily diplomacy, and with it international affairs, depended on both. A focus solely on the tasks performed by appointed diplomats, who were almost exclusively male in the period and places studied here, therefore skews our understanding of diplomatic relations.

Considering the importance ascribed to diplomatic wives by contemporaries, it seems crucial to understand the heterosexual couple as a diplomatic organizational unit and symbol, evidently important to diplomatic representation, in order to explain how twentieth-century diplomatic relations worked. That, in turn, will also put the challenges faced by the first female diplomats in new light. The aim is to fuse our growing knowledge on the political tasks performed by diplomats' wives with a broader narrative of how diplomacy was carried out in practice. Ultimately, the book seeks to tease out how everyday diplomatic practices and personal relations were connected to the big political structures of the postwar world. The focus on the couple has the advantage not only of including wives, but of bringing more people into view, as social networks and the diplomatic home take centre stage: staff, friends, family. To catch sight of mechanisms of inclusion and exclusion, noting in particular that Western

---

(Abingdon and New York: Routledge, 2015), 254–68; Kenneth Weisbrode, 'Vangie Bruce's Diplomatic Salon. A Mid-Twentieth-Century Portrait', in *Women, Diplomacy and International Politics since 1500*, ed. Glenda Sluga and Carolyn James (Abingdon and New York: Routledge, 2015), 240–53.

[12] Iver B. Neumann, 'The Body of the Diplomat', *European Journal of International Relations* 14, no 4 (2008): 671–95; Helen McCarthy, *Women of the World: The Rise of the Female Diplomat* (London: Bloomsbury, 2014); Nevra Biltekin, *Servants of Diplomacy: The Making of Swedish Diplomats, 1905–1995* (Stockholm: Department of History, Stockholm University, 2016); Susanna Erlandsson, 'Off the Record: Margaret van Kleffens and the Gendered History of Dutch World War II Diplomacy', *International Feminist Journal of Politics* 21, no 1 (2019): 29–46.

diplomatic couples were generally white, Christian, and upper class, the book takes an intersectional approach to the gendered history of diplomacy. Cultural affinity, wealth, and a sense of belonging to the same political elite played a role in diplomatic networks, and upholding those networks depended on a well-run diplomatic household that involved male and female staff of different cultural backgrounds, ethnicities, and nationalities. They too were part of mid-twentieth century daily diplomacy.

The micro study as method: background and materials

Trying to understand how a Western political culture of diplomacy – a set of shared attitudes and practices that shaped everyday diplomatic life – influenced the international relations of the postwar period is a macro level ambition that requires micro level research. To get at commonly held beliefs, feelings, values, norms, habits, presuppositions, and to understand why, when, how and which personal relationships were important to diplomatic work on an everyday basis, one cannot focus only on extraordinary events or just the most conspicuous diplomatic actors. The face-to-face meeting of Neville Chamberlain with Adolf Hitler on the eve of the Second World War, or the change in personal dynamics when Harry S Truman replaced Franklin Delano Roosevelt in talks with Winston Churchill and Joseph Stalin had important consequences and have rightfully been studied.[13] But what about the norms and presuppositions that caused the UK Foreign Office to hope for political results after a meeting between Clementine Churchill and Polina Molotov, or Margaret van Kleffens to connect her flirting with Alexandre Parodi with his veto in the Security Council, or her husband inviting Paul and Patricia Gore-Booth to dinner?

An up-close-and-personal study of one diplomatic couple, following their everyday movements, is a way to catch sight of these more generic personal–political relationships and collect enough of them to draw more general conclusions about Western diplomatic culture during and after the Second World War. The advantage of an in-depth study of one couple as opposed to a more sweeping survey of various couples over a longer period is that it enables a comprehensive study, rather than one of only those activities that, *a priori* seem

---

[13] Marcus Holmes, *Face-to-Face Diplomacy: Social Neuroscience and International Relations* (Cambridge University Press, 2018); Costigliola, *Roosevelt's Lost Alliances*.

politically significant. The more open-ended approach in this regard comes at the cost of limiting the reach of the research to the cultural tradition of the community to which this one couple belonged, in this case a transnational but distinctly Western diplomatic tradition. Nevertheless, insights far beyond personal preferences are possible. The couple chosen, Dutch top diplomat Eelco van Kleffens and his wife Margaret van Kleffens, née Horstmann, were not unusually powerful or extraordinary in the international context of their time. The aim is to uncover the everyday, the normal, not the exceptional. However, the couple were reasonably successful and well-positioned for their daily diplomacy to provide an insight into the diplomatic community as a whole. They are a good fit for identifying connections between everyday diplomacy and the political events that have made their way into history books, such as the shaping of the UN, Cold War, and decolonization. Finally, this couple left behind copious amounts of notes regarding their daily work, allowing insight into everyday life as it happened, not just as it was presented in retrospect.[14]

As representatives of the Netherlands, one of the smaller Western states, Eelco and Margaret van Kleffens had limited room for manoeuvre. They depended on an able use of diplomatic skills and networking more than might be the case with a couple from one of the bigger powers. The fact that they were appointed to positions that would not have been offered to a diplomatic couple considered controversial proves that they did well, in terms of displaying appropriate diplomatic behaviour. More importantly, they allow a close view of arenas that were central to the shaping of Western postwar policies, since the positions that Eelco van Kleffens held during and after the war placed the couple at the heart of world events, beginning with the exiled community in London during the Second World War. As Foreign Minister of the Netherlands, Eelco and Margaret van Kleffens flew to the United Kingdom on 10 May 1940, the day of the German invasion, to ask for help on behalf of their government, only to be joined a few days later by the rest of the ministers, when defeat and German occupation proved inevitable. Margaret van Kleffens was the only Dutch minister's wife to join her husband in exile and the couple played a central role in representing the Netherlands during the ensuing London years (1940–1945). As many researchers have pointed out, wartime London was a time and place crucial to postwar planning and the shaping of ideas on the postwar world

---

[14] For a discussion of how twentieth-century diplomats have used their memoirs to comment on diplomatic aptitude, see Biltekin, *Servants of Diplomacy*, 166–86.

order.[15] Eelco van Kleffens was actively involved in allied planning and became one of the early advocates for an Atlantic Pact as well as a staunch defender of the rights of smaller states in discussions on the future United Nations, pushing hard for basing its Charter on international law. He also negotiated and signed the Benelux customs union agreement with Belgian Foreign Minister Paul-Henri Spaak (sometimes nicknamed 'Mr Europe' for his important role in promoting European integration) and Luxembourg's Joseph Bech.[16]

Eelco van Kleffens remained Foreign Minister until 1946, but after a short postwar sojourn in the Netherlands, the couple went back to London and then to New York. Eelco van Kleffens represented the Netherlands, one of the first non-permanent members, in the brand-new United Nations Security Council, which meant that they moved in the social circles of the early United Nations. This position was followed by the ambassadorship to Washington, DC from 1947 to 1950, arguably the politically most important post for a Western country at that time. The important global issue of decolonization very much determined the couple's everyday activities in these years. In the UN Security Council, Eelco van Kleffens repeatedly had to defend the attempts by the Netherlands government to restore Dutch rule over the pre-war colony the Netherlands East Indies which, in 1945, had declared independence as the Republic of Indonesia. Decolonization was an ever-present diplomatic issue for the couple until December 1949, when the Netherlands recognized Indonesian independence. Eelco van Kleffens also played an important role in the preparation of the North Atlantic Treaty, finding compromise solutions and nuancing formulations to make the pact acceptable to the smaller signatories. In addition, Washington, DC was the posting with the most demanding social requirements and greatest media attention for an ambassadorial couple, so those years provide an excellent opportunity to gain insight into the postwar role of networks and public relations in the capital of the brand-new superpower.

In 1950, Eelco and Margaret van Kleffens became ambassador and ambassadress in Portugal having asked for a quieter post. Although Eelco

---

[15] Nikolaj Petersen, 'Danish and Norwegian Alliance Policies 1948-49: A Comparative Analysis', *Cooperation and Conflict* 14, no 3 (1979): 193–210; Martin Conway and José Gotovitch, *Europe in Exile: European Exile Communities in Britain, 1940-1945*, 1st edn (New York: Berghahn Books, 2001); Susanna Erlandsson, *Window of Opportunity: Dutch and Swedish Security Ideas and Strategies 1942-1948* (Uppsala: Acta Universitatis Upsaliensis, 2015); Julia Eichenberg, 'Macht Auf Der Flucht. Europäische Regierungen in London (1940–1944)', *Zeithistorische Forschungen/Studies in Contemporary History* 15 (2018): 452–73; Pavol Jakubec, 'Together and Alone in Allied London: Czechoslovak, Norwegian and Polish Governments-in-Exile, 1940–1945', *International History Review* 42, no 3 (2020): 465–84.

[16] Erlandsson, *Window of Opportunity*, 76, 97–103.

Figure 1.1 Eelco and Margaret van Kleffens with their dog Jansen, New York City, September 1946. Photo: private, MvK diary inv nr 396, 2.05.86, NL-HaNA, photographer unknown. Courtesy of the Netherlands National Archives, The Hague, with permission of the Van Kleffens family.

retained the ambassadorship in Portugal until 1958, the couple returned to New York City and the centre of world events in 1954, because of his appointment as president of the UN General Assembly for one year. The appointment is proof of a general recognition of diplomatic aptitude and diligence; the position required a candidate who was acceptable to all. From 1956 to 1958, Eelco van Kleffens became Permanent Representative of the Netherlands to NATO and to the Organisation for Economic Co-operation and Development (OECD), assignments that brought the couple to Paris. Finally, leaving the diplomatic service for a position as Permanent Representative of the Netherlands to the European Coal and Steel Community (ECSC), the couple returned to London in 1958 before retiring in Portugal in 1967.

Their background allows using a micro study of the Van Kleffenses as a prism through which to watch the macro developments of the early postwar years. They were part of the 'London moment', so important for Western postwar planning and moved to the United States just as Washington DC took over the role of the main Western diplomatic hub. The emphasis of the empirical study will be on those two locations, to enable comprehensive in-depth analyses. The fact that both spouses have left behind extensive contemporary papers makes them especially suitable for the kind of detailed, gendered study of a diplomatic couple envisioned here. In addition to all the preserved articles, diary notes, letters and public records of Eelco van Kleffens, for decades, Margaret van Kleffens-Horstmann kept a diary of daily work and experiences which she bequeathed to the National Archives of the Netherlands. This material links the political to the personal as the diaries offer detailed insight into the everyday life of the diplomatic household and community. In combination with her husband's notes and public material, they enable a systematic mapping of practices in the border area of public and private, secret and official, male and female. It is possible to identify the couple's shared and separate diplomatic activities and to discover patterns and connections between private and public arenas and personal and political relationships. The combination of papers enables an analysis of the spouses' views and uses of their contacts. Privately aired opinions or expressions of like or dislike can be compared to publicly held views, guest lists, correspondence, etc. The patterns found are placed in the context of macro political issues and developments, discussing concrete connections found between everyday practices and political events.

Although most of the source material revolves around two specific persons from the Netherlands, the study is not concerned with an analysis of them as individuals, but with their functioning in a context. Treating relations as the smallest unit of analysis (echoing Donna Haraway), the micro study reveals the gendered division of diplomatic labour and gendered diplomatic norms not only of Eelco and Margaret van Kleffens, but also of the transnational diplomatic community in which they functioned. The main focus of the study are the relations between people active in the diplomatic communities in the United Kingdom during the war and in the United States in the early postwar years. Notes on the interaction with others form the bulk of the diaries of both Margaret and Eelco van Kleffens. These inherently subjective descriptions of personal experiences are invaluable to identify historical norms and expectations, not least ideas of who could and could not be trusted. No matter how personal experiences noted in a diary may seem, the very notion of meaningful experience is socially produced so that the evidence of personal experience cannot but reflect the ideological system of the time and place in which a person writes.[17]

---

[17] Joan W Scott, 'The Evidence of Experience', *Critical Inquiry* 17, no 4 (1991): 773–97; Sidonie Smith and Julia Watson, *Reading Autobiography: A Guide for Interpreting Life Narratives*, 2nd edn (Minneapolis: University of Minnesota Press, 2010).

Nevertheless, to put the personal views of the story's main characters into perspective and to ensure their representativeness for a broader diplomatic culture, they will be placed in the context of others' views. To that end, three kinds of additional source materials are used. One is prescriptive materials, such as Foreign Office documents on the examination and evaluation of diplomats (and their wives), and handbooks on diplomacy. The second type of supplementary source material used is both published and unpublished material where one can find other diplomatic actors' subjective opinions and descriptions of diplomats and diplomatic practices: Foreign Office confidential personality reports, memoirs, personal notes, letters, and diaries of other members of the diplomatic communities to which Eelco and Margaret van Kleffens belonged. Although a comprehensive study of a large group of people is beyond the scope of this book, occasional samples will serve to check this representativeness and look for variations in diplomatic views and conduct. Finally, contemporary press clippings, mainly on Eelco and/or Margaret van Kleffens or on their embassy, reveal the media image of diplomatic practices.

Conceptualizing trust as a bridge between personal and political

To allow the analysis to oscillate between micro and macro, personal and political and to identify the political implications of everyday activities like diplomatic socializing, the book focuses on the personal trust necessary to carry out the core tasks of a diplomat – representation, negotiation, information gathering (reporting), promotion of friendly relations and protection of national interests. It is a working hypothesis that this trust building was a deeply gendered (as well as racialized and class-and-background-bound) activity.[18]

For trust to be conceptualized in an analytically rewarding way, the assumption that diplomats must build trust needs some clarification. Trust is a broad field of research, and not all types of trust are studied here. Systemic trust, in particular, is beyond the empirical scope of this book, which deals with the role of trust on a personal level (which is not to say that systemic trust does not influence whether we trust a person). Also, works on trust often engage with the question

---

[18] Susanna Erlandsson and Sari Nauman, 'Tillit och Diplomati. Ett Forskningsuppslag', in *Tillit och Diplomati: En Diskussionsbok om Personliga Relationer och Diplomatiska Processer 1670–1990*, ed. Susanna Erlandsson and Sari Nauman (Uppsala: Opuscula Historica Upsaliensia, 2019).

of how we determine who is trustworthy when we do not have enough personal information on which to base our judgement and to what extent we trust those we consider trustworthy based on stereotypes or group-based assessment.[19] For operationalizing purposes, however, this study focuses on the act of trusting itself.

Russell Hardin and others have pointed out that trustworthiness is a personal characteristic in the now while trust concerns an action in the future.[20] Inspired by their insights and building forth on a previous interpretation of those insights by Sari Nauman and myself, trust in this book refers to an expectation about a particular future action of, rather than a general feeling towards, someone. A careful and specific definition is needed not only for analytical purposes, but also to be able to empirically study the role of personal trust in political relations. When in daily life we speak of trusting someone, we often mean that we find someone trustworthy or reliable (in general). I use a narrower definition of trust, which differs from the everyday way in which we often use the word:

> Trust is a three-part relation between two subjects (A and B) and an object (x) in which one part (A) trusts the other part (B) to perform a certain action (x) in the future and A may blame B if B fails to do x.[21]

Using trust in this specific way means that trust regarding one matter does not necessarily mean trust in another. For example: a diplomat may trust his or her spouse to keep a political secret, but not to communicate the country's official stand on an issue to a fellow diplomat. The example makes the difference clear between trust and trustworthiness or reliability. While the latter two are personal characteristics in the present, the former concerns a future action, which always holds an amount of uncertainty and involves expectations that can depend on factors other than a person's trustworthiness. In the above example, the spouse's perceived trustworthiness is crucial for trust in the first instance, but insufficient in the second: not trusting a spouse to deliver a political message could be to do with expectations regarding the other diplomat's reaction to a spouse trying to talk politics, or with the spouse's lack of the necessary language

---

[19] Karen S Cook, Margaret Levi and Russell Hardin, *Whom Can We Trust? How Groups, Networks, and Institutions Make Trust Possible* (New York: Russell Sage Foundation, 2009), 5.
[20] Russell Hardin, *Trust and Trustworthiness* (New York: Russell Sage Foundation, 2002), 1–27; Cook, Levi, and Hardin, *Whom Can We Trust?*
[21] Erlandsson and Nauman, 'Tillit och Diplomati. Ett Forskningsuppslag'; Sari Nauman, 'Ordens Kraft: Politiska Eder i Sverige 1520–1718' (Lund, Nordic Academic Press, 2017) This is a schematic definition for analytical purposes. It does not mean that trust could not conceivably involve more than two subjects or an action in the past.

skills rather than their not being perceived as trustworthy. That said, trust and trustworthiness/reliability are connected in the sense that most people will be more inclined to trust someone to do a specific thing if they perceive that person to be trustworthy, as well as be more inclined to view someone as trustworthy if that person has repeatedly done what they trusted them to do – trust in one respect may lead to trust in another so this will be accumulative.

Considering a person trustworthy is not sufficient to trust that person with any and all matters. Conversely, personal trustworthiness is not necessarily a *sine qua non* for trust. We can choose to trust someone to do a certain thing despite insufficient evidence about a person's reliability or trustworthiness: a *leap of faith*. This leap might be facilitated by systemic trust. As Lisa Hellman has pointed out, however, even when downright suspicious of the counterpart's trustworthiness, diplomats have sometimes chosen to trust them on a specific issue because external circumstances have made cooperation absolutely imperative.[22]

This use of the concept of trust resembles what some political scientists call 'intention understanding'.[23] Both are to do with attempts to predict a future that always holds a measure of uncertainty. However, that term does not make use of the moral dimension that the definition used here includes. The reference to the right to blame someone who betrays our trust points to the role of emotions as well as to the effect on future trust and the estimation of a person's trustworthiness. But including the moral dimension also has a practical function: as a historian, blame gives me a specific indication of broken trust to look for in the source materials. Though historical sources may speak of trust, it is often hard to know whether these pertain to a sincerely felt emotion, and whether that feeling is general or specific. Trust may also be expressed as a rhetorical tactic. However, expressions of disappointment in a person's behaviour often reveal actors' more specific expectations. If an actor blames a person for acting in a particular way, we may assume that this actor had trusted that person to act differently. It reveals what the person expressing disappointment had expected, felt entitled to expect, or at least had reason to hope and so contributes to pinpointing social norms.

Studying the role of personal trust in diplomacy also requires a definition of whose trust building is relevant. A researcher studying non-officials as well as

---

[22] Lisa Hellman, 'När Tilliten inte är ett Val. Kinesisk-Ryska Relationer i Slutet av 1600-talet', in *Tillit och Diplomati. En Diskussionsbok om Personliga Relationer och Diplomatiska Processer 1670–1990*, ed. Susanna Erlandsson and Sari Nauman (Uppsala: Opuscula Historica Upsaliensia, 2019), 46–47; See also Karen S Cook, Russell Hardin, and Margaret Levi, *Cooperation without Trust?*, vol 10 (New York: Russell Sage Foundation, 2005).

[23] Holmes, *Face-to-Face Diplomacy*; Nicholas J Wheeler, *Trusting Enemies: Interpersonal Relationships in International Conflict* (Oxford: Oxford University Press, 2018).

appointed diplomats is faced with the problem of determining on what grounds a person should be considered a diplomatic actor. I have chosen a relationship-orientated definition that takes both performance and perception into account:

> Diplomatic actors are persons who credibly represent a state in a foreign context and work to promote that state's interests in a specific situation.[24]

Without fulfilling this definition of being a diplomatic actor, their building trust would not have diplomatic implications. Again, note that this might be different from how the term diplomatic actor is used elsewhere. It is designed to fit the purposes of this book, opening up the inclusion of many more people than appointed diplomats. The definition used here does not require a diplomatic actor to inherently be a state representative, nor to be credible or trustworthy in general: it is enough that they act and are perceived as representing a state in a particular situation. At the same time, the definition also limits the concept by making the function context bound. Although a person may act and be perceived as a representative of a state (that is, represent that state credibly) in one situation, that person might not be a diplomatic actor using that definition in another, depending on who else is present and on how they act and are perceived. Presumably, there are more specific situations in which officially appointed diplomats or ministers credibly represent a state in a foreign context as compared to non-officials. Still, this definition takes into account that their work also depends on interaction with others and that all individuals are fluid in their particular roles and identities.

The purpose of using these specified definitions is to make it possible to systematically analyze the relationship between the personal and the political in diplomatic culture in an attempt to integrate insights from separate fields like the History of Emotions, Feminist International Relations and New Diplomatic History into the narrative of so-called mainstream diplomatic history. As a whole, the book challenges the perception of big politics as impersonal. At the same time, it challenges the parallel tendency to focus on the personal influence of a few great men (and even fewer women) by shifting the focus to the context within which they were able to act. In part, this book redefines crucial political actors in diplomatic history. If we can pinpoint who could credibly represent a state under which circumstances in the mid-twentieth century and who was trusted to do what and why we will come closer to understanding how Western

---

[24] This is a slight variation of the definition given in Susanna Erlandsson and Sari Nauman, 'Tillit som Verktyg för Diakrona Jämförelser av Diplomati. Repliker, Slutsatser och Nya Frågor', in *Tillit Och Diplomati: En Diskussionsbok om Personliga Relationer och Diplomatiska Processer 1670–1990*, ed. Susanna Erlandsson and Sari Nauman (Uppsala: Opuscula Historica Upsaliensia, 2019), 129–42.

diplomatic culture helped shape the postwar world in practice. The scrutiny of everyday diplomatic practices brings to the surface the extraordinary historical significance of that which we tend to consider ordinary. To paraphrase John Updike, it gives the mundane its political due.[25]

Setting the scene

The set-up of this book is thematic rather than chronological. The time span of the research is too short to be able to draw conclusions about change over time, but the empirical study will continuously be placed in its temporal context with the help of existing literature. The analysis is not only concerned with the identified practices themselves, but also with the relationship between the micro and macro and how patterns on the personal level connect to diplomatic relations on the state level. To that end, the story is structured by concentric circles rather than by a neat timeline.

Following this introduction, Part I, The Diplomatic Couple, lays the groundwork for the rest of the book by addressing the importance of marriage in mid-twentieth century diplomatic relations while telling the story of how Margaret and Eelco van Kleffens met and married. In addition to delving into the division of tasks between a male diplomat and his female spouse, the part takes a broader look at diplomatic norms concerning marriage, gender and sexuality. It highlights the consequences of the heterosexual couple as a diplomatic organizational unit and symbol as mentioned above, looking at the implications not only for married male diplomats and their wives, but for unmarried male diplomats, homosexuals and unmarried female diplomatic actors. Prescriptive materials and literature on more recent periods are used to survey the long-lasting consequences of the norm of heterosexual diplomatic couples. The main focus remains on personal experiences in the mid-twentieth century, how diplomacy was gendered in practice and how personal and political relations overlapped.

Part II places The Diplomatic Home centre stage. It highlights the emotional work involved in the repeated diplomatic homemaking of Margaret and Eelco van Kleffens in different contexts and discusses the diplomatic importance and gendering of interior decoration. Domestic staff were essential to the daily

---

[25] The American writer Updike famously proclaimed as his duty 'to give the mundane its beautiful due'. John Updike, 'Smoke Signals', *The Guardian*, 10 January 2004. Available at: www.theguardian.com/books/2004/jan/10/biography.fiction (accessed 29 June 2021).

diplomatic work done at home. Family members and pets also had their place in that work. Discussing courtesy calls and house guests, special attention is paid to the role of homes and the personalizing of political relations in daily diplomatic practices.

Part III features the diplomatic practice of sharing food and/or drink, paying special attention to Dinner Diplomacy as a form of personal networking as well as formal representation. It surveys different types of social diplomatic events organized around eating and drinking, which means that lunches, teas, receptions and cocktail parties come into the picture as well as dinners. The gendered organization of these events is discussed, as is the mix of political purposes and personal preferences and prejudices that influenced who might be included or excluded at the diplomatic dinner table and on what terms. The discussion of food itself centres on its diplomatic uses and implications for diplomatic relations.

Part IV, under the heading Diplomatic Aptitude, uses daily diplomatic dinner practices to analyze how expectations and ideas about appropriate diplomatic behaviour were gendered, classed and racialized. Besides food, the two elements of dinner diplomacy that Margaret van Kleffens most frequently judged in her diaries in either positive or negative terms were looks (of both site and people) and conversation. Based on her frequent comments on appearances and discourse and against the background of its implicit presence in all previous chapters, it takes on the question what made whom a successful diplomatic actor in the mid-twentieth century.

The conclusion takes stock of what the focus on a diplomatic couple's daily diplomatic work has revealed about how mid-twentieth century Western diplomatic ideas, actors and actions were gendered, racialized and determined by affluence and cultural background and discusses the implications for our understanding of twentieth-century international history and the making of today's world. It recaptures results of the previous chapters in terms of power structures within the diplomatic corps as well as in international relations. By zooming in on some concrete diplomatic decisions of the day, it discusses the political significance of the many unseen events, people, and tasks that dominated everyday diplomatic life in the mid-twentieth century, demonstrating how micro studies can be placed within a wider context. Based on the results of this particular micro study, I argue that weaving a web of seemingly particular and personal stories can serve not only to bring into view persons and processes previously overlooked, but to make visible the very fabric of the macro world.

Part One

The Diplomatic Couple

And now I am going to the office – the office of a profession wherein, more than in almost any other one, the wife is at least as directly concerned and as important as the husband. How well you would do, with your beautiful clear head, as a diplomat's wife.
Letter from Eelco van Kleffens to Margaret Horstmann, 23 March 1934

[Mr Anderson] doit être considéré comme un "étranger de distinction" et placé immédiatement après les chefs de mission étrangers (ambassadeurs, ministres, chargés d'affaires en pied) et alors aussi après les danois qui ont préséance des chefs de mission.[1]
August Esmarch on the rank of the American ambassador's husband, 1949

§ 441. *Wives of diplomatists enjoy the same privileges, honours, precedence and title as their husbands. The wife of an envoy consequently is entitled to:*

1. *A higher degree of protection than what is assured to her in virtue of her birth and sex.*
2. *The same personal exemptions as belong to her husband.*
Satow's Guide to Diplomatic Practice, 4th edn, edited by Sir Nevile Bland, 1957

From the nineteenth century and until very recently, 'diplomatic couple' always stood for a male diplomat with a female spouse, even after an occasional female

---

[1] '[Mr Anderson] should be regarded as a "distinguished foreigner" and placed immediately after the foreign heads of mission (ambassadors, ministers, chargés d'affaires en pied) and hence also after the Danes who take precedence of heads of mission.' My translation from French. A *chargé d'affairs en pied* is a permanent chargé d'affaires, as opposed to a *chargé d'affairs ad interim* who only temporarily fulfils the tasks of an ambassador.

diplomat with a male spouse had appeared. The quotations above illustrate how, throughout the period studied, the idea of the diplomatic couple as a husband-and-wife unit working together permeated diplomats' personal relationships as well as their public guidelines. The first is from a love letter that Eelco van Kleffens wrote to Margaret Horstmann shortly after she had rejected his marriage proposal. Less than six months but over 80 letters later, she changed her mind and agreed to marry him. The prospect of their diplomatic partnership and the important work that would await her as a diplomat's wife was a recurring theme in her future husband's ultimately successful attempts to win her heart.[2]

The second quotation shows that a similar position did not await the husband of a married female diplomat (still a rare phenomenon). In 1949, the political appointment of Eugenie Anderson as United States ambassador to Denmark caused the Doyen of the Diplomatic Corps in Copenhagen, Norwegian ambassador August Esmarch, to specify to his colleagues that Mr Anderson did not hold the same rank as his wife. If the United States gave him a title of his own, they should treat him according to that rank and otherwise merely consider him a 'foreigner of distinction'.[3] Among other things, this meant that Mr Anderson was not seated anywhere near the ambassador at dinners and could not perform the duties that a female spouse performed, regardless of how supportive he was of his wife.[4]

As the third quotation shows, this treatment deviated from that of female spouses of diplomats, who enjoyed the privileges, honours, precedence and title of their husbands. British diplomat Ernest Satow first wrote the internationally influential *A Guide to Diplomatic Practice* in 1917, but the text cited is from the fourth revised edition of 1957 updated by the contemporary British diplomat Nevile Bland to 'ensure that all this information (appertaining to the present day) is accurate'.[5] Formally, the British Diplomatic Service had been admitting women to the profession since 1946, but none of the updated information accounted for the possibility of female diplomats and certainly not for diplomatic husbands – until 1973, the United Kingdom only allowed female diplomats who were unmarried.[6]

---

[2] Correspondance between Eelco van Kleffens and Margaret Horstmann 1934, inv nrs 434–437, 2.05.86, NL-HaNA.

[3] As cited by the Dutch legation in Copenhagen in a report to the Dutch Foreign Minister on 13 December 1949, inv nr 1929, Ministerie van Buitenlandse Zaken Code-archief 1945–1954, 2.05.117, NL-HaNA.

[4] Philip Nash, *Breaking Protocol: America's First Female Ambassadors, 1933–1964* (Lexington: The University Press of Kentucky, 2019), 120–21.

[5] Ernest Satow and Nevile Bland, *A Guide to Diplomatic Practice*, 4. (London: Longman, 1957), vi.

[6] Helen McCarthy, *Women of the World: The Rise of the Female Diplomat* (London: Bloomsbury, 2014), 284.

The chapters of this part explore how the central position of the diplomatic couple as invariably a male diplomat with a female spouse affected everyday diplomatic practices as well as personal lives in the mid-twentieth century with far-reaching and long-lasting consequences – for the men and women who conformed to expectations as well as for those who did not fit that template. Since the late 1960s, a few scholars – first anthropologists, then political scientists, then historians – have pointed to the important roles played by diplomats' wives.[7] Nevertheless, most studies of twentieth-century diplomacy, including those centring on diplomatic practices and networks, overlook the heterosexual couple as a fundamental diplomatic organizational unit with implications for how the whole system functioned.[8] Even studies of gender and diplomacy in the mid-twentieth century tend to focus more on mechanisms of exclusion than on the cooperation between husbands and wives in daily diplomacy. The focus on the struggles of women and their conflicts with men is understandable: this was, after all, a time in which formal changes to the admission system had led to the appearance of female diplomats who encountered a lot of overtly sexist opposition, whether in the shape of outright hostility or condescending benevolence. Nevertheless, diplomacy before the female diplomat was not an all-male world, but a world in which men and women worked together as a team far more often than as separate (let alone opposing) entities. Before women could become diplomats in their own right, men and women certainly did not have equal or the same tasks, but both were indispensable to diplomatic interaction. To understand the difficulties of female diplomats as well as how daily diplomatic work functioned in practice, a few separate studies of wives is not enough. It requires attention to the functions of masculinities and femininities in everyday diplomatic practices and to how men and women, as well as their employers, saw their separate spheres as part of a common endeavour.

---

[7] See A Hochschild, 'The Role of the Ambassador's Wife: An Exploratory Study'. *Journal of Marriage and Family* 31, no. 1 (1969): 73–87; C Enloe, *Bananas, Beaches and Bases: Making Feminist Sense of International Politics*. 2nd edn Berkeley, CA: University of California Press, 2014, 181–87; Hilary Callan, 'The Premiss of Dedication', in *Perceiving Women*, ed. Shirley Ardener (London; New York: Dent, 1975); Molly M Wood, 'Diplomatic Wives: The Politics of Domesticity and the "Social Game" in the U.S. Foreign Service, 1905–1941', *Journal of Women's History* 17, no 2 (2005): 142–65; '"Commanding Beauty" and "Gentle Charm": American Women and Gender in the Early Twentieth-Century Foreign Service', *Diplomatic History* 31, no 3 (2007): 505–30; Nevra Biltekin, 'The Diplomatic Partnership: Gender, Materiality and Performance in the Case of Sweden c. 1960s–1980s', *Genesis* XI, nos 1–2 (2012): 253–65; ; McCarthy, *Women of the World*; Nevra Biltekin, 'The Performance of Diplomacy: The Residence, Gender, and Diplomatic Wives in Late Twentieth-Century Sweden', in *Women, Diplomacy and International Politics since 1500*, ed. Glenda Sluga and Carolyn James (Abingdon and New York: Routledge, 2015), 254–68.

[8] On these separate spheres in research, see Susanna Erlandsson, 'Off the Record: Margaret van Kleffens and the Gendered History of Dutch World War II Diplomacy', *International Feminist Journal of Politics* 21, no 1 (2019): 29–46.

The first chapter exposes mid-twentieth-century gendered assumptions about diplomats and their spouses based on an analysis of diplomatic guidebooks and Foreign Office rules and regulations as well as debates on changing those rules to allow the admission of female diplomats. To give the reader an idea of the persistence of the pattern, references to a guidebook from the 1970s and some findings from recent research on present-day diplomats are included. With the lasting repercussions in mind, Chapter 2 then moves back in time and zooms in on the norm of the diplomatic couple in the shape it had before foreign offices started allowing female and (openly) homosexual diplomats. The love story of Eelco and Margaret van Kleffens provides an empirical lens through which to discuss the political and professional implications of the personal and intimate matter of marriage (and vice versa: the personal and intimate implications of aspiring a diplomatic career) in the 1930s. Chapter 3 proceeds to scrutinize the connection between marital trust and diplomatic secrecy in the 1940s and 1950s, drawing both on ego-documents that reveal what information diplomatic husbands actually shared with their wives and on British Foreign Office deliberations regarding wives as a security risk. Chapter 4 treats the question of how the diplomatic couple's division of tasks according to beliefs about male and female characteristics had consequences for unmarried diplomats, homosexuals and women in power too, noting how Margaret van Kleffens in her diaries reconciled the dissonances between personal experience and norm. Part I ends with a few concluding remarks positing the mid-twentieth century diplomatic couple as a cornerstone of everyday diplomatic work.

1 The persistent notion of the incorporated wife[9]

As this part's introductory quotations show, both individual diplomats and normative texts in the mid-twentieth century proceeded from the general assumption that (1) diplomats were men, (2) diplomats' spouses were women and (3) the position of the husband determined both his and her duties and privileges while the reverse did not apply. The first notion was very slow to change, the second slower yet, but the third has probably been the most persistent. In the face of a slowly growing presence of female diplomats in the second half of the twentieth century, the gendered perception of diplomatic

---

[9] See, for the concept of the incorporated wife (not only for diplomats but other professions too): Shirley Ardener and Hilary Callan, *The Incorporated Wife* (London: Croom Helm, 1984).

spouses did not change *pari passu* with the perception of the diplomat. The Netherlands, the country that Eelco and Margaret van Kleffens served and represented, formally allowed female diplomats from 1947.[10] Like other female civil servants, they had to be single: until challenged in parliament in 1955, leading to the decision to remove the stipulation on 1 January 1958, the honourable discharge of female state employees when they got married was automatic.[11] From the state's perspective, this made female diplomats bad business as it meant training diplomats who might soon have to leave their posts. Diplomacy was, in practice, a job best done by a couple and the bargain had been two for the price of one: most male diplomats married (and were encouraged to marry), their wives then became unpaid servants of diplomacy.

Though not phrased in terms of economic cost, mid-twentieth century objections to admitting women to the Service were clearly related to the roles played by diplomats' wives. Although, from 1947, a diplomat in theory could be either male or female, in that same year the Dutch Foreign Service Directorate introduced new evaluation forms that unequivocally presumed a male official. Modelled on existing British forms for the assessment of officials of the Foreign Service, the forms included questions evaluating the performance of the official's wife.[12] In practice, the powerful Head of Examinations and Committees, BWN Servatius, thwarted Dutch women's efforts to enter the Service for years to come, functioning as a gatekeeper. He consistently and determinedly discouraged female applicants, who were required to talk to him before they could take the exam. When questioned in 1957 by a member of parliament about the Service's systematic exclusion of women, Servatius defended his negative advice as being

---

[10] To put this year in the context of some other Western countries, in post-1815 diplomacy: the United States first allowed women diplomats from 1922, France from 1929, Denmark 1934, Norway 1938, the United Kingdom 1946, Belgium 1946, Sweden 1948, and Switzerland 1956. As in the Netherlands, these dates are no indication of when it became relatively common to admit women to the service. Norway, for example, did not admit the second woman until 1958 and, by 2007, only 14% of Belgium's diplomats were women, and most of those in the lower ranks. Iver B Neumann and Halvard Leira, *Aktiv Og Avventende. Utenrikstjenestens Liv 1905-2005* (Oslo: Pax Forlag, 2005), 351; Annemie Pernot, 'Vrouwen in de Diplomatie', in *Grenzen, Geweld En Gender. Internationale Betrekkingen Feministisch Bekeken*, ed. Joke Wiericx and Machteld de Metsenare (Brussels: VUB Press, 2009), 116-17.

[11] Exceptions were made for women older than 45 (who were not likely to become mothers). CC van Baalen, 'De Politiek en de Rechtsgelijkheid van Vrouwen op het Gebied van Arbeid (1955)', *Politiek(E) Opstellen* 18 (1998): 99-115; Els Kloek, *Vrouw Des Huizes : Een Cultuurgeschiedenis van de Hollandse Huisvrouw* (Amsterdam: Balans, 2009), 201; The marriage bar for female diplomats in the United Kingdom was not lifted until 1973, McCarthy, *Women of the World*, 284.

[12] Documents concerning the introduction of an appraisal system for officials in the Foreign Service (Stukken betreffende de invoering van een beoordelingssysteem voor ambtenaren werkzaam voor de Buitenlandse Dienst), 1945-1949, inv nr 624, 2.05.51, Directie Buitenlandse Dienst (Foreign Service Directorate) (1940) 1945-1954 (1955), NL-HaNA.

Figure 1.2 Women at work for the Netherlands Emergency Committee, London 1941. Photo: Anefo, London Series/HIE (Holland in England). Courtesy of the Netherlands National Archives, The Hague. The woman on the far right is Dutch London Ambassador's wife Henriëtte Michiels van Verduynen, and third from the right is Dutch Foreign Minister's wife, Margaret van Kleffens.

in their own interest. He was simply trying to prevent them from entering a profession that would be too taxing for them. The particular hardships for women that he mentioned included the harsh climate in some parts of the world (apparently more taxing for female diplomats than for wives who accompanied their husbands) as well as the misogynistic culture of countries, not as progressive as the Netherlands, which would make it difficult for female diplomats to function in all but a few likeminded countries. However, one of the most important objections to female diplomats, according to Servatius, was that they would lack the support of a spouse, which most male diplomats could count on.[13] Resistance to female diplomats was not only based on misgivings about a woman doing what was perceived to be a man's job, but also explicitly on the conviction that the job of a diplomat required the support of a spouse and that

---

[13] Letter by Mr BWN Servatius, Head of Examinations and Committees, answering a letter from First Chamber member Prof LJC Beaufort (a priest of the Catholic party KVP who, in his letter of 22 January 1957, referred to his experience with less discrimination against women in the United Nations), The Hague, 19 February 1957, inv nr 7, Vrouwen (Women) 1946–1957, 2.05.317, Ministerie van Buitenlandse Zaken, Examencommissie tot onderzoek naar de geschiktheid en de bekwaamheid voor de Buitenlandse Dienst (Archive of the Ministry of Foreign Affairs, Board of Examiners for investigation into the suitability and competence for the Foreign Service), NL-HaNA.

men could not do a spouse's job. These arguments against female diplomats were not specific to the Netherlands but were remarkably similar to those put forward in other Western countries.[14]

By the 1970s, most Western foreign services had begun to pay at least lip service to the idea of gender equality, recognizing that 'drawing on only half of the world's available brainpower' made no sense, as United States diplomat William Macomber put it in his 1975 handbook of modern diplomacy.[15] However, in the same book, Macomber went on to praise the work done by diplomatic wives and lament the fact that the annual evaluation report of her husband could no longer refer to a wife's performance. He found this regrettable because, as he saw it, that evaluation was one of the few ways to 'recognize the selfless contribution' of wives. However, since this was 'an era which attaches importance to wives' being independent, equal human beings in their own right', he concluded that the omission was inevitable. Any wife's help was voluntary, he emphasized, so the employer had no right to evaluate it as part of her husband's work. However, that did not mean that the functioning of a male diplomat no longer depended on the help of his wife. Macomber clarified:

> Social contacts play an important part in the work of all diplomats, and representational activities are a key part of the job for which he is paid.... A diplomatic service has a right to expect that this part of the job will be done well, and this in turn will often depend in no small part on the supporting performance of his wife. If his wife lets him down, this will not likely help his career because his performance may suffer in an important professional area. The degree of support, or lack of it, supplied by a wife to her diplomat-husband, however, is a private matter between husband and wife, not an official matter between employer and wife.[16]

In effect, the demands on wives remained the same. All Macomber did was shift the responsibility for the blame that was a failing wife's due, not remove it. The duty of control and right to reproach simply moved from the diplomatic service to the husband. Rather than letting the diplomatic service down, a woman who

---

[14] See, eg, for the UK, McCarthy, *Women of the World*, 136–50; and Susan Harris Rimmer, 'Women as Makers of International Law: Towards Feminist Diplomacy', in *Research Handbook on Feminist Engagement with International Law*, ed. Kate Ogg and Susan Harris Rimmer (Cheltenham, UK: Edward Elgar Publishing, 2019), 35–38; for Sweden, Biltekin, *Servants of Diplomacy*, 138; for Norway, Neumann and Leira, *Aktiv Og Avventende*, 350–51; for the US, Molly M Wood, 'Wives, Clerks, and "Lady Diplomats": The Gendered Politics of Diplomacy and Representation in the U.S. Foreign Service, 1900–1940', *European Journal of American Studies*, Vol 10: no 1 (2015): 5–9.

[15] William Macomber, *The Angels' Game: A Handbook of Modern Diplomacy* (New York: Stein and Day, 1975), 115, 117.

[16] Macomber, *The Angels' Game*, 127–29, long quote from p 128.

refused to do the unpaid work expected of her let her husband down. In effect, however, she thereby jeopardized his career: the service was still entitled to make demands on his representational activities that were difficult to fulfil without a wife's assistance. Political demands were simply disguised as personal ones.

Defending women diplomats, Macomber also called the traditional rule that women in diplomatic service must resign if they marry an 'absurdity'. To illustrate, he gave some examples of how a married female diplomat could continue to function, for example if she married another diplomat. Most diplomatic services had assignments enabling a post where both a husband and wife could serve. He was aware, he said, of the opposition to husband-and-wife officer teams on the grounds that 'a wife who has worked all day is not going to be as fresh and as helpful to her husband as a nonworking wife in the conduct of his evening responsibilities'. Rather than contesting the idea that a married female diplomat should also take on a diplomat's spouse's duties (in addition, presumably, to her own evening responsibilities as a diplomat), he argued that whether a female diplomat would be too tired to make a good diplomat's wife was 'subject to challenge, but even if true it is a small price to pay for a system which can so markedly broaden diplomacy's brainpower base'.[17] He appears unaware that the price he thought small to pay was charged not to him or to the service, but to the women who chose to offer the service their brainpower.

Despite the fact that the United States had already appointed a female ambassador in 1949 (and heads of mission with the rank of minister before then) and all the talk of female brainpower, it seems that the gendering of diplomatic practices had hardly changed in 25 years. Parallel to the rise of female diplomats and the recognition of (some) women as valuable additions to the workforce was the persistent perception of the diplomat as a man and of a woman in diplomacy as someone who assisted and complemented that diplomat. It is striking that, as late as in the 1970s, a diplomat like Macomber, who called explicitly and emphatically on diplomatic services to end discrimination against women, could not envision concrete everyday representational diplomatic work as anything but the social responsibility of a male diplomat supported by his female spouse. Nowhere did he even consider the possibility that a husband might give up his career to follow his wife or that the support might not solely be the wife's task in a couple comprising two diplomats. It seems never to have occurred to him that a change in the division of tasks between male and female spouses could even be part of the equation.

---

[17] Macomber, *The Angels' Game*, 116.

Research on gender and diplomacy in the mid-twentieth century has dealt with gender norms for male and female diplomats and diplomats' wives, but little attention has been paid to diplomats' husbands.[18] Yet, the way the latter were treated reveals gendered marital expectations as deeply intertwined with diplomatic work. The absence of husbands in present-day research reflects their perceived irrelevance to their wives' work. Before the female diplomat, wives played a pivotal role in diplomacy, so that the first female diplomats faced the need to play both the role of diplomat and that of hostess.[19] The entry of female diplomats neither ended the role of wives, nor saw the beginning of a similar role for diplomats' husbands. Even when female diplomats were allowed to and did marry (and they often did not), their husbands did not take on the tasks traditionally carried out by diplomats' wives. The fact that diplomatic wives' clubs started to appear from the 1960s and demands for financial compensation for work at the residences increased parallel to the overall societal emancipation of women in the 1970s, testifies to the influence of this development. However, the clubs asked for recognition for the important role of wives, rather than challenging it *per se*, and it took time before these diplomatic wives' clubs became spouses' clubs. According to Nevra Biltekin, in Sweden the 1960s to 1980s 'seems to have been a time characterized by both a growing articulation and formalization of the hostess role and an increasing awareness and questioning of performing the role without receiving any compensation and recognition'.[20] The second half of the twentieth century saw rising tensions between wives who took pride in the role and younger women who began to reject it.[21] Meanwhile, however, both employers and the men and women involved continued to assume wives, but not husbands, were to be incorporated into the career of their diplomat spouse.

Despite big changes in male and female labour participation and notwithstanding comprehensive reforms aimed at modernizing and democratizing the diplomatic service, a discrepancy between wives' and husbands' support of a diplomat spouse has persisted all over the Western world until the twenty-first century. For example, one of the conclusions of a 2009 article on why there were still so few female diplomats in Belgium was that it remained difficult

---

[18] An exception is Nash, *Breaking Protocol,* which explicitly deals with the 'spouse problem' of the first American female ambassadors.
[19] Birgitta Niklasson, 'The Gendered Networking of Diplomats', *The Hague Journal of Diplomacy* 15: nos 1–2 (2020): 13–42; McCarthy, *Women of the World.*
[20] Biltekin, 'The Performance of Diplomacy', 257.
[21] Neumann and Leira, *Aktiv Og Avventende,* 483.

for women to combine diplomatic work with having a husband and family. While male diplomats' wives still often gave up their own careers to support their husband and take care of children, it was less likely for female diplomats to find husbands who were prepared to do the same.[22] Getting married could be the best career move a male diplomat ever made, but long after the removal of the marriage bar, marriage was likely to prevent female diplomats from reaching high-ranking positions. In the United States, a study of all the 603 career ambassadors between 1993 and 2008 showed that female ambassadors were 'significantly more likely to be single and childless than their male counterparts'.[23] Interviews with Swedish diplomats between 2014 and 2019 show that female diplomats tend to do the combined work that male diplomats have traditionally shared with their wives: they access both diplomats' networks (by virtue of their appointment) and wives' networks (by virtue of being women).[24] Interviews with diplomats from Australia who were active between 1984 and 2020 show that the women diplomats who tended to be best equipped in terms of meeting the diplomatic double-burden – diplomatic work, in practice, being a two-person career, to borrow the phrase from Hanna Papanek – were those with same-sex female partners. Heterosexual women interviewees commented that it felt almost the same to be a single woman in post as when they were married with a male spouse. It was very rare for the male spouse to do the diplomatic housework that female spouses did or were expected to do.[25]

Though the patterns described here are not exclusive to diplomacy, their prominence in a world where formalized relationships and protocol are such important tools to regulate international interaction and avoid cultural clashes make them of central relevance to understanding the practices of postwar international relations. Considering how the norm of the diplomatic couple, as it looked before the Second World War, has lingered, it seems safe to conclude that it constitutes a supporting wall of the edifice of daily diplomacy. It is high time we took a closer empirical look at its construction.

---

[22] Pernot, 'Vrouwen in de Diplomatie', 115.
[23] Philip Nash, 'American Women at the UN: From Breakthrough to Dumping Ground?', Op eds by prominent historians, *History News Network* (blog), 19 April 2020. Available at: https://historynewsnetwork.org/article/175049 (accessed 29 June 2021).
[24] Niklasson, 'The Gendered Networking of Diplomats', 14, 36.
[25] Elise Stephenson, 'The Most Successful Female Diplomats? Women with Wives', *BroadAgenda* (blog), 10 August 2020. Available at: www.broadagenda.com.au/home/the-most-successful-female-diplomats-women-with-wives/?fbclid=IwAR34ipfaFLmFB32pIL7GOMPFRsUVlMHpIwesp4vLEm JFgZHNTconSFUbb7E (accessed 29 June 2021); see also Elise Stephenson, 'Domestic Challenges and International Leadership: A Case Study of Women in Australian International Affairs', *Australian Journal of International Affairs* 73, no 3 (2019): 234–53; Hanna Papanek, 'Men, Women, and Work: Reflections on the Two-Person Career', *American Journal of Sociology* 78, no 1 (1973): 852.

2 In love and diplomacy

Before the Second World War, the centrality of the diplomatic couple meant that a man who wanted a career in diplomacy would do well to marry and that a woman could become a diplomatic actor by marrying a diplomat. At the same time, it meant that a male diplomat who fell in love and wanted to marry had to take into account the substantial demands his work would place on his intended bride, and that those demands had to be a consideration for any woman who desired to marry a man who was a diplomat. Unsurprisingly, many diplomats married women who were daughters of diplomats or otherwise belonged to the inner circle of an international high society and who were, therefore, familiar with the kind of lifestyle that would be expected of them. Before the Second World War, the overwhelming majority of European diplomats came from families of diplomats; many of them came from the nobility. Whether noble or not, some personal wealth was a prerequisite to be able to fulfil the duties of a diplomat, which entailed the upkeep of a lifestyle well beyond the means provided by the Foreign Office.

The story of Eelco van Kleffens and Margaret Horstmann is particularly illuminating because while they were certainly from an upper-class environment – a *sine qua non* for reaching diplomatic posts in this period – neither of them came from a clear-cut diplomat background. They had to work consciously for a position that others may have found more self-evident and would therefore be less likely to articulate. While Eelco Nicolaas van Kleffens, born in 1894, came from a line of wealthy local administrators, he was not a nobleman and he was not so rich that he did not need his salary.[26] His father was not a diplomat, but Eelco van Kleffens ended up in the diplomatic world thanks to his interest in (and studies of) international law, a sharp wit, a talent for languages, and – last but not least – the recommendations of his well-connected mentor and PhD supervisor Willem van Eysinga.[27] He could never have achieved his position without a decent family background; the fact that his brother, Adrianus, became one of the first judges on the European Court of Justice strengthens the impression that family played a role in his career path. However, it was his personal abilities and friendships rather than his family connections that allowed

---

[26] Note that the Dutch 'van' is not a marker of nobility like the German 'von'.
[27] Eysinga worked at the Dutch Ministry of Foreign Affairs, had been an assistant delegate to the Second Hague Peace Conference in 1907 and, in 1931, became a judge on the Permanent Court of International Justice.

him to rise quickly through the ranks of the Ministry of Foreign Affairs from sous-chef of Juridical Affairs in 1922 to head of Diplomatic Affairs from 1929.[28]

It was in the latter capacity that he met Margaret Helen Horstmann. Born in 1912, she was the oldest daughter of August Carl Herbert Horstmann, a businessman of German descent (third generation), and American-born Catherine Pearl Horstmann (née van Cott). Besides having an American mother, Horstmann and her siblings – a younger sister and brother – had an English nanny so that, in addition to Dutch, she spoke English as a first language even though she grew up in the Netherlands. For six months in 1930, Margaret Horstmann went to study French and German (including German literature) in Switzerland, where she also did an elective course in typewriting. She also studied in France and possibly elsewhere, but the available sources are inconclusive as to her further education. Her diaries prove that she knew shorthand, that she was well versed in both classical and contemporary literature, art, and music and that her wit and language skills matched those of her husband. Margaret Horstmann's international background and social standing meant that she moved in the same social circles in The Hague as the diplomatic elite. Preserved letters from her sister from the early 1930s mention dances, parties, golf and other socializing with (the children of) both foreign ambassadors and Dutch diplomatic (often noble) families in The Hague.[29] Margaret Horstmann herself had neither a noble nor a diplomatic background and, although the family was well off, she did not bring any significant amount of money to the marriage.[30] At the time she met Eelco van Kleffens, she was working as a secretary at Petrolea, the headquarters of her father's company: he was managing director of the American Petroleum Company (an American-Belgian-Dutch branch of Standard Oil that would later become Esso).[31]

---

[28] EN van Kleffens, *Majesteit, U Kent Het Werkelijke Leven Niet: De Oorlogsdagboeken van Minister van Buitenlandse Zaken Mr. E.N. van Kleffens*, ed. MJ Riemens (Nijmegen: Vantilt, 2019), 9–10; EN van Kleffens, *Belevenissen I, 1894–1940* (Alphen aan de Rijn: AW Sijthoff, 1980).

[29] Letters from Aileen Emilie (Dicky) Horstmann to her parents August Carl Herbert and Catherine Pearl Horstmann, undated but postmarked [unreadable] 1931 and 29 September 1931 and to her mother Catherine Pearl Horstmann, undated but postmarked 12 April and 1 and [unreadable] October 1932, private archive of Clive Wilson (her son), London, UK (UK-Wilson).

[30] In 1983, the year of her husband's death, Margaret van Kleffens listed in her diary things that might have been a disappointment to him. Money – or rather lack of money – was one of the things she mentioned. 'At the time of our marriage it transpired that his hope had been that I had money. I had none whatsoever, no allowance, settlement or prospects.' MvK diary 8 December 1983, inv nr 423, 2.05.86, NL-HaNA.

[31] This information about Margaret Horstmann is pieced together from several sources: her own wartime account and diary 1941–1993 and the 1934 correspondence between Eelco van Kleffens and Margaret Horstmann, inv nrs 391–422 and 434–437 respectively, 2.05.86, NL-HaNA; letters of Aileen Emilie Wilson, née Horstmann (Margaret's sister), UK-Wilson; a family tree of the Horstmann family put together by Margaret's cousin Marion Van Aken-Fehmers (also in the possession of Mr Wilson who kindly shared it with me). An e-mail from Sandra Florinett of the Hochalpines Institut Ftan AG in Switzerland to the author on 11 February 2019 confirmed that, according to the school records, Margaret Horstmann studied these subjects in 1930.

The story of how Eelco van Kleffens and Margaret Horstmann met is a story of their falling in love, but also a story of how diplomatic work was organized along a gendered division of tasks in more ways than one. In October 1933, Eelco van Kleffens faced an urgent problem at work. A group of negotiators had just managed to conclude an important trade agreement with Germany, but now the Dutch mission in Berlin warned Van Kleffens that rumours were spreading locally that the deal was more favourable to the Netherlands than to Germany. If the Netherlands did not get the protocol signed as soon as possible, there was a risk of a last-minute German withdrawal. Alas, there was still only a German version of the document and it had to be signed in both German and Dutch for the deal to be binding. Aware of how difficult the negotiations had been and how crucial the agreement was for the Netherlands, Eelco van Kleffens undertook to translate the document himself. As he was a Doctor of Laws as well as the head of the department, doing it himself would save the time it would cost to outsource a translation and then adjust it to the specific legal needs of Diplomatic Affairs. There was, however, one fateful catch: besides his own expertise, he also depended on that of his multilingual secretary – and at that critical moment, she broke her leg and had to go to hospital.

Without his secretary, Eelco van Kleffens found himself in a somewhat desperate situation. Where could he, on very short notice, find a good typist who also commanded the nuances of economic German? He turned to his colleagues at the Ministry of Foreign Affairs, who were equally at a loss, but thanks to his personal network, their boss, Secretary-General Aarnout Marinus Snouck Hurgronje, found a solution. 'Let's see if Margaret Horstmann can help', he said. Margaret Horstmann was, like Snouck Hurgronje himself, a keen golfer and a friend and golf partner of his daughter Anne. Everyone who knew Horstmann agreed that she would be a splendid candidate for the job, so Snouck Hurgronje telephoned Herbert Horstmann, who consulted his daughter. She declined to come straight away because she had a golf match that afternoon, but agreed to come the next morning, a Saturday. When she punctually arrived, Eelco van Kleffens explained to her the nature and goal of their task, as was his habit (in his experience, people became more interested and did better work if they understood the purpose of what they were doing). After a long day of joint work, extending far beyond office hours and thanks to Margaret Horstmann's 'effective and generous help', the protocol had been translated, signed off by the Department of Finance, typed out and was ready to be signed. Van Kleffens helped her into her jacket and watched her walk away, 'a neat figure, but dressed without exaggeration'.[32]

[32] van Kleffens, *Belevenissen I, 1894-1940*, 267-68 though the detail of Snouck Hurgronje knowing Margaret through golf and his daughter has been added based on information from the letters of

The story of how Eelco van Kleffens met his future wife is recorded in his memoirs, which are dedicated to her. Despite its character of a retrospectively romantic 'how-we-met'-myth, undoubtedly polished and adjusted through being re-told many times, the account is telling. First of all, it shows that no single civil servant, however competent and hard-working, could function without complementing competences – competences that, in this case, were labelled as 'female'. Secondly, it shows the importance of personal networks: in any (political) emergency, a diplomat needed to know who to call upon for assistance and have the (personal) connections to convince that person to help. In this case, the need was for someone with secretarial and language skills, but the same principle would apply for a military expert or a friendly journalist. Thirdly, bearing in mind that diplomats tend to use their memoirs to convey their perceptions of diplomatic suitability and present themselves as successful diplomats, it gives us an idea of the ideals for a diplomat's wife in the 1930s. She should be modestly pretty (Horstmann had a neat figure but was dressed in an understated way); gently industrious (her help was effective as well as generous); well-liked and respected (everyone who knew her agreed she would be a good candidate); loyal and reliable (she would not abandon her golf partner and she showed up at exactly the agreed time and stayed as long as it took).[33]

The selection of facts for posterity left other things unsaid. After describing how they met and how afterwards he had sent her flowers and a book, Eelco van Kleffens emphasized how well Horstmann fitted into his social circles (another prerequisite for a diplomat's wife) and then jumped to how they married one-and-a-half years later. He summed up their marriage with one of the catchy expressions of which he was fond: 'Half a century, with bliss as the main dish.'[34] He did not mention that she was initially not as smitten as he was. When some five months after their first encounter he worked up the courage to tell her that at 39 he felt 'in a state I have not known before', Margaret Horstmann politely rejected him. She explained that 'while I feel admiration and sympathy for you, still my feelings for you are not at all the same as you say you have for me'. She pointed out that she knew him 'scarcely at all, and that mostly as your assistant who worked so pleasantly with you last October over State affairs'. Between October 1933 and March 1934, they had only met a few times

---

Aileen Emilie Horstmann, UK-Wilson, and the correspondence between Eelco van Kleffens and Margaret Horstmann in 1934, inv nr 434, 2.05.86, NL-HaNA.

[33] Nevra Biltekin also argues that in diplomatic memoirs, diplomats write about the occupation itself: they write the history of diplomacy and their craft. Biltekin, *Servants of Diplomacy*, 144–86.

[34] van Kleffens, *Belevenissen I, 1894–1940*, 269.

and those encounters had taken place at relatively big social occasions in The Hague.[35]

After Eelco van Kleffens had opened the letter that held Margaret Horstmann's reply to his (seemingly rather out-of-the-blue) proposal with 'fear and trembling', her answer triggered an intense courtship, because Horstmann did not shut the door completely. She would be glad to get to know him better, she said, 'if this is possible without binding ourselves in any way – simply to find out whether I am capable of a feeling of deeper friendship and sympathy for you, which alone could make for real happiness'.[36] Although he had hoped for a different answer, Van Kleffens wrote back, thanking her for her honesty: 'I *quite* agree that it is much the best for both to be entirely sincere and truthful about it.' He added that he was relieved that she had not 'said no in a final sort of way', but had left him with a 'situation which does not take away all hope'.[37] He then set out to win her over with a veritable flood of love letters in the coming months in which he tirelessly tried to convince her of his love, that he would take care of her and that life with him would be exciting and would make her happy, even though she was so much younger than him. A detail, but a striking one, is that he wrote to her in English even though they were both Dutch, albeit she with an American mother. He explained that it was because he could not bear using the strictly formal 'Zeer geachte' (very honourable) which would be the correct salutation for a person you were not on a first-name basis with in Dutch, while the English language allowed him to write 'Dear Miss Horstmann' without breaking any rules of etiquette.[38] It also seems likely that her international allure was part of what attracted him and that perhaps he wanted to emphasize that life with him would allow her to speak her mother tongue and have a more international and exciting life than any ordinary Dutchman could offer her. In any case and whatever the original motives, the couple kept corresponding in English after they began using first names.

---

[35] Letter from Eelco van Kleffens to Margaret Horstmann 18 March 1934, and from Margaret Horstmann to Eelco van Kleffens 20 March 1934, inv nr 434, 2.05.86, NL-HaNA. A draft copy as well as the final, posted version of Margaret's rejection letter is in the archive. The latter has a written error, "Sate affairs" instead of "State affairs" in the sentence quoted. In his letter, Eelco van Kleffens referred to the times they had met since October.

[36] Letter from Margaret Horstmann to Eelco van Kleffens 20 March 1934, inv nr 434, 2.05.86, NL-HaNA.

[37] Letter from Eelco van Kleffens to Margaret Horstmann 23 March 1934, inv nr 434, 2.05.86, NL-HaNA.

[38] Letter from Eelco van Kleffens to Margaret Horstmann 18 March 1934, inv nr 434, 2.05.86, NL-HaNA.

Besides sending her flowers and little presents – often books or notebooks – Van Kleffens kept emphasizing in his letters what an important position Horstmann would have as a diplomat's wife and he also introduced her to that life by inviting her to his diplomat's lunches. 'Dear Margy, It was awfully nice to have you to lunch this afternoon,' he wrote on 9 April 1934.

> If only you could have sat on my right instead of that incorrigible chatterbox, Mrs Raeder! But the Protocol is inflexible, and its iron hand assigned you your place.... I loved watching you in animated conversation with the Norwegian. Well done.[39]

He kept giving her compliments for her diplomatic abilities and furthermore emphasized how she had female proficiencies that he lacked, presenting himself as a man in sore need of a woman who could provide the female touch:

> And now I am sitting at my writing-table with your lovely narcissi in front of me, a fragrant promise of spring so like yourself in its naturalness, freshness and sincerity. They are arranged in a vase widening towards the top, in a way which no doubt you would think unutterably masculine, and yet I did my clumsy best. Were you only there to do it for me.[40]

Some letters were more specific about the future he envisioned for them and these reveal an ideal of a diplomatic couple as a natural centre of social activities. In early May 1934, he wrote:

> You know Margy my new ideal is to live with you at Oud Clingendaal; I suppose this could not be done right away because my present income would not suffice, but it might in times that must inevitably come some day.... Together we could be such a center (disinterested) to our diplomatic people, and bind the sympathies of foreigners to this country. Of course, you would have to pay calls! but you would do it, as I do, out of a sense of public duty, a sense few Dutch girls possess, and that is one of the reasons why so many of our diplomats marry girls of other nationalities.[41]

Eelco van Kleffens featured the diplomatic couple as an unselfconscious and dutiful glue tying people as well as peoples together and he emphasized how

---

[39] Letter from Eelco van Kleffens to Margaret Horstmann, 9 April 1934, inv nr 436, 2.05.86, NL-HaNA.
[40] Letter from Eelco van Kleffens to Margaret Horstmann, 28 April 1934, inv nr 436, 2.05.86, NL-HaNA.
[41] Letter from Eelco van Kleffens to Margaret Horstmann, 2 May 1934, inv nr 434, 2.05.86, NL-HaNA. Clingendaal is a historical luxurious neighbourhood on the outskirts of The Hague, today housing i.a. the prestigious think tank and academy on international affairs Clingendael – the Netherlands Institute for International Relations.

difficult and how important it was for a diplomat to find a wife suited for this line of work. He frequently shared stories about his work with her, making her complicit in his efforts and begged his sweet 'Pexy' – one of the many pet names he gave her – to become his partner not only in love, but also in diplomacy. He told her of his jealousy of other diplomats who had their wives with them (though careful to emphasize that it was not because any of those wives were anywhere near as desirable as Margaret was). During a stay in Berlin, where he (again) led a Dutch team which negotiated a treaty with Germany, he referred to the work of the Dutch envoy's wife there:

> I was much struck by the fact how much Mme de Stirum does here in the interest of our country in a great variety of ways. I know for certain how well you would do similar things, at The Hague or abroad. Pexy Pexy cannot you let your heart melt a little bit? How rich, how varied, how worth while, how interesting our life could be, so full of understanding for ourselves and for others. Do consider it, darling. I hope I may say I would never fail you, as I know you would never fail me, the divine miracle of being two, yet one.[42]

Again, there is an emphasis not only on marriage as a symbiotic union of two people who share everything and can always trust one another, but on his work as the sure provider of an exciting life for them.

Margaret Horstmann did gradually warm up to her suitor. However, although the exchange of letters shows how her answers went from politely friendly to more enthusiastic and from formal to increasingly personal, she remained more aloof than he almost up to the point where they got engaged. As soon as they moved to a first-name basis (a step taken in person sometime between the letters of 5 and 8 April 1934), he quickly went from 'Dear Margaret' to 'Dear Margy', 'Margy dear', 'Dear M.', 'Darling Margy', 'Carina mia', 'Carissima Miggs', 'My dearest everything', 'Perlita mia' and a variety of other creative pet names. She, however, kept referring to him as 'Dear Elcho' (opting for the Scotch version of his name) for another month and a half, switching to 'Dearest Elcho' towards the end of May and in June using 'Eelco dearest', 'My dear', 'My dearest Elcho'. She, too, finally introduced a pet name ('Dearest Van') at the end of June (by which time he was calling her 'My lovely little girl' or even 'Dear child'), and an occasional 'Darling' from July, though she only started using this greeting

---

[42] Letter from Eelco van Kleffens to Margaret Horstmann, 14 June 1934, inv nr 436, 2.05.86, NL-HaNA. Mme de Stirum was Catharina Maria ('Nini') van Limburg Stirum, born Lady van Coehoorn van Sminia, married to Johan Paul van Limburg Stirum (1873–1948), Dutch envoy to Berlin 1925–1936.

commonly after their engagement in September ('Darling Van', 'My darling pillar').[43]

This discrepancy may be something to do with what was considered appropriate or decent for a woman as compared to a man. However, a diary note from ten years later reveals that she was not just conforming to norms or playing hard to get: she seems to have been holding back because she was seriously considering marrying someone else, whether he was another admirer or a man she had unanswered feelings for – the sources are silent on this point. While Margaret van Kleffens's diaries are otherwise full of testimonies to her love and admiration for her husband, which seems to have kept growing over the years, a rare reference to this prior love appears on 4 August 1944. She wrote in her diary: 'It suddenly occurs to me that today ten years ago was the last time I saw Hans. I wept continuously for three days – and a month later was engaged to E.!'[44] Whatever role this elusive Hans might have played in her decision, he vanished from her life and Margaret Horstmann finally said yes to Eelco van Kleffens on 4 September 1934 – her 22nd birthday. When she did, she not only chose a partner for life and love; she chose a career in diplomacy. The couple married seven months later, on 4 April 1935. The sous-chef of Diplomatic Affairs, Willem van Bylandt, was best man.[45]

So how can this particular love story be representative of the average diplomatic couple's, if there even is such a thing? To avoid confusing specific contexts and personal circumstances with diplomatic norms, it is a useful exercise to compare the courtship of Eelco van Kleffens and Margaret Horstmann against that of Herman van Roijen and Anne Snouck Hurgronje, who married less than four months before they did. The couples moved in the same social circles in The Hague, but Herman van Roijen and Anne Snouck Hurgronje were both from prominent diplomatic families and Herman van Roijen was, as Margaret van Kleffens put it many years later in her diary, 'stinking rich'.[46] Anne Snouck Hurgronje and Margaret Horstmann were the same age (the former, born in 1913, a year Horstmann's junior) and – as already mentioned – they played golf together in their youth. Herman van Roijen and Eelco van Kleffens worked together at the Foreign Office, where Van Kleffens was something of a

---

[43] Correspondence between Eelco van Kleffens and Margaret Horstmann March–September 1934, inv nrs 434–437, 2.05.86, NL-HaNA.
[44] MvK diary 4 August 1944, inv nr 394, 2.05.86, NL-HaNA.
[45] Mentioned in MvK diary 20 December 1943, inv nr 393, 2.05.86, NL-HaNA.
[46] 'Herman is stinking rich, ce qui ne gâte rien [which does no harm] in his position as ambassador here in England, where money attracts people like honey attracts flies'. MvK diary 6 April 1964, inv nr 416, 2.05.86, NL-HaNA.

mentor and older friend to Van Roijen, who was born in 1905. According to the biographers of Herman van Roijen, he hesitated in asking Snouck Hurgronje to marry him because of the great sacrifice he thought it would be for her to follow him on his diplomatic postings around the world. Her friends knew Anne Snouck Hurgronje as a spontaneous, happy-go-lucky type of person who did not always conform to convention. However, she knew quite well what it meant to be a diplomat's wife, since she was the daughter of the boss of both Van Roijen and Van Kleffens, Secretary-General Snouck Hurgronje (who comes across as a veritable match-maker for his employees). In the love story of Anne Snouck Hurgronje and Herman van Roijen, it was she who pushed for an engagement and declared herself prepared to support her future husband in his career while he was afraid he might be asking too much of her and even broke off the relationship for a while for that reason.[47]

The differences between these two courtship stories show just how important the diplomatic partnership between husband and wife was. While the demands on a diplomat's wife were an asset in Eelco van Kleffens's courtship of Margaret Horstmann, the same demands constituted an obstacle in the love story of Herman van Roijen and Anne Snouck-Hurgronje. Van Kleffens's perception of Horstmann as a suitable diplomat's wife seems to have played a role not only in his falling in love with her, but also in his ultimately successful attempts to win her heart. Van Roijen's perception of Snouck Hurgronje as someone who might not find the role of diplomat's wife easy caused him to second-guess the relationship despite being in love with her. In both courtships, the fact that marrying would mean forming a diplomatic couple played a central role. The political and professional norm of the diplomatic couple could not be disregarded by anyone entering a marriage as or with a diplomat, however personal and private his or her feelings and whatever the particulars of the individual stories.

3 Carte blanche? Diplomatic secrecy and marital trust

The seemingly personal, intimate and romantic ideal of marriage as 'being two, yet one' (as Eelco van Kleffens put it in one of the love letters quoted above) surfaces both in Foreign Office documents and discussions about diplomatic

---

[47] Rimko van der Maar and Hans Meijer, *Herman van Roijen 1905–1991: Een Diplomaat van Klasse* (Amsterdam: Boom, 2013), 51–53 The image of Anne as a bit wild is also drawn from how she is described in letters from the early 1930s by Margaret's younger sister Aileen Emilie Horstmann ('Dicky'), UK-Wilson.

aptitude. From the state's perspective, the two-for-one advantage of male diplomats with wives was coupled with ideals and assumptions about marital trust. The fact that married women could not keep working for the state implies that the government considered a woman's first duties to be as wife and mother. She could only be trusted to put other duties first if she was unmarried and childless. In other words, the state expected a wife's duties towards her husband and children to take precedence over any other duties, or, more pointedly formulated, did not trust a wife to place the state's interests before her loyalty to her husband. However, that also meant that, ideally, the wife of a civil servant could be expected to be loyal to her husband and, therefore, by extension, to the state. This one-way marital loyalty was also part of why diplomatic husbands were considered a problem: it was feared that unlike wives, it would be impossible to control loose-lipped husbands.[48] In a profession where knowing what to say and what to keep secret was crucial, having an absolutely loyal and reliable confidant was not only personally but politically important. The following will provide a closer empirical look at the issue of marital trust and its role in diplomatic practice.

In his memoirs, Eelco van Kleffens painted the picture of a close and happy marriage. There are several references to his wife's loyal support, assistance and diplomatic usefulness. He accentuated how she, like he, put the interests of the state before her own preferences (for example by agreeing to his taking the job as Foreign Minister because the country needed him, even though she had her heart set on the embassy in Bern). The memoirs demonstrate his trust in her and her close involvement in his affairs by referring to her diary to verify details of his account and by citing her keen-eyed diary descriptions of both surroundings and political situations.[49] No matter how personal the account of Eelco van Kleffens may seem, it fitted a genre. Male diplomats often express gratitude to their wives in their memoirs, acknowledging their importance for their work and careers.[50] The commendations paint an image of a general trustworthiness, but it is hard to find diplomats explicitly stating in public that they shared state secrets with their wives. Nor are there records of Eelco van Kleffens explicitly saying in public that he trusted his wife unconditionally. Yet, he left behind evidence of his views of marriage and trust that shows not only that he did, but

---

[48] Harris Rimmer, 'Women as Makers of International Law', 35.
[49] See, eg, van Kleffens, *Belevenissen I, 1894-1940*, 161, 272-73, 290-91, 329-36; EN van Kleffens, *Belevenissen II, 1940-1958* (Alphen aan de Rijn: AW Sijthoff, 1983), 48, 50, 136, 166.
[50] Biltekin, *Servants of Diplomacy*, 183-85.

also that others silently assumed that trust and in general acknowledged marital trust as all encompassing.

After the Second World War, the Dutch parliament conducted an extensive survey to scrutinize the actions of the government at the outbreak of the war and in exile. During one of several interviews with Eelco van Kleffens, who was Foreign Minister between 1939–1946, the parliamentary commission questioned him about the restrictions on the freedom of action of the Commander-in-Chief on the eve of the German occupation in 1940. Should not the Cabinet either have trusted the commander and given him free reign or, if they did not trust him, have dismissed and replaced him? No, Eelco van Kleffens answered, you could not expect such a relationship between the Commander-in-Chief and the responsible Cabinet. He added: 'I believe that in human relationships there is only one relationship in which one gives someone a carte blanche, namely marriage.'[51] The purpose of his answer was not to express his views on marital trust or say something about his own marriage, but to illustrate how absurd it was to expect unconditional trust in the situation discussed. Yet, inadvertently, he did. The fact that he could refer to marital trust to make his point reveals that it was normal to see marital trust as exceptional – and his own marriage did not give him a reason to avoid that particular comparison.

The attitudes of several countries' Foreign Services at the time confirm this view of marital trust as a widespread Western phenomenon. That made it not only a personal but a political matter, at least as a concern of diplomats' employers, relevant to the political and professional trust that states showed their diplomats. Bear in mind that trust is not solely a positive thing: trust always means not knowing for sure, so misplaced trust can be dangerous. Besides the previously mentioned Foreign Office evaluation forms that included questions about the representational role of a diplomat's wife, there are records of discussions regarding whom a foreign officer should (not) marry, which prove that the Foreign Office considered both the representativeness and the reliability of their employees' wives their business. While marital trust could be an asset, it could also be a danger and appeared as such in discussions about foreigners. Potentially, a foreign woman was a serious security risk if her husband shared sensitive information with her and she did not conform to the ideal of putting her husband's interests before those of her (birth) state. Here, ideas about the

---

[51] My translation. Original, in Dutch: 'Ik geloof, dat er in de menselijke verhoudingen maar één verhouding is, waarin men iemand een carte blanche geeft, nl. het huwelijk.' *Enquêtecommissie Regeringsbeleid 1940–1945*, 2C, Verhoren (Gravenhage: Staatsdrukkerij, 1949), 324.

characteristics of different nationalities and ethnic groups intersected with ideas of typical female behaviour. The expectation that a diplomat's wife would support and be loyal to her husband did not extend to any female person but, as a rule, only to Western women of a certain class and complexion. A British Foreign Office minute from 1952 reveals that an existing clause that excluded officers with 'ex-enemy' mothers gave rise to a discussion on what nationalities officers should be allowed to marry. While the eventual decision was not to adopt any definite formula, this was not because the Foreign Office thought that the choice of a wife was not its business, or politically unimportant. On the contrary, the problem was that no formula could 'cover the dual problem of nationality and race'. The last sentence of the minute reads: 'Anything like a list of acceptable or unacceptable nationalities would tend to encroach upon the Secretary of State's right to exclude "unrepresentational" wives as well as wives likely to become "security risks".'[52]

Besides testifying to the assumption that wives would be deeply involved in their husbands' work and have access to sensitive information, the discussion reveals a racialized perception of reliability and representativeness, steeped in apprehensions about certain nationalities. Margaret van Kleffens showed her sensitivities to these perceptions when she started spelling her maiden name 'Horstman' rather than the more German-looking 'Horstmann' during the Second World War.[53] In 1948, her surprise at the decision to send a Dutch diplomat who was not entirely light-skinned and had an English wife who she believed was Jewish ('a Jewess or I'll eat my bonnet') to Japan shows how similar ideas permeated her thinking. 'It surely is the New Order that such people, however qualified, can be chosen to represent our country abroad, and that in a country where "face" counts for so much', she wrote in her diary.[54] As in the British discussion, the problem was not only 'ex-enemies' but also ethnicity – whether certain 'races' were considered more likely to be security risks or simply unrepresentative. Suspicion of foreigners was hardly a specifically British trait. In the United States, for example, President Franklin Delano Roosevelt in the 1930s considered all foreign nationalities undesirable as spouses of his country's

---

[52] Minute on Foreign wives of Foreign Service members: admissible nationalities for officers to marry, 1952, FO 366/2997, UKNA.

[53] 'I don't remember if I have put down yet in my diary that I have discarded the second "n" with which my maiden name ended, preferring to forget, and unwilling to allow strangers to realise, my German descent.' MvK diary 3 January 1944, inv nr 393, 2.05.86, NL-HaNA. Her paternal grandfather was a German immigrant to the Netherlands and her mother was American, but she was born and raised in the Netherlands.

[54] MvK diary 14 September 1948, inv nr 398, 2.05.86, NL-HaNA.

representatives. A presidential order of his first administration threatened American professional diplomats with dismissal if they so much as asked permission to marry a foreign woman.[55]

At the same time, in many countries diplomats frequently did marry foreign women, as Eelco van Kleffens pointed out in one of the letters quoted above (claiming that the reason was that Dutch girls lacked a sense of public duty) and few Western administrations were as adamant about preventing such marriages as the first FDR administration. Neither the Dutch nor the British ruled out marriages to foreigners. They did demand that the spouse adapt and integrate. In the United Kingdom, foreign women who married British subjects were automatically given British citizenship while British women who married foreigners were deprived of theirs. However, women from other countries (like the Soviet Union) did not necessarily lose their native citizenship upon marrying a foreigner. This circumstance in 1955 caused Secretary of State Anthony Eden to decide that foreign wives of Foreign Service officers should take British nationality only.[56] In the Netherlands, too, a foreign woman who married a Dutchman automatically became a Dutch citizen. Dutch women who married foreigners, however, lost their Dutch citizenship. This nineteenth-century law regulating the unity of nationality of spouses remained in place in the Netherlands until 1964.[57] Besides the formal transformation of foreign wives into Dutch citizens, the Dutch evaluation forms, mentioned earlier, included a question about the wife's nationality prior to her marriage with the follow-up question of whether she had learned the Dutch language and had adapted to a Dutch environment.[58] Similar questions about a diplomat's husband simply did not apply – even after the marriage bar was lifted, women married to foreigners no longer had Dutch citizenship and hence could not represent their country of origin.

The idea of unity in marriage, with spouses giving each other 'carte blanche' in Eelco van Kleffens's words, helps explain why Foreign Services viewed women of so-called races or nationalities that were considered more antagonistic or foreign than others as a potential security risk, but it does not reveal what role

---

[55] Charles Wheeler Thayer, *Diplomat* (United States, 1959).
[56] Letter 8 June 1945 from Archibald Clark Kerr to Soviet wives of British subjects, explaining the discrepancies between British and Soviet law and their dual nationality, FO 366/3107; Decision by Secretary of State that foreign wives of Foreign Service officers should take British nationality, 1955, FO 366/3107, UKNA.
[57] Corrie van Eijl and Marlou Schrover, 'Inleiding', in *Bronnen Betreffende de Registratie van Vreemdelingen in Nederland in de Negentiende en Twintigste Eeuw*, Broncommentaren 5 (The Hague: Instituut voor Nederlandse Geschiedenis, 2002), 10.
[58] Documents regarding the introduction of an appraisal system for civil servants working for the Foreign Service, 1945–1949, inv nr 624, 2.05.51, NL-HaNA.

marital trust played, in practice, in daily diplomacy. Diaries and correspondence give some clues, revealing at least in part what marital trust meant for diplomats' wives and what their husbands actually told them. The diaries of Margaret van Kleffens confirm that her husband trusted her to keep secrets, since the content proves that she had access to classified information. Many of the confidential things that turn up in her diaries do so in the shape of gossip about particular ministers or disagreements within the Cabinet, between Cabinet and Crown, or as reactions to exaggerated statements in the media, noting corrections.[59]

She often made remarks in passing that revealed that she was up-to-date on her husband's daily business. However, when she wrote about something that was about to happen but was not (yet) public knowledge, or if she perceived some piece of information as particularly sensitive, she had the habit of switching to shorthand, even though she was writing in her private, locked, diary. Margaret van Kleffens clearly took her role as her husband's confidante seriously and was careful not to break his trust. On 24 March 1944, for example, she used shorthand to write that according to Eelco, the British cabinet was very reluctant about the invasion, 'the inevitable', but were being pushed by the Americans to go ahead with it that year. A note made in shorthand on 9 June 1949 reveals that it was Eelco van Kleffens who authored the pro-Dutch speech that was shortly to be held in the American Senate by the American Senator Brewster (of whom she wrote that he was 'known to the knowledgable [sic] as "the most venal man" in Congress').[60]

Other information that she deemed so sensitive that it required shorthand, included damaging personal information, like the story of how a diplomat at the Washington embassy had treated his wife 'like a dog' and the wife would like to leave her husband but worried that it would end his career. 'This is a terrible problem', she wrote.[61] As wife of the ambassador, Margaret van Kleffens represented the nation together with her husband, but the behaviour of lower-ranked diplomatic couples reflected on the nation too. Moreover, personal problems of the staff and especially the welfare and behaviour of the wives were her responsibility.

---

[59] Erlandsson, 'Off the Record'.
[60] MvK diary 24 March 1944, inv nr 393; 12 May 1948, inv nr 397; 9 June 1949, inv nr 399, 2.05.86, NL–HaNA. I am indebted to Monique van Kessel of the Netherlands Institute for War Documentation (NIOD) who translated these shorthand passages for me.
[61] MvK diary 29 January 1949, inv nr 398, 2.05.86, NL–HaNA. These shorthand passages too were translated with the generous help of Monique van Kessel of NIOD. The couple, Otto and Aimée Reuchlin, did not end up getting a divorce, but the problem remained.

A few examples from other diplomats' wives' diaries from the same period show that they, too, had access to privileged information, confirming that the Van Kleffens marriage does not give a skewed view of marital trust, even if one reckons with the possibility that their marriage was exceptionally close. Other diplomats trusted their wives and they were as careful to be discrete as Margaret van Kleffens. For instance, in her book about her grandmother Elisabeth Knatchbull-Hugessen, wife of the British diplomat Sir George Peregrine (Gerry) Young, Lulah Ellender describes how her grandmother switched to Mandarin when writing about particularly secret matters in her diary.[62] The papers of Lady Theodosia Cadogan (a contemporary and acquaintance of Van Kleffens to whom she usually referred as Lady Theo) reveal that her husband confided in her as well. In Cadogan's 1938 diary notes, for example, she described internal conflicts in the British Foreign Office. Among others, she wrote about a disagreement between the Prime Minister, Neville Chamberlain and Foreign Minister, Anthony Eden, which was officially denied when a rumour about it appeared in the press.[63] Her husband, the British diplomat Sir Alexander Cadogan, at the time Under-Secretary for Foreign Affairs, seems to have shared the office gossip with his wife as readily as Eelco van Kleffens did with his. A salient detail: not on the phone. 'A. told me that there were a lot of "sharks" & that he had more or less cleared them all out', Lady Theo Cadogan wrote on 21 January 1938. 'When I asked who was he thinking of he said he couldn't say then – but would tell me later on.'[64]

Like Margaret van Kleffens, Theodosia Cadogan was involved in helping her husband keep track of events and write his diary. Besides Eelco van Kleffens using his wife's diary as memory support when he wrote his memoirs, Margaret van Kleffens noted in her own wartime diary that she took down her husband's diary every day in shorthand and that typing it out was one of her Tuesday jobs.[65] Lady Cadogan seems to have kept notes that her husband later used in his own diaries. In a notebook titled 'Jottings by T.C.' which she endowed to the Churchill Archives together with other family material after her husband's death, she wrote: 'not sure if A.C. had time to enter enclosed in his diary. Secret & interesting'.[66] While both Eelco van Kleffens and Alexander Cadogan had

---

[62] Lulah Ellender, *Elisabeth's Lists. A Life Between the Lines* (London: Granta Books, 2019).
[63] Diary of Lady Theodosia Cadogan (TC Diary) 21 January and 13 February 1938, inventory 8, Lady Theodosia Cadogan, nr 1: Diary notes 1914–1958, The Papers of Sir Alexander George Montagu Cadogan, ACAD, Churchill Archives Centre, Cambridge, UK (UK-CAC).
[64] TC diary 21 January 1938, ACAD 8/1, UK-CAC.
[65] MvK diary 23 March 1943, inv nr 392, 2.05.86, NL–HaNA.
[66] ACAD 8/4, UK-CAC.

secretaries at the office, their wives provided the secretarial assistance when it came to keeping their more private diaries. Cherish Watton has pointed out that the women whose scrapbooks she has studied (among others, diplomats' wives) often took on a role as family archivists, so were guardians of the family secrets.[67]

There are plenty of indications, then, that the personal, intimate trust between spouses in practice often involved the sharing of confidential information. That this remained off the record is hardly surprising: officially, wives were not supposed to know the details of confidential state matters. In 1967, when a Dutch journalist interviewed Anne van Roijen-Snouck Hurgronje about her life as the Dutch ambassador's wife in London, he asked her if she was afraid that she would accidentally let the cat out of the bag and reveal a diplomatic secret. Anne van Roijen laughed and told him no, because she had no beans to spill – her husband was not allowed to tell her anything and he abided by those rules.[68] This was unequivocally a lie. The couple's personal correspondence reveals that Herman van Roijen frequently used his wife as a sounding board and wrote to her about top secret political developments. He complained that she was not around so that he could discuss things with her, ask for her opinion or test his own opinion against hers. Herman van Roijen's biographers call his trust in his wife limitless – everything he knew, he was prepared to tell her.[69] The discrepancy between the archival evidence and the claims of Anne van Roijen in the media shows that a lack of public acknowledgements of diplomats' wives' roles as confidantes is no indication that their husbands kept them out of the loop. In fact, most diplomatic couples would probably be more likely to deny, than to admit to sharing, political secrets.

Historians have sometimes been all too ready to buy this version of the story. In fact, the idea that wives and homes had a private, apolitical character in some cases seems to have contaminated the assessment of work done by wives and/or at home. When Margaret and Eelco van Kleffens arrived in London after the German invasion of the Netherlands, one of the first tasks they accomplished together was writing the book *The Rape of the Netherlands*, to counter rumours that the Dutch people had not fought back with enough fervour. As usual, when

---

[67] Cherish Watton, 'Women's Scrapbooks of Political and Diplomatic Activity, c.1890-1939' (MPhil dissertation in Modern British History, Cambridge, University of Cambridge, Faculty of History, 2018).

[68] Proofs of article for Dutch paper *De Telegraaf* sent by journalist Tom Brouwer to Anne van Roijen on 24 January 1967, inventory number 58, Archive of Dr JH van Roijen 2.21.183.70, NL-HaNA.

[69] van der Maar and Meijer, *Herman van Roijen 1905-1991*, 191 See also; Susanna Erlandsson and Rimko van der Maar, 'Trouw aan Buitenlandse Zaken. Margaret van Kleffens, Anne van Roijen, de ambassade in Washington en de betekenis van het diplomatiek partnerschap voor de naoorlogse Nederlandse buitenlandse betrekkingen', *Tijdschrift voor Geschiedenis* 134, no 3 (2021).

wives helped their husbands write, it was published in his name only. That is not the only way her contribution has been hidden though. Historians who have been aware that the foreign minister wrote this defence of the Netherlands in his spare hours at home, aided by his wife, have instead played down the publication's significance, meaning that the importance of Margaret van Kleffens's work has been doubly denied.[70]

A relevant aspect of marital trust for diplomatic practices is that it seems to have made wives trustworthy to those other than their husbands. Besides more junior wives confiding in her, at least some male officials other than her own husband discussed inside diplomatic information with Margaret van Kleffens. It is difficult to say exactly what they told her, since she was so careful not to write secret matters down, even in shorthand. During the war, she simply noted 'talking shop' with the Dutch Ambassador in London, Edgar Michiels van Verduynen, who, during the Dutch government's exile, also served as Foreign Minister without Portfolio, assisting her husband in his work. In a diary note in September 1945 Van Kleffens said that she was 'flattered and felt honoured' that Alidius Tjarda van Starkenborgh Stachouwer, the last colonial Governor-General of the Netherlands East Indies (which had recently declared independence as Indonesia), on several occasions 'discussed matters with me which preoccupied him at the moment, and asked for my advice on some points – and took it!'[71] On another occasion, she mentioned talking to the visiting Adriaan Dijxhoorn, the Dutch exile-government's representative to the wartime Combined Chiefs of Staff in Washington. She was able to ask him 'direct and pertinent questions to my heart's content on such matters as the war's duration, the invasion of Europe and Hitler's biggest strategic mistake, gaining more satisfaction from his replies than my diplomatic spouse ever gives me!'[72] Although wives often, at some point, left their husbands alone with visiting officials to 'talk shop', it seems not to have been self-evident that they always would. Once when Crown Princess Juliana of the Netherlands visited, Margaret van Kleffens even seems to have found it a bit comical that Her Royal Highness – who was also a personal friend of hers – made a point of speaking to her husband alone: 'First we all had coffee and cake together and then I left her to talk business with E. Whether this "business" was secret or not, my withdrawal was obviously expected; rather strange and it made me laugh!'[73]

---

[70] For a discussion of this, see Erlandsson, 'Off the Record'.
[71] MvK diary 16 September 1945, inv nr 395, 2.05.86, NL–HaNA.
[72] MvK diary 19/20 June and 28 October 1943, inv nr 393, 2.05.86, NL–HaNA.
[73] MvK diary 14 October 1944, inv nr 394, 2.05.86, NL–HaNA.

The above testifies to her keen interest in world events, but the last two quotes and especially the complaint about a lack of spousal information also illustrate the fact that Margaret van Kleffens did not learn everything her husband knew – far from it. This does not seem to have been the consequence of a lack of trust though. Whenever Eelco van Kleffens wanted to share things with his wife, he clearly felt free to do so, as did others. However, the sharing was their privilege, not hers. She did not have a right to political updates or involvement, as is visible from her frustration with the lack of information from her husband and her evident pleasure and pride at a male official discussing events with her and taking her advice. Still, it is worth noting that Dutch officials seem to have felt at liberty to talk openly to her about matters that they would have shared with her husband but would probably not have discussed outside the inner diplomatic circle of compatriots and allies. Primarily, Dutch diplomats confided in Margaret van Kleffens, but foreign diplomats with whom the couple was on good personal terms sometimes included her in their confidences. According to Van Kleffens, who described some of the political discussions in her diary, even if in general terms, the British diplomat Alexander Cadogan, was usually 'very outspoken' with her.[74] A relevant circumstance is that foreign diplomats with whom the couple were on friendly personal terms were always representatives of countries with whom the Netherlands had good relations. Political trust might not always have led to personal trust, but personal trust without political trust appears to have been unthinkable. The book's final part will return to the ways in which this made personal trust-building and the roles that wives played therein, politically expedient.

4 The diplomatic couple as template

Margaret van Kleffens dutifully performed her tasks as a diplomat's wife from her marriage in 1935 until her husband retired in 1967 (and in many ways long after that). In the privacy of her diary, she occasionally complained about her role – 'My role is little more than a harassed housekeeper, and every day is too short'[75] – but she did not question it or seem to consider it anything but natural. That was not changed by the fact that, over the years, she encountered people who were able to function (sometimes extraordinarily well) as diplomats without conforming to the model of diplomats being men married to women – women

---

[74] MvK diary 27 June 1946, inv nr 396, 2.05.86, NL-HaNA.
[75] MvK diary 16 September 1945, inv nr 395, 2.05.86, NL-HaNA.

who were diplomats in their own right, or male diplomats who were single. As Marcus Tullius Cicero put it more than 2,000 years ago, *exceptio probat regulam in casibus non exceptis* – the exception proves (or verifies) the rule in cases not excepted. Looking at those exceptions is one way to discern the norm of male-diplomat-with-female-spouse since it influenced everyday diplomacy and determined the margins for manoeuvre of those who deviated from it too.

Take Thanassis Aghnides, the Greek ambassador to London during the war, who was divorced. There is no evidence that Eelco and Margaret van Kleffens or others in the diplomatic community thought him lacking in the formal competences of a diplomat, such as education and language skills and his Dutch colleagues clearly found him both intelligent and sympathetic. Yet, the diary comments of Margaret van Kleffens speak of the Greek ambassador with pity, because he was so unfortunate as not to have a wife. Her comments are those of someone confident of having female expertise that he lacked and needed.

> Poor Aghnides has got possession of his own Embassy at last, having almost forcibly turned out Mme Simopoulos, widow of his predecessor ... It is a large, unpractical, Victorian and quite frightful building in Upper Brook street. I say "poor" Aghnides – he is *so* helpless, and obviously being diddled + robbed on all sides by his domestics. Man-like, he has arranged *one* room as his den, and there he sleeps, works and sits. I'll try and find him a butler + housekeeper of which he's in sore need.[76]

Aghnides comes across as having had difficulty asserting himself vis-à-vis both his predecessor's widow and his domestic staff. Since he was too 'man-like' to make appropriate living arrangements, Margaret van Kleffens decided to lend him a hand. The fact that she took it upon herself to assist him shows that it was not his emotional well-being or love life that concerned her (even if she may have worried about that too) but his ability to manage his everyday social diplomatic life.

The effects of the gendered division of tasks in diplomatic practices become even more visible in relation to other forms of help that Margaret van Kleffens offered Thanassis Aghnides. On a couple of occasions, the wife of the Foreign Minister of the Netherlands acted as hostess at Greek embassy lunches, to help out her friend.[77] Evidently, Margaret van Kleffens could temporarily represent

---

[76] MvK diary 8 February 1943, inv nr 393, 2.05.86, NL-HaNA. For more on Thanassis Aghnides, see Haakon A. Ikonomou, *The International Bureaucrat in the Twentieth Century – A Global Biography of Thanassis Aghnides*, London: Palgrave Macmillan (forthcoming).

[77] MvK diary 16 June 1944, inv nr 393, and 17 August 1945, inv nr 395, 2.05.86, NL-HaNA.

another state without anyone objecting. Besides giving away how indispensable they were for the display of hospitality, this shows that women had a more fluid position in the diplomatic world than men did. Even a permanent switch of allegiance seems to have been unproblematic for at least some women. Certain nationalities or a complexion that did not match that of their husbands could be an obstacle, but most upper-class women could, by marrying a diplomat, become readily accepted as a trustworthy representative of their husband's country. The ex-wife of Aghnides, Hellé née Zervoudaki, remarried Henri Bonnet, the French politician who between 1944 and 1954 was ambassador to the United States.[78] This example is particularly interesting since Hellé Zervoudaki was not only of Greek origin herself, but had also represented Greece as the wife of a Greek diplomat. With her divorce and remarriage, her switch from representing Greece to representing France seems to have been readily accepted. In July 1946, the French magazine *Elle* wrote that Madame Hellé Bonnet was not only the wife of the French ambassador in Washington; she was also 'the ambassadress of French taste in the United States'.[79] The former Greek was not merely tolerated, she was seen to have embodied French taste and excelled at representing her new country. According to Margaret van Kleffens, Hellé Bonnet was the most efficient ambassadress in Washington, DC.[80]

As long as a woman was perceived as loyal to her husband, a change in her national loyalty seems to have been unproblematic – perhaps even irrelevant. Apparently, Margaret van Kleffens could temporarily step in as hostess at the Greek embassy without casting doubts on her loyalty either to her husband or her country. Hellé Bonnet's permanent switch of loyalty to France seems to have been taken for granted after her marriage to a French diplomat. Partly, this says something about the transnational character of the diplomatic elite. On the one hand, diplomats represented different national governments. On the other hand, Western diplomatic culture transcended national borders, giving diplomatic communities an identity of their own. Diplomats were part of an international upper-class community, one to which the Zervoudaki family belonged. However, transnational ties between elite families and the international character of the diplomatic community did not allow men to change their national allegiance.

[78] MvK diary 3 April 1946, inv nr 395, 2.05.86, NL-HaNA.
[79] My translation. 'Mme Hellé Bonnet n'est pas seulement la femme de M. Henri Bonnet, ambassadeur de France à Washington, elle est l'ambassadrice du goût francais aux Etats-Unis.' Hélène Gordon-Lazareff, ed., 'Mme Bonnet a Emporté Paris Dans Sa Valise-Avion', *Elle – L'hebdomadaire de La Femme* 1946 (23 July 1946): 4. Thanks to Haakon Ikonomou who shared this article with me.
[80] MvK diary 24 & 26 February 1949, inv nr 400, 2.05.86, NL-HaNA.

The possibility to transcend national barriers was gendered. It would have been unthinkable for a man of a different nationality to join Margaret van Kleffens during one of her husband's absences to help her represent the Netherlands; a man who married a foreign woman retained his own nationality.

To put it crudely, women were indispensable but replaceable. Although the lack of a wife was a handicap in everyday diplomatic practices, widowed, divorced or unmarried men could still have careers as diplomats, as long as they did not challenge the template of the heterosexual couple. Among other things, that meant that they needed some other woman to step in as hostess, usually a female relative or a colleague's wife.[81] As shown above, even a foreign woman married to someone else could do the honours if required. The situation was similar if a married diplomat's wife became ill or, for other reasons, could not fulfil her hostess duties. For instance, right before a tea she was supposed to give in honour of Javanese princess and actress Maria Soenario Wiranata Kusuma, Margaret van Kleffens came down with a bad cold and had to stay in bed.[82] Without further ado, Aimée Reuchlin, Norwegian-born wife of another high-ranking diplomat at the Netherlands Embassy in Washington took her place as hostess, assisted by Margaret van Kleffens's sister, Dicky Wilson, British by marriage, who happened to be visiting. Mrs Wilson also went to a lunch in her sister's stead. A salient detail is a newspaper clipping that Margaret van Kleffens pasted in her diary (name and date of paper not visible) which reported that 'Princess Soenario was honored at a tea by Mme. van Kleffens, wife of the Netherlands ambassador'.[83] In public, it apparently did not always matter if a wife was present in person or by proxy.

For female diplomats, the strength of the heterosexual couple-norm had other consequences. Many countries had a marriage bar which forced women to leave the service if they got married and even those who were married could not rely on their husbands to help them with their social tasks. The heterosexual norm was not only about reserving sexual and marital relations for persons of the opposite biological sex, but about the appropriate gendering of those relations. In the world of mid-twentieth century diplomacy women could, in exceptional cases, be perceived as suitable for a man's job, but a man could never

---

[81] Biltekin, *Servants of Diplomacy*, 183.
[82] I have opted to maintain the Dutch spelling used at the time of all Indonesian names but would like to note here that the 'oe' has later often been replaced by 'u', Sunario in this case. There may be different spellings of her other names too. This is good to know for anyone who wants to do an Internet search, for example.
[83] MvK diary 24 May 1948, inv nr 398, 2.05.86, NL-HaNA.

take on the tasks normally done by a woman. Consequently, as already discussed in Chapter 1, a female diplomat had to take on the role of both diplomat and spouse. Any assistance in household duties would have to come from another woman (whether staff or family) and could never include acting as a dinner partner. Couples were always male–female and a man accompanying a woman was not seated according to her rank – not even if he was married to her (as in the case of the American ambassador to Denmark 1949–1953 Eugenie Anderson and her husband mentioned in Chapter 1).

The different consequences for men and women who did not fit the template of the diplomatic heterosexual couple (male diplomat with female spouse) reveal a few things about the view of homosexuality in mid-twentieth century elite transnational circles. For one, it points to the fact that female homosexuality was a non-topic. Single female diplomats did not cause rumours regarding their sexuality, while single male diplomats were often suspected of being gay. While male diplomats needed a woman at their side not only for her assistance but also to counter such rumours, female diplomats did not need a man as a heterosexual alibi. Another point worth making is that homosexuality was not necessarily viewed as problematic, as long as men kept their sexual preferences private and in public acted according to the heterosexual norm. In 2003, Sverker Åström, a Swedish career diplomat from 1939 to 1982, publicly came out as a homosexual at the age of 87. According to him, he had lived between two worlds and had been able to function well as a diplomat by acting as if the gay world did not exist as long as he was among diplomats. The bigger problem, according to Åström, was that homosexuals could become security risks: in a world where homosexuality was not only considered morally wrong but was also illegal, they could be vulnerable to extortion. In his own case, Åström said in an interview, he had neutralized the threat of blackmail by telling his superiors – Swedish foreign minister Östen Undén and the consecutive Prime Ministers Tage Erlander and Olof Palme – that he was gay.[84]

While it is conceivable that other diplomats' superiors would have reacted differently, the fact that Undén, Erlander and Palme were aware of Åström's sexual orientation and did not make a problem of it is in line with the attitude towards homosexuality that comes across in Margaret van Kleffens's diaries: it was fine as long as it was kept out of sight. By 'fine' I do not mean approved of, just that it was accepted as a fact of life. In her diaries, Margaret van Kleffens often referred to homosexuals – in her world always men – as 'pansies', a

---

[84] Thomas Lerner, '"Mina chefer visste att jag var gay"', *Dagens Nyheter*, 24 January 2006.

derogatory expression that she used as a matter-of-fact term, regardless of whether she liked them. That a person was (believed to be) homosexual did not necessarily influence her professional judgement of him individually in a negative way, nor did it, as a rule, result in a personal sense of superiority or the desire to keep her distance. Even though, officially, homosexuality was cause for exclusion from public service, she never coupled her comments about (possible) homosexuality to comments about unsuitability for the job. In her diary she just occasionally mentioned that she had heard, or suspected herself, that a particular politician or diplomat was 'of the wrong direction'.[85]

Men who never married were often suspected to be homosexuals, especially if they also displayed good taste and an interest in interior decoration or clothes. One example is Dag Hammarskjöld, for whose competences Margaret van Kleffens had little but praise, calling him 'sunny, engaging and brilliantly clever'.[86] Having dined at his New York apartment in 1954, she noted in her diary that he had decorated his apartment himself 'in modern Swedish style', adding in shorthand – her language for secrets – that she suspected him of being 'one of pansies'. Returning to normal English, she went on to say that he was 'charming, cheerful, gifted, sporting, highly intelligent'.[87] Clearly, her high opinion of him was not negatively influenced by her belief that he might be homosexual, but it did cause her to be very careful not to express her suspicion openly. Hammarskjöld was not the only man suspected of homosexuality because he was single in combination with having abilities that were coded as feminine. In 1953, Margaret van Kleffens noted with surprise that their Belgian former colleague in Washington, DC, the 59-year-old ambassador Baron Robert Silvercruys, had married. 'He was generally thought to be a pansy', she wrote in her diary, 'on account of his uncommonly exquisite taste and his long bachelorhood'.[88]

In the period treated in this book, same-sex sexual intercourse was still criminalized in many Western countries and treated as an abnormality that was condemnable. However, Margaret van Kleffens and many of her upper-class contemporaries seem to have viewed homosexuality simply as a fact of life. Even if many people did not personally have a problem with homosexuals though, they did speak of them as being on the 'wrong' side in a matter-of-fact way. It

---

[85] Margaret van Kleffens quoted her husband saying this in Dutch – 'van de verkeerde richting' – about American former diplomat Clarence Bussey Hewes, MvK diary 26 July 1946, inv nr 396, 2.05.86, NL-HaNA.
[86] MvK diary 22 June 1948, inv nr 398, 2.05.86, NL-HaNA.
[87] MvK diary 30 September 1954, inv nr 405, 2.05.86, NL-HaNA. Steno deciphered with the generous aid of Monique van Kessel at the Netherlands Institute of War Documentation (NIOD).
[88] MvK diary 25 September 1953, inv nr 404, 2.05.86, NL-HaNA.

went without saying that those in office who were homosexual must behave according to the heterosexual template. People who were openly homosexual or whose homosexuality became a known fact (rather than remaining a public secret) could not hold office. That does not mean that Eelco and Margaret van Kleffens privately rejected individuals who were known homosexuals. One of Eelco van Kleffens's oldest friends, Leopold Ries, had been a successful Treasurer General at the Ministry of Finances until a scandal in 1936 publicly revealed his homosexuality, which cost him his job and caused him to decide to leave the Netherlands in 1937 (considering that he was also Jewish, this might have been a blessing in disguise). In 1941, he ended up in New York City, where Eelco van Kleffens got him a job at a Dutch-language radio station broadcasting from the United States during the war. While barred from being a civil servant, behind the scenes Ries remained a frequent and appreciated visitor who advised his old student-friend Eelco van Kleffens on all sorts of matters. During the Van Kleffens's stays in New York (1946–1947) and Washington (1947–1950), Ries also became a close friend of his wife, who grew very fond of him and praised his erudite wit. Both Eelco and Margaret van Kleffens corresponded with Leopold Ries after they left the United States until his death in 1962.[89] In the lengthy, grief-stricken diary entry that Margaret van Kleffens wrote about him after the news of his passing, there is no mention of his homosexuality.[90]

The naturalness of the norm (diplomats and other officials were males supported by female spouses) seems not to have been shaken by Margaret van Kleffens's occasional encounters with (and respect for) people who did not fit the template. That went for closeted homosexual men as well as for women in positions of political authority of their own, such as Eleanor Roosevelt and Vijaya Lakshmi Pandit. It is well to remember that these women, too, at least in part owed their position to their relationship with a man and, therefore, perhaps did not threaten but rather confirmed the idea of how women could reach a position of power: Mrs Roosevelt was married to the American president and Mrs Pandit was the sister of Jawaharlal Nehru, the Indian prime minister. The way these women advanced in their careers was certainly thanks to their own abilities but, as in the case of Eelco van Kleffens or anyone else, getting the chance in the first place required a certain background.

While gender was an important dividing line in the diplomatic world and one that determined the behaviour of everyone within that world (even powerful

---

[89] Letters from Leopold Ries, some addressed only to her, some to her and her husband together, can be found in MvK diaries, inv nrs 402–413, 2.05.86, NL-HaNA. Ries also visited them in Portugal.
[90] MvK diary 10 July 1962, inv nr 414, 2.05.86, NL-HaNA.

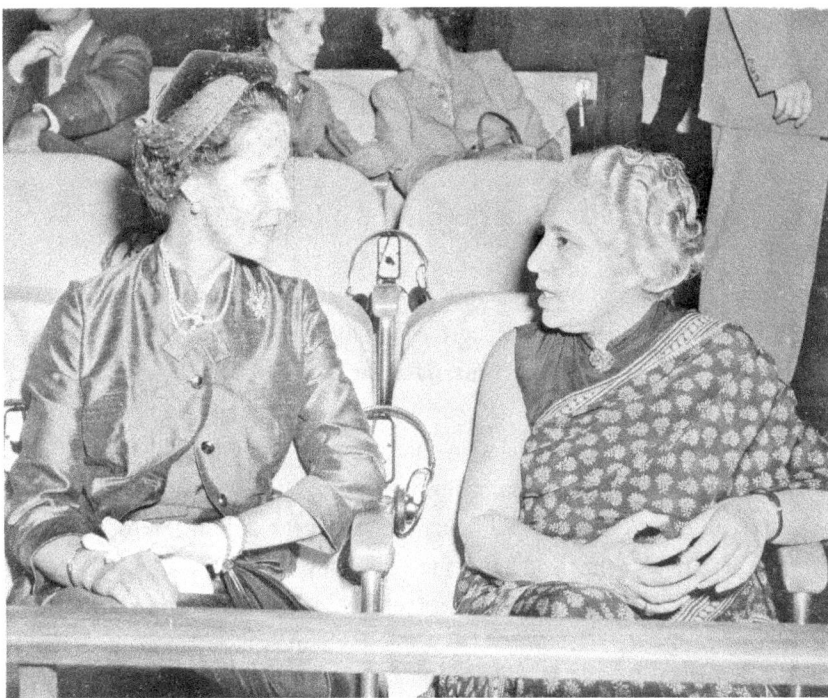

Figure 1.3 Margaret van Kleffens with Vijaya Lakshmi Pandit at the United Nations General Assembly of 30 September 1954. Photo: Bettman/Getty images. From the original caption: 'Mrs. Eelco Van Kleffens (left), wife of Holland's Dr. Eelco Van Kleffens, president of the UN General Assembly, and Madame Vijaya Lakshmi Pandit of India, sit together during a meeting of the United Nations General Assembly at New York. Madame Pandit served as General Assembly President before Van Kleffens took over for the current session.' Diary description by Margaret van Kleffens: 'I sat beside Mme Pandit and we had to face a battery of floods + cameras for several minutes, making (strained) conversation as requested.' MvK diary, 30 September 1954, inv nr 405, 2.05.86, NL-HaNA.

women like Roosevelt and Pandit could not act the same way as powerful men), racialized and classed norms were even stronger mechanisms of exclusion and inclusion (more on which later). Tracing women who gained power in diplomacy means to 'start royal and work your way down' as Susan Harris Rimmer puts it: the first women to make it to independent positions of power in the diplomatic world gained their legitimacy from their aristocratic status or other connections and, in most countries, the first women ambassadors were political appointments while it took much longer for female career diplomats to reach higher ranks.[91]

---

[91] Harris Rimmer, 'Women as Makers of International Law', 33–34.

The existence of female figures of power, then, did not in itself necessarily challenge the general rule that women could gain influence by virtue of their specific feminine qualities and their relation to men.

Concluding remarks on the diplomatic couple

Rather than criticizing the division of tasks between men and women, Margaret van Kleffens, like many wives, took pride in doing the work well that she accepted as her duty. Although before her marriage she had worked as a secretary at her father's company and during the war was occasionally bored and considered getting a job, she always concluded that it would be impossible to combine outside work with her tasks as a diplomat's wife. It is worth noting that she apparently did not count the voluntary work that she did during the war. Like many other Dutch women in exile, she actually worked quite a lot outside her own household, at the Dutch Red Cross refugee clothing depot on North Row.[92] Still, she wrote in her diary in 1943 that she was 'acutely aware of my uselessness in the war-effort. But – what can I do? I feel strongly that my first duty is to provide a well-run house for E.'[93] What a well-run diplomat's house meant in practice and why the home was crucial to diplomatic work is the theme of Part II. Suffice it here to say that daily diplomacy in the mid-twentieth century could not have functioned as it did without the efforts of women like Margaret van Kleffens. The acceptance of women's roles as different from and, at least in some ways, inferior to the roles played by men did not imply a conviction that all men were better or more competent than women, only that male and female competences involved different characteristics. When Margaret van Kleffens did find a way to make herself more useful to the war effort, only a few months after the note quoted above, it was in the shape of more unpaid work at 'a Lady Russell's, who has a sub-contract from a war factory for making teleprinter terminal units and other electrical gadgets for bombers and tanks'.[94]

Margaret van Kleffens often distanced herself from other women, writing in her diary for example that 'the company of my sex, unless friends, means little to me as such, being largely lacking in grey matter'.[95] This reveals how she reconciled

---

[92] First mentioned in MvK 1941 account, inv nr 391; see also MvK 4 & 15 January, 19 February, 5 March, 16, 19, 27 & 30 April, 21 May 1943, inv nr 392, and also in inv nr 393 and 394, 2.05.86, NL-HaNA.
[93] MvK diary 18 March 1943, inv nr 392, 2.05.86, NL-HaNA.
[94] MvK diary 8 July 1943, inv nr 393, 2.05.86, NL-HaNA.
[95] MvK diary 15 August 1947, inv nr 397, 2.05.86, NL-HaNA.

Figure 1.4 Margaret van Kleffens (left) at work for the Dutch Red Cross at North Row in London during the war, together with two other wives of important Dutch officials: Henriëtte Michiels van Verduynen (in the background), wife of the Dutch ambassador (first name Edgar) and Helen Zorab (right), wife of a judge of the Java High Court in the Netherlands East Indies (first name also Edgar). November 1943. Photo: Anefo. London Series/HIE (Holland in England). Courtesy of the Netherlands National Archives, The Hague.

a personal character that indicated otherwise with the notion that women, in general, were not suitable for intellectual work. She painted a picture of herself as different from most women, the exception that confirmed the rule in cases not excepted. There was no doubt an element of pragmatism, accepting things that seemed unchangeable (for example, inequality being part of how the world worked). Looking back in 1987, Van Kleffens wrote in her diary that the idea of equality was a myth, born during the Second World War and dear to many, but a myth nonetheless. The comparison she made testifies to her roots in the world of international relations. 'Wherever we are in today's world,' she wrote, 'we are all supposed to be equal. Not just as to opportunity, or before the law, but in every way. Naturally this is as much balderdash as it is to give Mali the same vote in the United Nations as the U.S.A.'[96]

While most people would agree that small states have less power and play their roles in international relations differently than big ones, few would argue that they are therefore irrelevant to international relations. When it comes to women, however, it is very common to dismiss their roles in diplomacy on the grounds that they were less powerful than men or did not have access to particular political arenas. But analyses of diplomacy that do not take gender into account miss not only women's influence by sheer numbers. They miss a fundamental aspect of how the whole system of diplomatic relations was organized, which limits their explanatory reach. Research on diplomacy that does take gender into account must not limit its focus to the exceptional women who were able to exercise power in public rather than behind the scenes. Helen McCarthy points out that while well-connected aristocratic women had previously been able to wield political influence, by the late nineteenth century the diplomatic profession excluded women.[97] While that is true, it does not mean that women disappeared from diplomatic practices until the female diplomat appeared in the mid-twentieth century or, that after that, women only played a diplomatic role as diplomats (as McCarthy indeed also points out in her book). Relegating women to the private sphere did not mean that they could play no role in diplomacy, but that they could play a certain role – one that men, in turn, could not play. Recognizing the political importance of the (ostensibly) private is crucial to understanding how diplomacy worked in practice in the mid-twentieth century as Part II will show. That recognition makes visible the couple as a fundamental unit of diplomatic practices and gender as a cornerstone of day-to-day diplomacy. The rest of this book unpacks how diplomatic practices were structured as personal politics around the heterosexual couple as a unit of male diplomat–female spouse.

---

[96] MvK diary 13 August 1987, inv nr 422, 2.05.86, NL-HaNA.
[97] McCarthy, *Women of the World*, 5–6.

Part Two

The Diplomatic Home

Figure 2.1 Drawing room of the Dutch embassy/residence in Washington, DC, May 1948. Photo: private, MvK diary 20 May 1948, inv nr 398, 2.05.86, NL-HaNA. Photographer unknown, but possibly Margaret van Kleffens herself. Courtesy of the Netherlands National Archives, The Hague, with permission of the Van Kleffens family.

Throughout the modern era, the homes of envoys have been important sites of diplomatic work, but research on twentieth-century diplomats seldom treats them as diplomatic arenas. Biographical works which pay attention to diplomats' personal assets and efforts sometimes mention homes – pointing out the size, stylishness and neighbourhood of a residence, for instance, or exhibiting it as a stage for family matters – but analyses of the diplomatic functions of homes are rare, even if servants, houseguests, and dinner parties come up as matters of fact.[1] Why? Studies of Early Modern diplomatic practices recognize homes as sites of political work.[2] Do changing perceptions and presentations of the home reflect complete changes in its functions?

Yes and no. In Iver Neumann's study of diplomats' daily work, which focuses primarily on the late twentieth and early twenty-first centuries, the homes of diplomats only appear in a discussion of the tensions between home and work: the difficulties of combining diplomatic work with caring responsibilities for example, and the necessity of upholding boundaries between work life and private life.[3] These concerns seem to distinguish modern diplomats clearly from those of the Early Modern period (when it would rarely have made sense to separate work life from private life). However, while separate spheres did rise as an ideal among some people in some places in the eighteenth century, that ideal was not all-encompassing nor were its effects clear-cut.[4] When it comes to diplomacy, Rogério de Souza Farias has pointed out that, as late as the early twentieth century, the dichotomy between work and home as gendered spaces was less straightforward than in other areas because diplomatic residences and embassies were often housed in a single building. At the same time, in his study of 1920s Brazilian diplomacy he asserts that an increasing separation of home as a shielded, private space and the office as an impersonal one led to 'a spatial culture of social circulation that relegated women to apolitical roles'.[5]

Considering the general image of nineteenth century homes as increasingly private and women as their apolitical inhabitants, it is unsurprising that twentieth century diplomats' homes share the fate of diplomats' wives: if research on diplomats' work mentions them at all, it is usually only in passing. No surprise either that twentieth-century studies on diplomats' wives tend to highlight the diplomatic value of work done in diplomats' homes.[6] Being married to a diplomat

---

[1] See, eg, van der Maar and Meijer, *Herman van Roijen 1905–1991*, 271, 276.
[2] See, eg, Peter Lindström and Svante Norrhem, 'Diplomats and Kin Networks: Diplomatic Strategy and Gender in Sweden, 1648–1740', in *Gender and Political Culture in Early Modern Europe, 1400–1800*, edited by James Daybell and Svante Norrhem] (Abingdon & New York: Routledge, 2017), 68–86.
[3] Iver B Neumann, *At Home with the Diplomats: Inside a European Foreign Ministry* (Ithaca: Cornell University Press, 2012), 102–7.
[4] For an instructive overview and discussion of the intertwined history of private and public, both as realities and as theoretical concepts, see Sari Nauman and Helle Vogt, 'The Private in the Public: Scandinavia in the Eighteenth Century', in *Private/Public in 18th-Century Scandinavia*, ed. Sari Nauman and Helle Vogt (London: Bloomsbury Academic, 2021), 1–16.
[5] Rogério de Souza Farias, '"Do You Wish Her to Marry?" Brazilian Women and Professional Diplomacy, 1918–1938', *Diplomacy & Statecraft* 28, no 1 (2 January 2017): 46.
[6] Molly M Wood, '"Commanding Beauty" and "Gentle Charm": American Women and Gender in the Early Twentieth-Century Foreign Service', *Diplomatic History* 31, no 3 (2007): 505–30; N Biltekin, 'The Diplomatic Partnership: Gender, Materiality and Performance in the Case of Sweden c. 1960s–1980s'. *Genesis* XI, no 1–2 (2012): 253–65.

did not bring access to negotiating tables and spouses did not sign any of the treaties and declarations that make up the dominant paper trail for descriptions of the international reorganization of the post-war world. The vast majority of spouses, however, were the undisputed rulers of diplomatic homes. Sometimes, that home was located in the embassy building, which played an official and public role as a setting for social events. This applies to the Dutch Washington embassy, where Eelco and Margaret van Kleffens lived from 1947–1950. Often though, diplomats' residences were separate from their official workplaces. This part focuses on the diplomatic functions of the diplomatic home and the behind-the-scenes work those functions required.

Whatever the variations, which depended on the post, the type of residence and the circumstances of the day and place, all mid-twentieth century diplomatic homes were sites of work which had a bearing on diplomatic relations. Sometimes, that work involved obvious public relations management associated with soft power diplomacy, such as receiving journalists at home or giving embassy tours. However, in addition to those high-profile functions, all diplomats' homes were centres of diplomatic activity for which the wives were primarily responsible: the decoration and equipment of a representative home, the administration of invitations and hosting of house guests, the heading of a household staff, and (overseeing) the care and training of any children and pets. I argue that it is a mistake to dismiss these tasks and the sphere of home as politically irrelevant. For some crucial diplomatic work, there was no place like home.

Placing the daily life of the Van Kleffenses under the microscope enables an understanding of what it took to run a diplomat's house and why it was crucial to diplomatic relations. It reveals patterns of everyday concerns and behaviour and features well-known, as well as overlooked, actors, allowing an assessment of the functions and value of homes in mid-twentieth century diplomacy. The part has three empirical focus points. To begin with, a survey of what preoccupied the couple – him, her, or both – as they planned and moved to their first home sheds light on determining characteristics of diplomatic homemaking. Chapter 5 engages with the ideas and realities of separate male-female spheres. Chapter 6 discusses the role of domestic staff, an overlooked but critical factor for the functioning of daily diplomatic practices. It touches on how servants could play symbolic as well as practical roles, while attention for wives as heads of staff complicates the notion that women were kept out of leadership roles. Chapter 7 analyzes the empirical evidence for the ways in which the home became an arena for diplomatic interaction. Who visited whose house and what diplomatic significance did an invitation to someone's home have, as compared to a meeting somewhere else? This chapter explores the interaction between the public and private spheres; between formal diplomatic actors and pronouncedly informal, non-political actors and aspects of a diplomat's life, such as children and other family members and pets.

5 Homemaking for diplomats

During the courtship described in Chapter 2, when Eelco van Kleffens wooed Margaret Horstmann with images of the exciting future they would have together, he evoked an idyllic picture of the couple's future home. In one of his letters, he described how he dreamed that they would live at Oud Clingendaal – an upper-class neighbourhood in The Hague associated with the international elite – where together they would entertain Dutch diplomats as well as 'bind the sympathies of foreigners to this country'.[7] Though breathing the allure of a romantic daydream this proved a realistic ambition. Even Eelco van Kleffens's proviso that it would probably take some time to realize (for financial reasons) seems to have been overly cautious: the newlyweds moved into a flat right on the corner of the Clingendaal Park.[8] The modern and luxurious apartment building, built just a few years earlier in the Dutch architectural style called The New Hague School (Nieuwe Haagse School), was characterized by straight lines and cubist shapes.[9] For the head of Diplomatic Affairs, it meant abandoning his bachelor's abode on Daendelstraat 10, where he had rented a floor in a tailor's house. The tailor doubled as Van Kleffens's valet.[10]

Between her 22nd birthday on 6 September 1934, when Margaret Horstmann agreed to marry him, and their wedding day on 4 April 1935, the dreamy visions Eelco van Kleffens had painted of their future home turned into down-to-earth discussions regarding its practical arrangements. The number of letters exchanged between them dropped significantly after their engagement – presumably, the couple from then on discussed most of the arrangements in

---

[7] Letter from Eelco van Kleffens to Margaret Horstmann, 2 May 1934, inv nr 434, 2.05.86, NL-HaNA.
[8] Home address (Duinwijck flat 116, van Alkemadelaan 350 in The Hague) found on letters from 1937 and 1938, inv nrs 439 & 440, 2.05.86, NL-HaNA.
[9] The building is described on the site of The Hague Monumentenzorg (responsible for the conservation of monuments in the Netherlands) as a typical example of the New Hague School. 'Van Alkemadelaan 350, Ruychrocklaan 171', in *Monumentenzorg Den Haag*, 19 December 1993. Available at: www.monumentenzorgdenhaag.nl/monumenten/van-alkemadelaan-350-ruychrocklaan-171 (accessed 29 June 2021).
[10] E N van Kleffens, *Belevenissen I, 1894–1940*, (Alphen aan de Rijn: AW Sijthoff, 1980), 232.

person.[11] However, the couple continued to correspond by letter when they were apart for a few days (to the historian's delight). As the date of their wedding drew nearer, his letters (hers of this period are unfortunately lost) testify not only to their discussions on bridal wear, wish lists, and nuptial administration and arrangements, but also to counting pots, pans and trivets and renovating and importing suitable furniture and fabrics.[12]

A month before the wedding, Margaret Horstmann went to Brussels with her mother, where her fiancé joined them a few days later. Between her departure from The Hague on 3 March and his arrival in Brussels on 7 March, he wrote her five letters. Besides giving his fiancée the names and addresses of two diplomats' wives in Brussels whom she should contact if she wanted help, Eelco van Kleffens kept her in the loop on the ongoing refurbishment of their future home, told her what bills had been sent and what he had paid, and mentioned a variety of other household issues. A request that she make sure to get the required 'certificate d'origine' for the items that were subject to import restrictions reveals that the goal of the trip to Brussels was to shop for home furnishings. He even attached a list of the tariff rules 'with reference to those kinds of articles you are most interested in'. This included blankets, furniture, carpets, bedding, table linen, many different kinds of fabrics, lace and embroideries, and specified that there was no quota for lamps and mattresses.[13] The other letters are full of comments on furniture, curtains, table- and glassware, as well as carpentry issues and the overall renovation of their future home. These extensive and specific reports reveal that together, they planned a household which would be nicely decorated down to the last detail and which anticipated the demands of diplomatic entertaining. For instance, Eelco van Kleffens wrote about having been dissuaded from indoor thresholds (on account of their being serving obstacles, it would seem), suggested a Meissner crockery set for 18 people as suitable for their needs and worried about how to decide which cook to pick out of the no less than six who had responded to their advertisement. He identified one of them as 'my Minister's cook'.[14]

---

[11] The exception is a surge of letters in September 1934, since Eelco van Kleffens had to go away for work immediately after their engagement and they did not officially announce it until he was back. After that, the archive only contains three more letters from 1934. Inv nr 437, 2.05.86, NL-HaNA.
[12] A total of seven letters from Eelco van Kleffens to Margaret Horstmann January to March 1935, inv nr 438, 2.05.86, NL-HaNA.
[13] Second letter from Eelco van Kleffens to Margaret Horstmann (of two) on 5 March 1935, inv nr 438, 2.05.86, NL-HaNA.
[14] Letters from Eelco van Kleffens to Margaret Horstmann 3, 4, 5, and 6 March 1935, inv nr 438, 2.05.86, NL-HaNA.

This archived fragment of an evidently ongoing discussion provides enough information to draw at least three conclusions. First, the household was a matter of high importance; it took hard work as well as a substantial amount of money to create a good diplomat's home. The reference to asking other diplomats' wives for advice testifies to this being the normal state of affairs among diplomats, showing that the Van Kleffenses conformed to a pattern. That the cook of the Foreign Minister (Andries Cornelis Dirk de Graeff) had apparently applied for the job as the Van Kleffens's cook also indicates that they had similar sorts of household. Second, good homemaking was important to men as well as women and the future spouses shared all the different types of concerns about the household. Eelco van Kleffens paid the bills, but he kept his fiancée up-to-date on the financial side of things and his own involvement was by no means restricted to financial concerns. He wrote to his future wife about the pros and cons of specific pieces of furniture and told her that he had personally counted the delivered glassware, for example. There is no indication that his interest in the specifics of the household was out of the ordinary – on the contrary. His matter-of-fact account of how his boss, Secretary General Snouck Hurgronje, had tipped him off about an available set of crockery shows that it was perfectly normal for tableware to come up in a conversation between two male diplomats. Third, although the couple acted as a team, there were gendered divisions of the practical tasks concerning the home and household. The letters show that while Eelco van Kleffens was deeply involved in and concerned about household matters, he treated them as an area of expertise where his future wife had the final say. The comment that he had adjusted his tariff list to the items that most interested her points to her privilege in choosing household items, as does the fact that he left it up to her to decide whether to get the Meissner or a Rosenthal set of crockery. That she would be in charge of household staff is indicated by his complaint that the procedure for making sure one hired the best cook was 'quite beyond me'.[15]

That Eelco van Kleffens valued the importance of running a home and recognized that it needed female expertise is consistent with the image of the divorced diplomat that surfaced in the previous chapter: if we are to believe Margaret van Kleffens, running a household was a job that male diplomats without wives were notoriously bad at. Her 1943 diary comments on Greek ambassador Thanassis Aghnides described him as easy prey for disloyal domestics and his poor residence organizing as 'man-like'. She perceived her own

---

[15] First letter from Eelco van Kleffens to Margaret Horstmann (of two) on 5 March 1935, inv nr 438, 2.05.86, NL-HaNA.

skills as superior in this particular regard.¹⁶ The comments of both Eelco and Margaret van Kleffens not only point to a gendered division of tasks, but to another crucial fact about the diplomatic home: it required personnel. As a bachelor, Eelco van Kleffens had a landlord who acted as his valet, and a fully-fledged diplomatic home had several household staff members. The important diplomatic role of servants is discussed below and the importance of a good cook is a topic for Part III. Before moving on to the people of the household, however, the story of homemaking is not complete without a few words on housing and moving.

The available sources do not reveal how Eelco van Kleffens and Margaret Horstmann found their first flat on the Alkemadelaan, but there is plenty of information about their subsequent house hunting, which, despite its particulars, provides an insight into the conditions of diplomatic housing in general. Sometimes, the house came with the job. In 1938, the couple was preparing for the ambassadorship to Switzerland, where they would have taken over the residence from the previous ambassadorial couple, Alexander and Betty Loudon.¹⁷ However, on the verge of their departure in August 1939, Prime Minister Dirk Jan de Geer asked Eelco van Kleffens to become Minister of Foreign Affairs, a fateful turn of events. His acceptance not only meant that the couple moved to the Foreign Minister's official residence at the Voorhout 38 in The Hague instead of to Berne, but also that, only a few months later, they found themselves in exile in the United Kingdom. On 10 May 1940, the day of the German attack on the Netherlands, the government decided to send the Ministers of Foreign and of Colonial Affairs (Eelco van Kleffens and Charles Welter) abroad to ask for British and French help. In the considerable chaos of that day, Eelco van Kleffens was able to locate his wife in time for their hurried departure and bring her along. After a short but dramatic flight under German gunfire, ending in their fuel-leaking seaplane making an emergency landing off the coast of Brighton, the couple reached the United Kingdom with only half of their hastily packed suitcases.¹⁸ There, the matter of housing became a recurring theme.

When they first arrived in London, Eelco and Margaret van Kleffens stayed at the hotel Carlton in Brook Street. Only a few days later, the rest of the ministers

---

¹⁶ MvK diary 8 February 1943, inv nr 393, 2.05.86, NL-HaNA.
¹⁷ Letter from Eelco van Kleffens to Margaret van Kleffens, 3 October 1938, inv nr 440, 2.05.86, NL-HaNA.
¹⁸ The couple told the story of their dramatic flight in Eelco Nicolaas van Kleffens, *The Rape of the Netherlands* (London: Hodder and Stoughton, 1940), 144–49; see also, among others for a comparison with other accounts of the event, S Erlandsson, 'Off the Record: Margaret van Kleffens and the Gendered History of Dutch World War II Diplomacy'. *International Feminist Journal of Politics* 21, no 1 (2019): 29–46, 38.

joined them. The Netherlands surrendered and a government-in-exile was established in London. Realizing that their stay was not likely to be brief, the Van Kleffenses decided to obtain a flat. At first, they moved to Queen Anne's Mansions, on the South side of St. James' Park, where service was included – good service, Margaret van Kleffens wrote in her 1941 account of their first year in exile, though the food was 'unfortunately very indifferent'.[19] They entertained at Queen Anne's 'in a small way': Eelco van Kleffens's colleagues occasionally came to dinner, as did 'other friends and acquaintances' and once Prince Bernhard (husband of the Dutch Crown Princess Juliana, who had moved on to Canada with her two young daughters). However, it was not ideal and, after only six weeks, the couple moved to a London flat lent to them by Margaret van Kleffens's sister Aileen Emilie Wilson (who, in her sister's diaries, went by the pet name 'Dicky'[20]) and British brother-in-law Raymond Wilson, who had themselves acquired a house in Virginia Water, outside London. The flat came complete with nice furnishings and a cook, saved expenses and was nicer for entertaining, Margaret van Kleffens wrote; yet, having a household of their own again depressed her. Being surrounded by other people's personal belongings reminded them of what they had lost: news had come that their property in the Netherlands had been confiscated by the Germans so that 'mentally we had taken a wretched leave of all our lovely things, collected with such love and care ever since we were married'.[21]

The circumstances of Eelco and Margaret van Kleffens were extraordinary because of the war but leaving things behind and starting over was part of ordinary diplomatic life. Even losing everything was not unique for people who moved every few years. In the only published memoirs by a contemporary Dutch diplomat's wife, Dé Buma describes how she and her husband, the Dutch diplomat Han Buma, lost all their belongings twice when moving from one posting to another – right after the war because the ship that carried their belongings hit a mine and was destroyed and a few years later because of a warehouse fire. Like Margaret van Kleffens, Dé Buma described a sense of devastation bordering on defeatism. After the second incident, she and her husband could hardly bear the idea of starting all over again and even decided to

---

[19] Margaret van Kleffens, 44-page typed account of experiences since 10 May 1940, dated January 1941, inv nr 391, 2.05.86, NL-HaNA. The introduction reveals that she wrote it on the suggestion of her husband, 'as a sort of private sequel' to *The Rape of the Netherlands*. The importance of good food is treated in more depth in the next chapter.

[20] Sometimes spelled Dickie, often simply D. According to Dicky's oldest son Clive Wilson, the nickname had to do with his mother having been a chubby child – 'dik' (pronounced 'dick') in Dutch meaning fat or chubby. E-mail from Clive Wilson to the author, 18 December 2019.

[21] Margaret van Kleffens, January 1941 account, inv nr 391, 2.05.86, NL-HaNA.

only rent furnished houses in the future.[22] They did not stick to that plan. As Margaret van Kleffens said: a private home was nicer for entertaining, and being able to entertain was important, even for a lower-ranked diplomatic couple like the Bumas in the 1940s. After only a month on their first posting after the second loss, in Stockholm, Sweden, Han and Dé Buma gave up the furnished house they had just rented and moved to a bigger house where they took on a new process of interior decoration, in order to be able to entertain more. The reason, Buma writes in her memoirs, was that the ambassador expected his embassy personnel to get to know all the important people quickly. To achieve that, you not only had to accept all invitations, but also invite people yourselves.[23]

Whatever their sentiments about it then, there were professional reasons to put great effort into homemaking. At the same time, what made homes a better place to entertain than full-service flats or hotels was precisely the fact that they were also personal, as the last empirical chapter of this part will highlight. In diplomatic homes, the sincerely personal and emotional was thoroughly entangled with the politically and rationally opportune. That made homemaking diplomatic work, hard work – all the harder because it was invested with personal emotions. A note that Margaret van Kleffens made after a day of housework with her sister in July 1945 gives an idea of how stressful that life could be.

> I was wondering today, as we rushed around, our hair tumbled and our noses sadly in need of powder, whether there will ever be leisure again in life. Shall we ever again live for at any rate part-time pleasure, make plans, have time to spend our days with some measure of grace, instead of being forever out of breath + trying to catch up, and always, moving, moving, moving – six months here, two years there, one year in the next place, ceaselessly on the go. When I find myself with an hour to spare, what do I do? I fritter it away, because I no longer can sit still on a chair and enjoy a book, having lost the habit of such gentle pursuits.[24]

The personal pressures of a diplomatic life did not only affect Margaret van Kleffens. Four months later, her husband on his 51st birthday had a breakdown so severe that his doctor ordered him to 'stop working at once and go away for a month'.[25] The couple went to Switzerland and eventually, Eelco van Kleffens resigned as Foreign Minister. Initially, her husband being overworked meant

---

[22] Dé Buma, *Donderdag Komt de Koerier. De Kleurrijke Levensreis van een Diplomatenvrouw* (Amsterdam: Van Soeren & Co, 2000), 81–82, 115.
[23] Buma, *Donderdag Komt de Koerier*, 120.
[24] MvK diary 12 July 1945, inv nr 395, 2.05.86, NL-HaNA.
[25] MvK diary 17 and 18 November 1945, inv nr 395, 2.05.86, NL-HaNA; Kleffens 1983, Belevenissen II, 124.

more work for Margaret van Kleffens. Since her husband's illness was announced publicly to explain his absence, she was faced with the added task of receiving all the people who made sympathy calls and explaining his 'enforced rest on medical advice'.[26] She also had to make travel arrangements and organize the care of the household during their absence. Once in Switzerland, however, she was elated. 'How infinitely pleasant is this life, without worry, servants, telephones and all the rest', she wrote in her diary.[27]

This much-needed slowing of pace was only temporary. By January, Eelco van Kleffens was back at work. Even though he exchanged his position as Foreign Minister for one as Minister without Portfolio, his work was soon as stressful as ever. From March 1946 he represented the Netherlands on the brand-new United Nations Security Council in New York and, from July 1947, he took on the arguably most important diplomatic post for the Netherlands of the postwar years: Washington, DC. Caught in the vortex of international criticism of the Netherlands' handling of the declaration of independence of their former colony Indonesia – the Netherlands' government decided to intervene militarily in July 1947 and again in December 1948 – this was hardly the calm posting Margaret van Kleffens would have wished for and which both she and her husband would have needed. Unsurprisingly, Eelco van Kleffens had a second breakdown in 1949 – only this time, the couple kept it a secret.[28] It is instead Margaret van Kleffens's health problems that have gone down in history as the sole cause for her husband's forfeiting a brilliant career by asking for a calmer post: in 1950, the couple left Washington for the ambassadorship to Portugal.[29]

The US ambassadorship had taken a toll on both of them: during their stay in New York City in 1946, she had been diagnosed with so-called essential hypertension (meaning that the hypertension had no identifiable cause), and her blood pressure rose dangerously when they were stationed in Washington.[30] If stress had anything to do with it, it is easy to understand why. Running a mid-twentieth century embassy in the United States was demanding and the couple did not get off to an easy start as the first Dutch military intervention in Indonesia

---

[26] MvK diary 20–21 November 1945, inv nr 395, 2.05.86, NL-HaNA.
[27] MvK diary 4 December 1945, inv nr 395, 2.05.86, NL-HaNA.
[28] MvK diary 2 October 1949, inv nr 400, 2.05.86, NL-HaNA.
[29] Erlandsson, 'Off the Record', 38; Bert Zeeman, 'Jurist of Diplomaat? Eelco Nicolaas van Kleffens (1939–1946)', in *De Nederlandse Ministers van Buitenlandse Zaken in de Twintigste Eeuw*, ed. Duco Hellema, Bert Zeeman, and Bert van der Zwan (Den Haag: SDU Uitgevers, 1999), 149.
[30] She was diagnosed in April 1946 and went from a systolic blood pressure fluctuating between 160–170 during April 1947, before leaving New York City, to 190 the day after arrival in Washington, DC and surging to 218 a few months later. MvK diary 11 April 1946, inv nr 395; 1, 8, 15, 22 & 29 April 1947, inv nr 396; 23 July and 6 December 1947, inv nr 397, 2.05.86, NL-HaNA.

was announced during their very journey to Washington. 'The place was like a madhouse', Margaret van Kleffens wrote, describing the hectic days of moving into the Washington residence:

> The Hague ringing up ten times a day; our house phone not functioning properly; our furniture arriving, with attendant breakages and losses; the servants, all eight of them, asking questions; the carpenter, the electrician, milling around, wanting instructions, Jansen barking furiously.... A blessing it is that Rosa [the cook] works on her own, so I don't have to think about meals and only need to see her as occasion offers.[31]

This image of setting up a diplomatic home shows it as an intersection of dealing with politics, practical housekeeping and private family matters (here represented by Jansen the dog). Household staff, depicted in this diary entry both as a management burden and as providers of relief, played an indispensable role in this mix.

6 Domestic staff

Considering the frequency with which servants are the topic of diplomatic actors' letters and diary notes, the lack of research on household staff as a factor of diplomatic culture is astonishing.[32] In Margaret van Kleffens's diary, comments about servants range from articulations of indignant despair about their incompetence or inappropriate behaviour and complaints about the difficulty of finding good staff to expressions of grateful admiration for servants' excellence and family-like concern for their welfare. Descriptions of, and stories about, servants make up a constant in her diary over the years, whether they had only a cook and a maid, as in that first flat of their own in London, or a fully-fledged permanent domestic staff including butler, cook, chauffeur, footman and several maids, as at the Washington embassy. Judging by the amount of attention they

---

[31] MvK diary 28 July–5 August 1947, inv nr 397, 2.05.86, NL-HaNA.
[32] I speak of servants when I am giving voice to the concerns and views of the actors I study since that is the word they used. In more analytical reasoning, I refer to the same group of people as domestic or household staff. There are many differences between the people lumped together in this category – big positional differences between a chauffeur, the cook, and the gardener, for example, in addition to gendered and racialized differences often tied to rank. Those differences are significant and their implications for the functioning of diplomacy deserve more scholarly attention. However, in this context, separate functions of household staff will only come up when specifically relevant to the broader argument that is made here about the importance of diplomats' homes for the functioning of diplomacy.

Figure 2.2 Household staff, plus Jansen the poodle, 'minus chauffeur Mac, and the laundress (Gonzalez)' on the steps of the Dutch Washington embassy/residence in 1950, shortly before Eelco and Margaret van Kleffens left the United States for Portugal. Far left and far right are Willy and Nelly, the Dutch maids. The cook, Rosa de Zepeda, is standing in the middle with her hand on the shoulder of the woman in front of her. Behind her is Vladimiro Caponetti, the Italian butler. Photo: private, MvK diary 10 June 1950, inv nr 401, 2.05.86, NL-HaNA. Photographer unknown, possibly Margaret van Kleffens herself. Courtesy of the Netherlands National Archives, The Hague, with permission of the Van Kleffens family.

spent on them, servants were of paramount importance to the diplomatic couple. No matter how much effort they put into finding the right house, furnishings and decoration of the residence's interior, no troubles surpassed those taken to find suitable servants. Not that the issues were separable: finding the right house was closely linked to the domestic staff-issue, as a continued overview of the Van Kleffens's homes in exile in London shows. There were servant-less flats like the one they first took in exile, that is, apartments where cooking and cleaning was included so you did not need to employ your own servants. However, convenient as this might seem, it was clearly a second-rate solution in Margaret van Kleffens's view: as soon as they had the chance, the couple moved to a borrowed flat where they could have their own household. Besides the Hungarian cook Maria, who was already in place ('a first-rate cook but temperamental in the extreme') they tried to get a house-parlour maid but had to manage with a temporary maid – Gladys, who was 'an excellent girl' but a lower-ranking type of maid.[33]

Finding, assessing, and supervising servants was a big and constant part of providing a well-run diplomat's house, and something that time and again had to be done all over, not only because servants quit or were fired, but because diplomats tended to move house frequently. Although some servants stayed with a diplomatic couple and accompanied them to new postings, others could or would not. Hiring servants was chiefly a wife's task but notes and letters show that husbands certainly had an eye for servants too and were often actively involved in the search for staff. When looking for a new flat in London in 1940 (sharing with the Wilsons, who used the flat on weekends, had proven untenable), the servants that came with the flat were as important as it having the necessary facilities for entertaining. In her account of their first year in exile, Margaret van Kleffens wrote that after considerable difficulty, they found a flat in Grosvenor Square where 'the housekeeper, the servants and even the food made an excellent impression' (and in her notes, her husband has inserted in pencil that 'there was an old, very dignified yet humorous butler looking exactly like Gladstone').[34] Eelco and Margaret van Kleffens thought that they had found the place to stay for the duration of their exile, but they soon had to think again: their moving in (on 3 September 1940) only just preceded the beginning of the Blitz (on 7 September). With bombs falling incessantly over London after dark, the couple had to spend night after night in the basement restaurant of the building together with a number of other people. Soon lack of sleep became a problem, as did the fact that they could no longer entertain. 'Dining out, or having friends to dinner, now were things of the past; everyone hurried to be under cover before dark',

---

[33] Margaret van Kleffens, January 1941 account, inv nr 391, 2.05.86, NL-HaNA. A house parlour maid would have had a higher status and more guest-orientated tasks (such as cleaning the parlour and serving) than an ordinary maid.

[34] Margaret van Kleffens, January 1941 account, inv nr 391, 2.05.86, NL-HaNA. This account is full of little additions and corrections made in pencil by Eelco van Kleffens – the handwriting is distinctly different from that of Margaret van Kleffens and corresponds to that of his handwritten notes. The archive inventory also states that it is an account by Margaret van Kleffens with additions in her husband's hand.

Margaret van Kleffens wrote. Her husband added: 'Luncheons became the only meals to which one could invite guests.'[35]

It might seem odd that even in the midst of war, with bombs falling and people dying around them, the ability to entertain guests was at the forefront of their minds. However, considering that it was a war in which the Dutch depended on allied help to restore their independence, there is a logic to it. Entertaining was part of a strategy to create personal goodwill for the Netherlands – a regular part of diplomats' work, as the previously cited reference to 'bind[ing] the sympathies of foreigners to this country' reveals – and as such an even more pressing concern for the Foreign Minister and his wife in war than in times of peace.[36] It was in line with the publication of *The Rape of the Netherlands*, a book written as a matter of urgency by Margaret and Eelco van Kleffens together during their stay at Queen Anne's Mansion (though published under his name only). It appealed to emotions by describing how the innocent, honourable Dutch were overrun by the much stronger and treacherous Germans despite the Dutch people's civilized behaviour, peaceful nature and heroic resistance, making use – as the title shows – of a gendered war rhetoric that had proven efficient in stirring public opinion during the First World War.[37] The book, which had quite an impact if evidence of circulation is anything to go by, has been ridiculed in Dutch descriptions of the period as an undertaking devoid of a sense of reality or priorities.[38] It is easy to imagine a similar dismissal of the couple's preoccupation with entertaining guests during the Blitz. In both cases though, a dismissal implies the assumption that the well-educated Van Kleffenses were foolishly naïve and/or arrogantly misguided and that emotional pleas and personal feelings of friendship did not influence foreign policy behaviour. That is contrary to the available evidence, as a more thorough discussion of house guests (in the next chapter) and other forms of entertaining and networks (in Part III of the book) will show.

---

[35] Margaret van Kleffens, January 1941 account, inv nr 391, 2.05.86, NL-HaNA.

[36] Letter from Eelco van Kleffens to Margaret Horstmann, 2 May 1934, inv nr 434, 2.05.86, NL-HaNA; see first paragraph under 'Homemaking for diplomats' above.

[37] E N Kleffens, *The Rape of the Netherlands* (London: Hodder and Stoughton, 1940); On gendered war rhetoric see Nicoletta F Gullace, 'Sexual Violence and Family Honor: British Propaganda and International Law during the First World War', *The American Historical Review* 102, no 3 (1997): 714–47; Ruth Harris, 'The "Child of the Barbarian": Rape, Race and Nationalism in France during the First World War', *Past and Present*, no 141 (1993): 170–206.

[38] Meyer Sluyser, -, *daar zaten wij: impressies over 'Londen '40–'45'* (Kosmos, 1965), 15; Cees Fasseur, *Eigen Meester, Niemands Knecht: Het Leven van Pieter Sjoerds Gerbrandy Minister-President van Nederland in de Tweede Wereldoorlog* (Amsterdam: Uitgeverij Balans, 2014), 188; For a discussion see S Erlandsson, 'Off the Record: Margaret van Kleffens and the Gendered History of Dutch World War II Diplomacy'. *International Feminist Journal of Politics* 21, no 1 (2019): , 38–39.

In light of the personal danger and of the impossibility of entertaining in London anyway, Eelco and Margaret van Kleffens moved to the Chalfont Park Hotel outside London. On 1 November 1940 they definitively gave up their London flat. Only in 1942, after two (of what would eventually become more than five) years of exile, one-and-a-half of which were spent living in hotels, the couple moved to a more permanent place of their own again. They rented a house close to Margaret van Kleffens's sister and brother-in-law in Virginia Water, a 35-minute train ride or one-hour drive by car from London.[39] When she started keeping a regular diary in December 1942, Margaret van Kleffens began by describing the servants of the house, even before describing the house itself: 'Since May 14 of this year, we live at "Velsheda", Wentworth, in Surrey', she wrote. '"We" includes, besides Byntie [her nickname for her husband] and me, our servants: Mrs Wiltshire (from Wiltshire!), cook; Mabel, house-parlourmaid; and Popham, chauffeur, who has now been with us since November 1940 and has been "house-trained" since we took this house'.[40] The joke about the chauffeur having been house-trained is exemplary of the unthinkingly condescending jargon used for servants and other lower-class people. In practical terms, it probably meant that he doubled as a manservant and is consistent with a higher status of in-house servants. The diaries also reveal that Mr Wiltshire, the cook's husband, did work for them as a gardener on his day off from the National Fire Service. Like diplomats, many servants, especially those of higher rank such as butlers and cooks, worked together as couples (although unlike with diplomats, it was usually not just one of them who was officially employed). At the Dutch ambassador's residence in Berne, for example, the male head servant's wife was First Maid.[41]

When, in late 1944, the Van Kleffenses were asked by their landlord to vacate 'Velsheda', the servants and especially the married cook who could not be expected to leave her husband behind were a central concern in Margaret van Kleffens's diary summary of the inconvenience this caused them:

> What to do with the servants, to each of whom special problems are attached; what to do with the chickens, (just about to begin laying!), with Vicky [the dog], if we have to go to an hotel or servantless flat; the car; our packing-cases, and so

---

[39] In 1942, according to Margaret van Kleffens, MvK diary 31 December 1942, inv nr 392, 2.05.86, NL-HaNA. It is almost exactly the same in 2020 (even a little faster in 1942 by train, though it might have been to a different station).
[40] MvK diary 31 December 1942, inv nr 392, 2.05.86, NL-HaNA.
[41] Letter from Eelco van Kleffens to Margaret van Kleffens, 3 October 1938, inv nr 440, 2.05.86, NL-HaNA.

on – one damn difficulty after another. Above all there is the question of finding other accommodation, which must be short-term, and, for Mrs. W's sake (or rather, in order to keep her), in this district.[42]

How to keep the cook was a consideration that influenced the search for a new house. The impression that a house was considered useless without well-functioning servants is strengthened by the fact that, although they finally found a house in the right area and Mrs (and Mr) Wiltshire to her relief decided to go with them, Margaret van Kleffens worried that the house was not nice enough for the servants. She complained in her diary that it was filthy, worn-out, badly planned, and lacked equipment which meant more work for her as well as for the servants. Worse, the house had a 'dreadful' kitchen, which was a drawback especially for Mrs Wiltshire. Moreover, while the Van Kleffens's own living room was fine (after cleaning), Margaret van Kleffens lamented that there was no servant living room in the new house. She wrote that she felt sorry for the servants whose only place to sit was in 'that beastly kitchen'. When the servants indeed grumbled and displayed their dissatisfaction, their discontent was a reason for the couple to consider giving up the house, as they would 'prefer even life in a hotel to the present atmosphere of endless difficulties'.[43]

Finding a home and finding servants remained intertwined operations. When the war ended, Eelco van Kleffens as Foreign Minister immediately had to get to work in the Netherlands, travelling back and forth from their home in the UK (by then a London flat). Meanwhile, his wife was charged with finding and staffing a home for them in The Hague. Joining her husband on one of his trips to the Netherlands in June 1945, she returned to her native land for the first time after more than five years in exile. Despite emotions running high on seeing all the material and personal devastation and reuniting with her visibly aged and broken father – her mother had died during the war – she efficiently used the few days at her disposal to find them a suitable residence. She was able to acquire the former Japanese legation, which had been inhabited by 'Nazi-crooks' during the war, she wrote in her diary after returning to London. 'Now for the staff to run it', she added.[44]

In the following months, her diary entries testify to the rollercoaster of efforts, hopes, successes, frustrations and problems that this involved. One day she

---

[42] MvK diary 23 October 1944, inv nr 394, 2.05.86, NL-HaNA.
[43] MvK diary 5 and 24 December 1944, 4–6 and 8 January 1945, inv nr 394, 2.05.86, NL-HaNA.
[44] MvK diary, account under the heading 'Journey home' following the entry of 25 June 1945, inv nr 395, 2.05.86, NL-HaNA.

was overjoyed that she had found an excellent servant couple (butler with wife), the next her hopes were dashed by his failing the obligatory post-war test of political reliability (allegedly, the intended butler had voluntarily gone to work in Germany during the war). Then there was their pre-war chauffeur-annex-footman Gerard who first offered them his services, then got another job offer with more security and then eventually joined them after all. A cook was found who then abandoned them before even beginning, another was hired but fired again for turning out to be a 'regular she-devil' (another testimony to what was considered normal treatment of servants), a third was found but could not start in time for an important dinner party, so finding and hiring a temporary cook became necessary, and so on.[45] The servant troubles were endless, and not specific for the immediate post-war period in the Netherlands either (though food and material scarcity made the running of that particular residence extra troublesome). Soon they had to start again from scratch, as in March 1946, the couple was sent to New York City, as Eelco van Kleffens had been appointed as the Dutch representative to the brand-new UN Security Council.

Like diplomatic house-hunting, servant-hunting was usually the wives' primary responsibility, but it was clearly a concern that also involved their husbands and drew on all sorts of contacts within a wider diplomatic network. As with diplomatic houses and furnishings, male diplomats exchanged tips regarding servants, or even exchanged the servants themselves. When Eelco and Margaret van Kleffens were hit by what she in her diary called their 'first domestic crisis' at the Washington embassy, namely losing the '*super*-excellent' butler Vergeer ('no small calamity'), the solution came in the shape of the butler of the Dutch diplomatic couple Van Bylandt at the embassy in Rome – thanks to the intervention of Eelco van Kleffens's former secretary Elly van Alphen.[46] When the Van Kleffenses left Washington in 1950, their successors and old friends Herman and Anne van Roijen took over several of their servants. Among them was the same Italian butler, Vladimiro Caponetti, who remained at the Dutch embassy in Washington for many years.

The 1950 correspondence between the departing and the arriving Dutch ambassador includes repeated consultations regarding servants. Incoming ambassador Herman van Roijen, for example, thanked his predecessor for

---

[45] MvK diary 24, 25, 26 July, 21 August, 2, 5 September 1945, inv nr 395, 2.05.86, NL-HaNA.
[46] MvK diary 12 January and 4 May 1948, inv nr 397, 2.05.86, NL-HaNA.

sending back Capponetti's contract and asked Eelco van Kleffens's advice about the passage of both Vladimiro Capponetti and a new male servant from Italy to the United States. Eelco van Kleffens also wrote to his successor to tip him off that the Washington chauffeur of the Portuguese ambassador was available because of the ambassador's return to Portugal. He attached a letter of recommendation from the Portuguese Chargé d'Affairs emphasizing that the chauffeur, James Redwing, was a devoted and reliable employee and 'a capable driver who knows the city and who takes excellent care of the cars entrusted to him'.[47] Though that letter gives some clues as to what made a good diplomat's chauffeur, Eelco van Kleffens's accompanying letter shows that it lacked one piece of information that he apparently thought relevant: 'This man makes a good impression', he wrote to his friend and colleague, 'but I don't know if you consider it an objection that he is black as ebony'.[48]

Although local knowledge would seem like an important advantage for someone hired to drive around Washington ('I don't think I have ever known a place so hard to find the way in as W', wrote Margaret van Kleffens about the city in 1947[49]), Van Roijen did not hire Redwing. Instead, he brought his own chauffeur from the Netherlands to Washington. It is impossible to say for sure whether Redwing's skin colour played a role in that decision. The archive holds no record of Van Roijen's reaction to that particular piece of information or reasons for bringing his Dutch chauffeur. However, the fact that Eelco van Kleffens brought it up shows, at the very least, that he thought it was a potential issue. Regardless of all the other implications and questions this raises about how race might have played different roles for diplomats from different countries in the hiring of (different types of) domestic staff – a topic worthy of a book of its own – it shows that not only the skills, but also the appearances of staff were factored in. Staff were not only needed to drive, to keep the diplomatic home clean and representative, to wait on guests, and to be able to serve excellent food (the importance of which returns as a topic in the next part). Their value was also symbolic, which made factors like gender and skin colour part of a person's qualification for a position. A good chauffeur brought you to the right place at

---

[47] Letter of recommendation by Manuel Rocheta, Chargé d'Affairs ad interim, Portuguese Embassy in Washington 18 May 1950. Correspondence between Eelco van Kleffens and Herman van Roijen, inv nr 305, 2.05.86, NL-HaNA.
[48] My translation from Dutch: 'Deze man maakt een goede indruk, maar ik weet niet of je het een bezwaar vindt dat hij zwart is als ebbenhout.' Eelco van Kleffens to Herman van Roijen, 19 May 1950, inv nr 305, 2.05.86, NL-HaNA.
[49] MvK diary 21 August 1947, inv nr 397, 2.05.86, NL-HaNA.

the right time, but his (never her in this period) appearance was a matter both of status and of conveying the desired national image.⁵⁰

A case in point is an October 1949 article in the American weekly *The Saturday Evening Post*. It provides an unusually clear illustration of how the composition of diplomatic household staff could play a role in public diplomacy. The article featured the 'exotic and wonderful' food served at different embassies in Washington, even claiming that it was the Washington legations rather than the city's restaurants that had Washington's best gourmet food. One of the cooks featured was the cook of Eelco and Margaret van Kleffens, Rosa de Zepeda. A photograph of her smiling in the Dutch embassy kitchen was one of four article photographs – the others were from the British, French, and Portuguese embassies. The caption read: 'Rosa de Zepeda, of Guatemala, offers the Dutch Embassy's guests stuffed peppers – native style.' The exotic image invoked continued in the article itself, which told the reader that the Netherlands embassy probably had 'the most spectacular domestic staff in Washington', with among others – besides the Guatemalan cook – 'an Argentine kitchen maid, two British parlor maids, a Dutch footman named Piet, a Scotch-American chauffeur called Mac, and an Italian butler romantically named Vladimiro for a character out of Dostoevski.' The political implication of the description becomes clear with the next sentence. 'Such below-stairs internationalism is not tolerated, of course, at the Soviet embassy, which may be what is wrong with the food.' The article went on to describe a Soviet dinner: cold soup, burnt meat, a glum atmosphere, and drunk Russians, adding that not even caviar was served.⁵¹

The article, which at first sight seems to be about lifestyle, food and glamour, had a clearly political angle and one which benefitted the Netherlands more than is perhaps immediately evident. As the chapter on food will feature in more detail, the international style of the kitchens of several of the Western embassies was emphasized, setting them off against the Soviets. The Netherlands came across as one of the club, a loyal Western ally, something that was deeply

---

⁵⁰ In the case of Redwing, the recommendation letter's emphasis on his reliability and devotion hint at (an awareness of) racialized perceptions of who could be trusted, in line with the discussion about suitable wives recounted in Chapter 2. However, the simultaneous racist belief that blacks had a special talent for serving whites and the fact that the American Washington political elite often preferred African American servants, complicates the idea that this was some general diplomatic attitude. Moreover, there might be different ideals for different types of staff within the same diplomatic household. Understanding what role gendered and racialized considerations played when diplomats assessed and hired staff requires more targeted studies.
⁵¹ Elise Morrow and Mary van Rensselaer Thayer, 'We Toured the Embassy Kitchens', *Saturday Evening Post* 1949 (29 October 1949): 32–33 An inaccuracy in the article's description made the staff seem even more diverse than it was: in reality, the parlour maids, Willy and Nelly, were not British but Dutch.

important to the government of the previously neutral state. Even more importantly though, when it came to the Netherlands in particular, the *Saturday Evening Post* described the ethnically and nationally diverse staff of its embassy as 'a small experiment in international harmony'.[52] This is striking considering the timing: two months before the Netherlands recognized Indonesian independence. The UN Security Council had condemned the Dutch military interventions of 1947 and 1948/49, and American public opinion was a major concern for the Netherlands' ambassador in Washington. Eelco van Kleffens had to defend the international reputation of his country in the face of heavy criticism of its colonial policies (policies of the Dutch government with which, incidentally, he privately disagreed).[53] In this light, it was no small diplomatic triumph that a widely circulated magazine for the American middle class described the Dutch as promoters of international harmony. That was precisely the image Eelco van Kleffens preferred.

Domestic staff could contribute to a country's standing directly, as in the example above, and indirectly, by the way in which they ensured a smooth running of the household and hosting of successful parties. Events at Washington embassies often made the paper, so that the successful entertaining of important guests as network building and the image of that entertaining as public diplomacy intersected. On 29 January 1948, for instance – one of numerous similar notices that Margaret van Kleffens has pasted into her diary – the *Washington Post* reported that a 'dinner party was given at the Netherlands Embassy last evening by the Ambassador and Mme. van Kleffens' and proceeded to name all the illustrious guests. Of that same party, Margaret van Kleffens wrote in her diary:

> What can give greater satisfaction, a warmer glow of pride, than to know that your house looks beautiful, that your dinner is good, that you look pretty yourself – and your table lovely – that the servants work like clockwork, and that everyone is admiringly appreciative of your party?[54]

Servants' role in public relations cannot be separated from the everyday role that they played in keeping the residence clean and presentable, cooking and serving excellent food and making house guests feel welcome and comfortable. Without them, the home could not function as a diplomatic arena.

---

[52] Morrow and Thayer, 'We Toured the Embassy Kitchens', 32.
[53] As several of Margaret van Kleffens's diary entries show, but most explicitly MvK diary 18 December 1948, inv nr 398, 2.05.86, NL-HaNA.
[54] MvK diary 28 January 1948, inv nr 397, 2.05.86, NL-HaNA.

7 The home as a diplomatic arena

What can homes tell us about the functioning of international relations? What can micro history add to macro theories? On a systemic level, realist views of international relations as a competitive system have been challenged by scholars who have argued for a shift towards understanding power in international relations in terms of the ability to cooperate.[55] At the practice level, the concern of ambassadorial couples for the décor and household management of their residence testifies to an environment which, on an everyday basis, was both competitive and aimed at cooperation. The competitive aspect is visible in countless diary comments by Margaret van Kleffens – some to be highlighted shortly – on how other embassies were run or comparing her own home to the homes of people she visited. It is confirmed as a more general phenomenon by her contemporary (a decade younger) British colleague Beryl Smedley, who claims in her book *Partners in Diplomacy* that 'the status of a diplomat abroad, and therefore of his spouse, is to some extent defined by the standard of his housing, which must also reflect well on the country he represents'.[56] However, a competitive status was not the only goal of a well-furnished, well-run house: so was creating a pleasant environment for entertaining guests, a crucial ingredient in building networks and fostering goodwill to improve cooperation.

To study how diplomatic competition and cooperation played out at the micro level of diplomatic homes, it seems crucial to include another aspect of international relations that is increasingly receiving scholarly attention: the fact that diplomatic actors are human beings with personal feelings that cannot be distinguished from political feelings.[57] Jonathan Mercer, who has pointed to the emotional component of all beliefs (whether believing in aliens or in Iran's intention to build nuclear weapons) has argued that international prestige – the matter of status – is an illusion because (1) rational actors use their feelings as

---

[55] The classic realist account is Hans Morgenthau, *Politics Among Nations: The Struggle for Power and Peace* (New York, NY: AA Knopf, 1948); critics are a.o. J. Ann Tickner, 'Hans Morgenthau's Principles of Political Realism: A Feminist Reformulation', in *Gender and International Relations*, ed. Rebecca Grant and Kathleen Newland (Milton Keynes: Open University Press, 1991), 27–40; Robert Keohane, 'International Relations Theory: Contributions of a Feminist Standpoint', in *Gender and International Relations*, 41–50; see also Helen Milner, 'International Theories of Cooperation Among Nations: Strengths and Weaknesses', *World Politics* 44, no 3 (1992): 466–96.
[56] Beryl Smedley, *Partners in Diplomacy* (Ferring: The Harley Press, 1990), 92.
[57] Barbara Keys, 'The Diplomat's Two Minds: Deconstructing a Foreign Policy Myth', *Diplomatic History* 44, no 1 (January 2020): 1–21; Barbara Keys and Claire Yorke, 'Personal and Political Emotions in the Mind of the Diplomat', *Political Psychology* 40, no 6 (2019): 1235–49; F Costigliola, *Roosevelt's Lost Alliances: How Personal Politics Helped Start the Cold War* (Princeton, NJ: Princeton University Press, 2012).

evidence of whether they have prestige and (2) policymakers tend to discount the prestige of others so that, in the end, the pursuit of prestige does not bring increased power but is merely based on a misguided emotional belief in the possibility of obtaining the admiration of others.[58] In my view, though, that does not make competition itself – the pursuit of status – irrelevant. Even if an actor's sense of being admired does not necessarily cause the presumed admirers to act differently, it might still affect his or her own behaviour and feelings of goodwill. The quote that rounded off the previous chapter conveys a sense of the personal investment and pleasure at having hosted a successful party. Its emotional quality points to what the feeling of success does to a person who believes he or she has prestige, regardless of whether other actors express admiration out of sincerity or simply out of politeness (or even calculated flattery).

The role of emotions in beliefs about both status and the possibility of cooperation raises the question of whether and how policymaking was influenced by diplomatic interactions taking place at homes – places of emotional attachment for diplomats as for most people. Pointing to the importance of the spatiality of diplomacy, Iver Neumann has argued that the mundane and everyday work of creating and maintaining sites is 'at the very heart of diplomatic work', since sites shape the event and vice versa.[59] Based on the evidence of diplomatic actors' inability to separate political and personal feelings, I argue that the emotional, personal and at least semi-private character of a home made it a site of potential personal influence on diplomatic relations – and vice versa for that matter – par excellence. To be sure, the diplomatic work of entertaining guests and building personal relations took place at other sites too: restaurants, theatres etc. The next part will deal with the general rules and purposes of entertaining as a diplomatic practice. First, however, a closer look at the diplomatic interactions that took place at homes, and the significance ascribed to them, will expose some interesting overlap both between personal and political competition and between personal and political cooperation.

Homes are (still) explicitly included in diplomatic protocol. The private residences of diplomatic agents (ie, mission staff members) enjoy the same inviolability and protection as the premises of the mission.[60] Mid-twentieth

---

[58] Jonathan Mercer, 'The Illusion of International Prestige', *International Security* 41, no 4 (2017): 134–35; see also Jonathan Mercer, 'Emotional Beliefs', *International Organization* 64, no 1 (2010): 1–31.
[59] Iver B Neumann, 'Sited Diplomacy', in *Diplomatic Cultures and International Politics: Translations, Spaces and Alternatives*, ed. Jason Dittmer and Fiona McConnell (Abingdon: Routledge, 2015), 79–92.
[60] See Article 30, § 1 of 'The Vienna Convention on Diplomatic Relations' (1961). Available at: https://treaties.un.org/pages/ViewDetails.aspx?src=TREATY&mtdsg_no=III-3&chapter=3&clang=_en (accessed 29 June 2021).

century diplomatic practices also emphatically involved visiting diplomats at their homes. The stories of both the Van Kleffenses and the Bumas have already shown how hard it was to manage diplomatic responsibilities without using a private, personal home. Besides visits as the result of invitations, diplomats and their wives paid numerous calls to, and received calls from, other diplomats and their wives at their homes – those representing other nationalities, but also colleagues from their own country. Making so-called courtesy calls, usually short visits of no more than half an hour, was a regular part of diplomatic protocol. The 1957 edition of Satow's *Guide to Diplomatic Practice* (edited by Nevile Bland) makes a distinction between official calls, bound by specific rules and regulations and private calls, which a diplomat 'can freely make'. Both, however, were understood to be social calls and were emphatically not supposed to involve political discussions. This does not mean that social calls never involved mentioning things for political purposes (see Chapter 8 and the concluding remarks of Part III), only that the purpose had to be masked as personal. Neither was paying these calls as such a non-political matter: despite speaking of 'private' calls being made 'freely', Satow and Bland went on to say that it was 'advisable to call privately on the *doyen* of the diplomatic body'.[61] For all the non-committal language, a newly arrived head of mission could not freely decide whether he felt like paying certain so-called private social calls. Failing to do so might be taken as a personal insult – and because the person in question was a state representative, it would be interpreted as a political statement which might harm relations between the two countries.

For lower-ranked diplomats, who joined an embassy in the mid-twentieth century, a failure to duly pay a first call to the head of mission would likely have jeopardized their career. Depending on the post, other calls would be expected too. Wives were emphatically included in this practice. They both joined their husband on his official calls and paid calls separately to other diplomats' wives. The wife who had the highest-ranking husband was entitled to receive the first call. Failure to pay a first call or to return a call speedily could be perceived as an insult by wives too and was a serious matter. Dé Buma recounts in her memoirs how, in 1949, when her husband was posted to Stockholm, she had to end her vacation with the children on an island off the Swedish coast to come to the capital to pay a call to Betty Teixeira de Mattos, wife of the Dutch envoy. Buma's husband had urged her to hurry because the envoy had already asked

---

[61] E Satow and N Bland, *A Guide to Diplomatic Practice*, (London: Longman, 1957), 145.

him if she had arrived in Sweden yet.[62] Margaret van Kleffens's diaries confirm that he was right to believe that higher-ranking diplomats' wives kept a keen eye on the behaviour of other wives. In 1943, for example, Van Kleffens noted indignantly that a Dutch diplomat's wife's call was 'about six weeks overdue!'[63] On the other hand, in 1949, when she recorded that one of the embassy employee's wives had come by for a cup of coffee, she added: 'Specific purpose of visit unknown', which makes it sound as if it slightly annoyed her to be disturbed for no good reason.[64]

That the home was a purportedly private space did not make it less important for diplomatic relations. If anything, a visit to someone's home seems to have been more politically charged than an office appointment, for foreign visitors paying their respects but also as a site where domestic diplomatic relations and hierarchies were established. Yet, the rules were largely unwritten and as the comment above reveals, not always easy to master for the beginner. Calls could be made for different reasons, but, it appears, preferably not for no reason at all. The call that Buma made to the wife of her husband's boss had at least two motives: it was a sign of deference but also a first meeting with a supervisor. There was no official training for diplomats' wives but, in practice, senior wives were supposed to both mentor and monitor more junior ones. Writing about her memories of that first call to Teixeira de Mattos, Buma added that she had always been grateful to have her as a teacher and described how the envoy's wife had taught her how diplomatic protocol worked and the social codes of entertaining.[65]

Part III will revisit the importance of the women's networks that were created and entertained in this and other manners. Here, it is sufficient to point out that already the established habit of making calls made all diplomats' homes sites of diplomatic activity. Moreover, the home was given a political value, even if the calls were allegedly social and private: going to someone else's home was a way to show personal respect to the country and position that person represented. An adherence to this practice seems to have been part of what established individuals as trustworthy members of the diplomatic corps. The calls then facilitated future cooperation, but they also gave diplomats and their wives a chance to gauge each other, compare homes and, since they were, in fact, not made 'freely' (as in guided

[62] Buma, *Donderdag Komt de Koerier. De Kleurrijke Levensreis van een Diplomatenvrouw* (Amsterdam: Van Soeren & Co, 2000), 119.
[63] MvK diary 22 August 1943, inv nr 393, 2.05.86, NL-HaNA.
[64] MvK diary 9 November 1949, inv nr 400, 2.05.86, NL-HaNA.
[65] Buma, *Donderdag Komt de Koerier*, 119–26.

by personal preference), they brought them into contact with the wives and homes of representatives of all countries, regardless of feelings of friendship.

Margaret van Kleffens's descriptions of calls to the wives of officials of different countries provide a peek into the connection between the personal and the political landscape as they tend to mirror political Dutch sentiments. Though it may well have been unconscious and unintentional, she seems to have been out to confirm politically induced preconceptions. A general Western European opinion of Europe as more civilized than South America, for example, seems reflected in the sense of superiority that Margaret van Kleffens expressed vis-à-vis her Venezuelan and Columbian counterparts when she noted in her diary that she had called on them 'and was able to draw smugly favourable comparison between their embassy and ours, both as to décor and running'.[66] Her description from exactly four years earlier, a few months after the end of the Second World War, of a return call in The Hague to Madame Valkova, wife of the Soviet ambassador to the Netherlands Vasily Valkov, is so much in line with the image painted by the *Saturday Evening Post* mentioned above that it is worth citing in its entirety. Moreover, it shows how servants, as well as children, were part of the image conveyed.

> This afternoon I returned Mme Valkova's call, at the Russian Embassy in Zorgvliet. The whole mise-en-scène was exactly what you would expect: a shabby, shady individual, in a navy blue suit, opened the front door, peered at me suspiciously and ushered me into a drawing room where, at this early hour, the curtains were drawn. No carpet graced the floor, and we sat – Mme Valkova dressed in blue velvet – on stiff chairs while the cook, in a red pullover and felt slippers, plunked down the tea on the mantelpiece. Pressed caviar and creams tarts were pressed on me as I tried to converse in pidgin-English. Presently the two young daughters of the house came in, dressed alike in thick, bright red material, and with plaits sticking out at the back of their heads. They giggled awkwardly and dutifully answered my questions as to where they most liked to live: 'We like Moscow best.'[67]

The servants, the interior decoration, the wife, the children – all were interpreted as what one could expect from the Soviet Union. The description stands in sharp contrast with a description of a call paid to Clementine Churchill during the war that also features tea and snacks, servants, a hostess not very forthcoming in conversation and a daughter doing her best. Despite many factual similarities,

---

[66] MvK diary 23 November 1949, inv nr 400, 2.05.86, NL-HaNA.
[67] MvK diary 23 November 1945, inv. nr 395, 2.05.86, NL-HaNA.

the interpretation is radically different. Van Kleffens rather gleefully recounted how the British policemen from whom she asked directions 'eyed me with suspicion' (compare 'peered at me suspiciously') until she dropped 'the magic name of Churchill'. The 'elderly maid' who received her at the door took her to 'a medium-sized, pleasant room'. The fact that Clementine Churchill failed to 'ask any even remotely personal question' so that the conversation threatened to become 'somewhat sticky' was 'rather to my surprise considering Mrs C's experience'. The shortcoming did not prevent Margaret van Kleffens from praising her hostess's 'charming, delicate face', adding that she 'looks young for her age in spite of white hair'. Instead of tea being pressed on her, she was offered 'cake, cheese-puffs and currant-bread, to which I did but little justice'. And on this occasion, the daughter saved the day: Mary Churchill enlivened the visit with her stories of her experiences in the Auxiliary Territorial Service, the women's branch of the British Army.[68]

There were no doubt particular circumstances in each case that influenced Margaret van Kleffens's assessment (eg personality, age, language and social skills, etc). Other aspects of creating feelings of likeminded-ness or alienation, of the (conscious or unconscious) mixing of personal and political networking and of judging different people's diplomatic aptitude return as topics in the following chapters. In the context of this chapter, however, I want to draw attention to the fact that the attitude towards and descriptions of the homes and hospitality of supposedly apolitical inhabitants – women, servants, children – corresponded with expectations and hierarchies entirely in line with diplomatic relations. The Dutch depended heavily on their British allies, while Soviet–Dutch relations were strained and marked by Dutch distrust of Soviet intentions.[69] This overlap is not only visible in descriptions of the comparatively superficial (because brief and at least semi-formal) house calls, but all the more in the making and accepting of invitations to homes for events like dinners or weekend stays.

Other than courtesy calls, going to somebody's home for a pre-arranged social event required an invitation. That made having dinner and weekend guests a more personal and intimate matter than making and receiving calls. For example, Margaret van Kleffens would not have brought her sister along when making a required social call, but she very often invited her to attend diplomatic dinners she and her husband gave at home or to join them when they had weekend guests. The more personal character of home invitations does not mean

---

[68] MvK diary 26 October 1943, inv nr 393, 2.05.86, NL-HaNA.
[69] S Erlandsson, *Window of Opportunity: Dutch and Swedish Security Ideas and Strategies 1942–1948*. (Uppsala: Acta Universitatis Upsaliensis, 2015), chs 5 and 6.

they were optional and they were certainly no less politically important than courtesy calls. Ambassadors had a special duty to house royalty or other prominent compatriots visiting the country where they were posted. However, as Dé Buma wrote in her memoirs, diplomats of all ranks were expected to get to know all the important people where they were posted; to do that, you had to both accept home invitations and have others accept yours. It was of considerable political importance to make a name as a host of good parties, an endeavour that placed diplomats' wives in crucial positions and to which end access to competent servants was indispensable.

Some home dinners had the express purpose of informal political discussions (though they took place after eating). In August 1943, for instance, Margaret van Kleffens noted in her diary that Queen Wilhelmina had 'affairs to talk over with the great one [Winston Churchill], + was invited to dinner for the purpose'. That Churchill invited the Dutch queen to his home in her capacity of Head of State and on business is further evidenced by the fact that she wanted her Foreign Minister to attend, which she, according to Margaret van Kleffens, had 'tactfully intimated' so Churchill had invited Eelco van Kleffens.[70] The example highlights the difference between a formal meeting and meeting at someone's home. As a house guest, the queen could not request that the foreign minister be present, she had to hint at it, allowing the host to take the initiative. Visiting people's homes was an obligation, having house guests was an obligation, but an invitation into someone's home was also a personal privilege. The more important the person whose home it was, the more coveted an invitation. Conversely, the more important the guest, the more of a social diplomatic triumph it was to have him or her accept an invitation. As already mentioned, the post-war American press tended to report on these embassy events so that networking and public diplomacy interests intersected. For example, the *Saturday Evening Post* article mentioned above referred to a dinner party at the Netherlands Embassy as Mme van Kleffens having 'achieved a social-diplomatic triumph by lining up for dinner the foreign ministers of the Benelux countries, plus Secretary of State Dean Acheson'.[71]

Since the American press often mentioned embassy events, they served as very visible sites for exclusive receptions and dinners, hosting high-ranking political guests. A certain fame in the shape of frequent media appearances was good both for networking (more people would be likely to accept an invitation

---

[70] MvK diary 3 August 1943, inv nr 393, 2.05.86, NL-HaNA.
[71] Morrow and Thayer, 'We Toured the Embassy Kitchens', 32.

if you were known as a good hostess) and for general publicity and public diplomacy, with elements both of competition and of (exhibiting) cooperation. The American press relished the more personal stories, so that homes, wives, children, dogs etc. became public diplomacy assets. When Dicky Wilson visited her sister in Washington, DC, Margaret van Kleffens wrote that '[t]he photographers are all over us with D. here'.[72] The children of ambassadors, too, were favourite topics of Washington's society columnists; the children of their successors, Herman and Anne van Roijen, featured prominently in American press.[73] Eelco and Margaret van Kleffens did not have children of their own, but newspapers in Washington paid attention to the Christmas parties Margaret van Kleffens threw for the embassy personnel's children in 1947, 1948 and 1949. The 1948 article described the children as 'unmistakably Dutch … towheads with apple-red cheeks' and recounted how they 'dressed in native costume, ended the party with a folk dance and song'. The 1949 article also paid a lot of attention to Jansen, the 'miniature French poodle who is well liked everywhere' and emphasized the homey atmosphere of the embassy. Though government property, the embassy had 'touches unmistakably Mme. van Kleffens' and while it was 'spotless and fresh' it 'at the same time looks lived in'.[74] Jansen was sometimes photographed together with his mistress and was very often mentioned in articles about her or the embassy.[75]

Family members and pets were not only good assets for publicity, but also for enhancing the image of the diplomatic home as a private arena with their presence. When being on the receiving end, as a guest, it is striking that the value ascribed to an invitation seems not only to have increased in proportion to the fame and/or perceived political importance of the inviting person, but also in proportion to its private character. If invited by someone perceived as equal or higher in rank, being entertained at home outranked being entertained at a restaurant. The more exclusive, the more private and intimate, the greater the privilege and political value, as a sign both of status and of amicable cooperation.

[72] MvK diary 4 May 1948, inv nr 397, 2.05.86, NL-HaNA.
[73] S Erlandsson and R van der Maar, 'Trouw aan Buitenlandse Zaken. Margaret van Kleffens, Anne van Roijen, de ambassade in Washington en de betekenis van het diplomatiek partnerschap voor de naoorlogse Nederlandse buitenlandse betrekkingen'. *Tijdschrift voor Geschiedenis* 134, no 3 (2021).
[74] Elizabeth Maguire, 'Mme. van Kleffens Entertains for Children', *Washington Post*, 28 December 1947; 'Magician Entertains Tiny Tots at Netherlands Embassy Fete', [?], 26 December 1948, MvK diary inv nr 398, 2.05.86, NL-HaNA; Elizabeth Maguire, 'Mme. van Kleffens Assists Santa: Dutch Get Yule Treat at Embassy Party', *Washington Post*, 25 December 1949.
[75] See newspaper clippings in her diary, eg, MvK diary 14 March 1946, inv nr 395; 27 August 1947, inv nr 397; 7 September 1949, inv nr 399, 25 December 1949, inv nr 400, 2.05.86, NL-HaNA. I have not been able to include these published images of Jansen for copyright reasons, but he can be admired on the private photograph in the introduction.

Figure 2.3 Margaret van Kleffens with her nephew, Clive Wilson, during the war, probably 1941. Photo: private, photographer unknown but possibly A.E. Wilson. Courtesy of Clive Wilson.

In 1946 in New York, when Eelco van Kleffens represented the Netherlands on the UN Security Council, his wife proudly described a farewell party for the American banker and diplomat Winthrop Aldrich and his wife, who were leaving on a trip to Europe, noting that 'as so often before, it was striking and gratifying to find Theo and we were the only foreigners present – besides the chief attraction: the Duke and Duchess of Winsdor'.[76]

The following year, having just arrived as the Dutch ambassadorial couple to Washington, DC, the Van Kleffenses were guests of the influential Vandenbergs.

---

[76] MvK diary 13 November 1946, inv nr 396, 2.05.86, NL-HaNA. Theo = Lady Theodosia Cadogan, wife of UK diplomat Sir Alexander Cadogan.

Figure 2.4 Margaret van Kleffens with Jansen's predecessor, the Cairn terrier Vicky (short for Victory), in the summer of 1943. Photo: private, photographer unknown, but possibly AE Wilson. Courtesy of Clive Wilson. A copy of the photo is also available in MvK diary inv nr 393, 2.05.86, NL-HaNA.

Arthur Vandenberg was chairman of the US Senate Foreign Relations Committee, an important person to befriend for any diplomat in the post-war United States and most certainly for a representative of a smaller European country very dependent on American aid. Margaret van Kleffens's diary testifies to her interpretation of the invitation as an even greater achievement because of its personal and intimate character:

> The Vandenberg party was nice and a great compliment to E. for us to have been invited, as it was her birthday and we the only foreigners in a company of 20

mostly consisting of Senators (Taft, Milliken, repr. Derksen + others), very informal, with everyone serving himself and the sitting at little card-tables, with beer or water to drink after the usual more serious imbibing. I sat next to the burly and genial host, who is a nice and clever man of humble Michigan (Dutch stock) origin.[77]

The seat next to the host was the place of honour, and the status of that proximity was only enhanced by the party's personal and informal character. Relative to a person's political importance, it seems that the more personal and private, the more valuable: if you could get a group of important people to visit you at home, it was considered a 'social-diplomatic triumph'. The more private and intimate a gathering an important person invited you to, the better. This means that family members, children, dogs, etc. could be valuable assets since they would reinforce a sense of informality and intimacy. Conversely, not being personal enough when inviting someone to your home was a diplomatic *faux pas*. After a dinner at the home of the British ambassador Baron and Lady Franks in Washington, DC, Margaret van Kleffens commented not only on the 'unstylish reception', but on their '*most* impersonal, bare and unhomelike house'.[78] It was its personal, even private character which made the home useful as a diplomatic arena.

Even more intimate than inviting guests for dinner was having visitors stay overnight. This, too, was an obligation for a diplomatic couple and one of the first things mentioned by Margaret van Kleffens when she started to keep a diary (on 31 December 1942). At the time, Eelco van Kleffens was Foreign Minister-in-exile. The information that they invited 'weekend guests regularly once a fortnight' was preceded by an emphasis on how the couple loved their Sundays, Eelco van Kleffens always being very busy at the office, therefore would 'keep every other week-end for ourselves', which conveys the obligatory character of having house guests.[79] That does not mean that all guests were people they would not have socialized with regardless of their diplomatic job. Most house guests that Eelco and Margaret van Kleffens hosted during the war were either compatriots or foreigners with whom they entertained particularly close (collegial) relationships. Some of the more frequent guests, like the British envoy extraordinary and minister plenipotentiary to the Netherlands, Nevile and Portia Bland, were more obviously relevant to their country than others, such as Greek Ambassador Thanassis Aghnides, who was an acquaintance of Eelco van

---

[77] MvK diary 28 July–5 August 1947, inv nr 397, 2.05.86, NL-HaNA.
[78] MvK diary 20 October 1948, inv nr 398, 2.05.86, NL-HaNA.
[79] MvK diary 31 December 1942, inv nr 392, 2.05.86, NL-HaNA.

Kleffens from the time they both served at the League of Nations. While sometimes the guests (in this case Dutch Minister of Finances Johannes van den Broek and Swedish envoy to the Netherlands government-in-exile Erik Sjöborg) were described as 'both cheerful, interesting + full of conversation' with whom one could pass 'a very pleasant evening',[80] another visit (in this case the former Dutch envoy to Berlin Haersma de With and his wife) could be described as 'a trial. As charming and pleasant as he is, so artificial and affected is she.... This morning, praises be, they left us!'[81]

The couple's choice of weekend guests was clearly based on a mix of (perceived) obligation coupled with their official function and personal preference. It could even be both such as when Prince Bernhard in 1943 said that he would like to come and stay for the weekend.[82] He was the husband of Dutch Crown Princess Juliana, whom Margaret van Kleffens knew quite well from her youth.[83] Juliana spent the war years in Canada with her young children. On the one hand, turning down the royal request would have been unthinkable. If the Prince indicated that he would like to come and stay, inviting and hosting him was an obligation for a couple working for the Foreign Office. It had the character of work in the sense that they could not opt out of it and it meant a lot of extra household labour.[84] On the other hand, besides the personal connection between Margaret van Kleffens and Princess Juliana, a royal visit was a personal honour and a privilege. The couple went to great lengths to make sure the prince would enjoy himself, in the process enjoying themselves as well. Work and leisure, professional need and personal pleasure overlapped. What is more, professional contacts and personal friends and family members were deliberately mixed. When diplomatic couples had weekend guests, one of the ways to entertain them was to invite additional guests to lunch or dinner. These could be other diplomats, but they did not need to be, since a more important criterion was that they were perceived as compatible with the guest(s) of honour and/or had the desired

---

[80] MvK diary 16/17 January 1943, inv nr 393, 2.05.86, NL-HaNA.
[81] MvK diary 13–15 February 1943, inv nr 393, 2.05.86, NL-HaNA.
[82] MvK diary 23 July and 25 August 1943, inv nr 393, 2.05.86, NL-HaNA.
[83] Well enough for them to exchange occasional letters and for Margaret van Kleffens to buy the princess underwear as a Christmas present. Letters from Juliana are mentioned or kept in several of her diaries, eg, a condolence letter on the death of her mother, dated Ottawa January 1942, kept in MvK diary inv nr 392. Notes on her Christmas shopping and a thank-you letter from Juliana can be found in MvK diary 28 October 1949 and 5 January 1950 respectively, inv nr 400, 2.05.86, NL-HaNA. 'For Juliana I bought the most luscious lace- and plissé-trimmed white nylon slip, quite unknown in Holland, which will delight her, I know. This I did for the pure and simple reason that I think she is a dear and unselfish thing.'
[84] There are several diary mentions of preparations and worries in the weeks leading up to the visit, as well as tidying up after. MvK diary 13, 18, 19, 22, 24 and 28 September 1943, inv nr 393, 2.05.86, NL-HaNA.

social skills to make the main guest(s) feel at home. Moreover, including family members allowed them to emphasize personal friendship.

The visit of Prince Bernhard is an illustrative example. The prince, who was 32 at the time, liked filming and photography and was interested in airplanes. He had 'gotten his wings' (his pilot's licence) in 1941 in the British Royal Air Force (RAF). The prince was known for a rather overt preference for beautiful women, his extra-marital affairs a public secret. Both dinners hosted during the weekend were kept small and intimate, in line with the non-public character of the visit. For the first dinner, Margaret van Kleffens invited two couples whose ages matched the prince's: a Dutch diplomatic couple and an RAF squadron leader and his wife.[85] For the second night, she invited a good friend of theirs, Greek Ambassador Thanassis Aghnides, and her sister Dicky Wilson, who lived nearby and whose husband was serving abroad for much of the war. Mrs Wilson was a frequent guest to the Van Kleffens's home. She and her sister were close, and Margaret van Kleffens liked having her around for personal reasons, but she was evidently a diplomatic asset too. As a family member without a diplomatic position of her own, her presence enhanced the intimate allure of a private dinner. Moreover, Dicky Wilson was considered a beauty and had plenty of a highly valued diplomatic social skill: female charm. An added bonus in this particular case was that she, like her husband, had studied photography.[86]

Both evenings were very successful. Margaret van Kleffens noted, clearly pleased, that on the second night, the prince had initiated a game of dice, which had led to a late night of 'childish' fun rather than the 'solemn evening in exalted company' that Aghnides had expected. It contributed to the success that 'D. looked lovely in black velvet and lace, with the family jewels, and H.R.H. [His Royal Highness] showed signs of falling under her spell'. The prince even 'went with E. to take her home, and to inspect her movie-camera, which is the same as his' and 'promised to serenade her by flying his Spitfire' over her home. While from a twenty-first century perspective this might seem like inappropriate behaviour, there is no indication that Margaret van Kleffens interpreted this flirtatious 'boyishness' as she called it, as anything but a great compliment and sign of her success as a hostess.[87] Though in this case the Dutch prince had a reputation as a

---

[85] Pedro Désiré Eduard Teixeira de Mattos, Esq and his wife Elisabeth Arnoldine Clothilde Leonie Marie Josèphe Ghislaine de Bassompierre (known to their friends as Epi and Betty) and John de László, son of the famous painter Philip de László, and his first wife Peggy Cruise, daughter of Sir Richard Robert Cruise. MvK diary 26 September 1943, inv nr 393, 2.05.86, NL-HaNA.
[86] Letters from Dicky Horstmann to her family written in 1937 describe her photography studies in Los Angeles, UK-Wilson.
[87] MvK diary 27 September 1943, inv nr 393, 2.05.86, NL-HaNA.

Figure 2.5 Aileen Emilie 'Dicky' Wilson, née Horstmann. Date unknown but probably around 1947. Photo: Raymond Wilson, her husband. Courtesy of their grandson Edward Wilson.

philanderer, later examples will show that a degree of (modest) flirtation between men and women was a regular part of socializing, regardless of their marital status.

The practice of inviting important guests to stay the weekend and trying to charm them as much and in as personal a way as possible was by no means limited to the Dutch Foreign Minister and his wife. Many foreign ministers (and other diplomatic actors) entertained in similar ways, and not only during the war. The organization of weekend visits of the Dutch couple during their exile seems fairly improvised compared to the networking of the foreign secretary of the United Kingdom and his wife in the following decade, but the aims appear similar. In February 1955, for example, Anthony Eden received a request, which he forwarded to his wife Clarissa Eden, for himself and Lady Eden to spend a weekend in April at the estate of Lord Robert ('Bobbety') and Lady Elizabeth Salisbury, Hatfield House. The occasion was the 'courtesy visit to this country' of Admiral Lewis Strauss, the Chairman of the United States Atomic Commission and his wife Alice Strauss. Admiral and Mrs Strauss were going to be entertained as weekend guests by Lord and Lady Salisbury (the Lord President of the Council and his wife). They were already going to be joined by Mr Harold and Lady Dorothy Macmillan (she a famous socialite and he, at the time the note was written, Defence Minister), but the Department hoped to get the Eden's to join too. 'As you know,' the request said, 'Admiral Strauss is a very influential person and we hope to make rather a fuss of him during his visit.'[88]

Empirical evidence from different settings indicates that inviting influential people to stay over as house guests was a widespread practice, used to deepen a relationship or imply a special friendship. It was more intimate and more exclusive than the many other forms of dinner diplomacy but, however personal, it was a professional obligation. The formal request in the British example shows how it was part of the work of foreign secretaries and other high-ranking government officials to personally pamper politically important international contacts, and their wives were included in this effort. For Eelco and Margaret van Kleffens, having weekend guests remained an obligation for the rest of their career, even if exactly who they were obliged to entertain and what logistical support they had to do so varied depending on the post and position. As diplomats abroad after the war, personal entertaining was an even bigger part of everyday diplomatic work; having house guests was only one small part of it.

Concluding remarks on the diplomatic home

Even when physically separated from the embassy or office, the homes of especially top-ranking diplomats were significant sites of diplomatic work: the empirical material studied has yielded not a single exception to the rule that diplomats did work-related entertaining at home. The separation of spheres of home (in which women played crucial roles) and office (as an exclusively male environment) therefore did not make diplomats' homes more private or less

---

[88] Note to the Secretary of State 4 February 1955. AP/3/2/3 Lady Avon: Correspondence, etc, relating to entertainments, Avon Papers, Cadbury Research Library, Birmingham, UK (UK-CRL).

politically important. In fact, quite the contrary. Homes were diplomatically expedient precisely because of their private status and as a domain where women ruled. An extra dimension was added in the rising superpower, the United States, where newspapers treated ambassadors as celebrities of sorts. According to Cold War historian Michael Hopkins, post-war Washington, DC was a city that had only just started to adapt to its position as a great power centre of government, with the American system being still quite open to foreign influence.[89] In 1950, the American capital housed 55 embassies and offered an intense social life and close contacts between diplomats, journalists and politicians.[90] When talking of how embassies played a role in shaping foreign policy, historians rarely recognize their importance for their role as places of personal residence. Nor, as a general rule, do other diplomatic or politicians' homes feature as important sites of social diplomatic interaction. Yet a lot of the social interaction in Washington, DC took place within these homes. After half a year as ambassadress to the Unites States, Margaret van Kleffens exclaimed in her diary that a lunch she had been invited to at the Mayflower was 'the first time I lunch outside a private home, I believe, in Washington!'[91]

In 1969, Arlie Hochschild wrote in a study of (contemporary) ambassadors' wives, that 'public behavior even in apparently private places is "diplomatically significant" and carries with it messages which have less to do with personal feelings than with the decisions of higher state department officials in Washington'. One way to communicate diplomatic messages was by '"formalizing" and "informalizing" diplomatic occasions'.[92] The strong evidence in Margaret van Kleffens's diaries that receiving, accepting and refusing invitations to someone's home – an 'informalized' occasion – was interpreted as political, is entirely in line with what Hochschild claimed more than 50 years ago. And yet, most research – as referenced in the introduction to this Part – tends to underestimate the political role of the diplomatic home as a consequence of seeing it as an increasingly private, apolitical sphere in the twentieth century.

The empirical findings presented here show that the home was at the heart of daily diplomatic work. As a (semi-)private arena, it played an inescapable role in mid-twentieth century diplomatic relations. Though it was connected to

---

[89] Michael F Hopkins, 'Focus of a Changing Relationship: The Washington Embassy and Britain's World Role since 1945', *Contemporary British History* 12, no 3 (1998): 105–6.
[90] R van der Maar and H Meijer, and Hans Meijer. *Herman van Roijen 1905–1991: Een Diplomaat van Klasse*. (Amsterdam: Boom, 2013), 271–72; Hopkins, 'Focus of a Changing Relationship'.
[91] MvK diary 30 January 1948, inv nr 397, 2.05.86, NL-HaNA.
[92] A Hochschild, 'The Role of the Ambassador's Wife: An Exploratory Study'. *Journal of Marriage and Family* 31, no 1 (1969): 73–87 at 73.

Figure 2.6 Margaret and Eelco van Kleffens giving the press an image of domestic idyll by playing a game of Scrabble, 1954. Original caption: 'President of the United Nations General Assembly Dr Van Kleffens relaxes with his wife, in their Waldorf Astoria suite in New York.' Photo: Orlando/Three Lions/Getty Images.

previous diplomatic traditions, like the nineteenth-century salons, the use of the home in the twentieth century shows novel patterns. It was by then possible to imagine the home as a private, apolitical place, so that inviting someone home could be used as a gesture of intimacy, implying friendship and trust that served as important diplomatic assets. Though gendered in different ways, the dichotomy between home and work remains an illusion, since well-functioning diplomacy required both.

Part Three

Dinner Diplomacy

I have more need of casseroles than of written instructions.
Talleyrand to King Louis XVIII, leaving for the
Congress of Vienna[1]

At the Dutch Cabinet meeting of 2 January 1946, Prime Minister Wim Schermerhorn summarized the recent Netherlands–United Kingdom talks on Indonesia (in the Netherlands still better known as the Netherlands East Indies). After the Japanese occupation of the Dutch colony in 1942, followed by the Indonesian declaration of independence on 17 August 1945, the Dutch were not able to recover and hold on to their former territory without British military assistance. Knowing this and believing that the loss of the colony would be disastrous for the Netherlands' economy as well as overall international position, the consultation with the British was an important agenda item for the Cabinet.[2] The talks were 'not exactly smooth' to begin with, Schermerhorn reported. But then, he said, British Prime Minister Clement Attlee 'interrupted the discussions for tea. Afterwards, the discussions were conducted in a significantly better tone'. Things went even better following dinner. 'After that, they quickly proved prepared to take over practically our whole statement.'[3]

---

[1] As cited in B Keys, 'The Diplomat's Two Minds: Deconstructing a Foreign Policy Myth'. *Diplomatic History* 44, no 1 (January 2020): 1–21, 12.
[2] Frans Glissenaar, *Indië Verloren, Rampspoed Geboren* (Hilversum: Verloren verleden, 2003); John Newsinger, 'A Forgotten War: British Intervention in Indonesia 1945-46', *Race & Class* 30, no 4 (1989): 51–66.
[3] As recorded by secretary P Sanders during the Dutch Cabinet meeting of 2 January 1946, inv nr 388, Archive of the Council of Ministers (Ministerraad) 2.02.05.02, NL-HaNA. My translation from Dutch. Original quote in context: 'Het gesprek verliep niet bepaald vlot.... Attlee onderbrak de besprekingen voor de thee. Nadien werden de besprekingen in een aanzienlijk beteren toon gevoerd.... Men werd het eens over de uitgifte van een gemeenschappelijk statement. Er werd toen een ontwerp gemaakt door ons en één door de Engelschen. Voordat deze ontwerpen werden vergeleken, werd er eerst gedineerd. Daarna bleek men vrij snel bereid om practisch ons statement geheel over te nemen.'

The prominent mention of tea and dinner as factors of influence on the negotiations of a matter as politically significant, sensitive and complicated as the Dutch–British coordination of military activities in Indonesia is striking. Of course, when it comes to daily life, most people would probably recognize the simple truth verbalized by Virginia Woolf in 1928 and proved by neuroscience in many different ways since then:

> The human frame being what it is, heart, body, and brain all mixed together, and not contained in separate compartments as they will be no doubt in another million years, a good dinner is of great importance to good talk.[4]

It is hard to see why diplomatic talks would be an exception. Indeed, the wining and dining diplomat is not only a well-established public image but is also a well-documented fact of diplomatic life.[5] Nevertheless, I have yet to come across an account of the history of Dutch decolonization that considers commensality as a factor in negotiations or political decision making. Much like wives and homes, the sharing of food and drink seldom appears in political analyses of diplomatic relations. Indeed, more often than not they are analyzed as if heart, body and brain were, in fact, contained in separate compartments.

Testimonies to eating and drinking together as a way to break the ice or promote mutual goodwill are ubiquitous both within and outside a diplomatic context. Commensality, the act of sitting down at the same table to share a meal, is considered one of the most important ways to create and manifest a sense of community in all cultures of all times.[6] No wonder, then, that, in practice, international relations entail so much eating and drinking. What better tool to transcend the differences between peoples and cultures than a phenomenon that is truly universal, to engage in an act so fundamentally human? Alas it is not that simple. As anybody with any substantial experience of family dinners knows, commensality does not always create one big happy family. Eating and drinking together is a way to establish closeness, but it can also help to expose hidden enmity or distrust.[7] Breaking the (often unwritten) rules of behaviour at a shared meal can also damage interpersonal goodwill: arriving over- or underdressed; not eating the right thing at the right time in the right manner; or by drinking or talking too much, or too little. Moreover, the rules of commensality differ

---

[4] Virginia Woolf, *A Room of One's Own* (London: Penguin Books, 2004), 21.
[5] I Neumann, *At Home with the Diplomats: Inside a European Foreign Ministry* (Ithaca: Cornell University Press, 2012) 18.
[6] See, eg, Claude Fischler, 'Commensality, Society and Culture', *Social Science Information* 50, no 3–4 (2011): 528–48.
[7] Maurice Bloch, 'Commensality and Poisoning', *Social Research* 66, no 1 (1999): 133.

considerably between different social, political, religious and economic contexts. It is not only an inclusive practice, but also one that often creates a community at the expense of people excluded, whether they have not been invited to begin with or fail to act according to group norms. Food cultures differ, tastes differ and table manners that are unfamiliar or perceived as being rude may reduce rather than enhance feelings of goodwill. At the same time, even bad food or broken rules might lead to bonding – depending on the setting, existing relationships or other circumstances. In short, to be useful, the diplomatic role of sharing food and drink needs to be studied in its particular historical context. The need to be specific is all the greater because commensality is such an omnipresent feature of daily diplomatic life and one to which all human beings are inescapably susceptible. Whether a minister as famous for his diplomatic skills as Talleyrand really said to King Louis XVIII that casseroles were more useful to him than instructions, the fact that the quote has survived testifies to the reputation of hosting dinners as a longstanding and efficient diplomatic method.

This part is not just about dinners. It takes a closer look at how eating and drinking together was employed as a diplomatic method in the mid-twentieth century. The primary focus is on the Western diplomatic hubs London (during the war) and Washington DC (in the early postwar years). I use the phrase 'dinner diplomacy' to signify any diplomatic interaction (ie, interaction between persons perceiving each other as representatives of states in that situation) taking place under the auspices of eating and/or drinking together. I have not adopted the existing term 'culinary diplomacy' because the focus is not exclusively on the diplomatic role of food and cuisine but on other aspects of the practice as well.[8] At the same time, though the overlap with what others have called the 'sociability of diplomacy' is considerable, I have opted for a term that explicitly includes food, because sharing meals was such a strikingly dominant feature of daily diplomatic life.[9]

While that means that occasional other social activities like playing golf or going to a concert are left out, the following chapters host a motley collection of lunches, tea parties, receptions, cocktail parties and dinners, big and small, both formal and informal. Framing these widely diverse occasions as different expressions of dinner diplomacy allows me to bring them together under one

---

[8] For the use of 'culinary diplomacy', see Sam Chapple-Sokol, 'Culinary Diplomacy: Breaking Bread to Win Hearts and Minds', *The Hague Journal of Diplomacy* 8, no 2 (2013): 161–83.
[9] For sociability in diplomacy, see, eg, Naoko Shimazu, 'What Is Sociability in Diplomacy?', *Diplomatica* 1, no 1 (2019): 56–72; Deepak Nair, 'Sociability in International Politics: Golf and ASEAN's Cold War Diplomacy', *International Political Sociology*, no Generic (2019).

analytical framework while posing open questions. What purpose did dinner diplomacy fulfil in the diplomatic practices of the mid-twentieth century? Who played what roles in that diplomacy and what were the elements that made it successful? The goal is not to show how particular dinners had particular political consequences – though some examples, like the introductory one, do seem to indicate that they could have – but to analyze the practice of eating and drinking together as a diplomatic method and to consider what it meant for the functioning and development of postwar international relations. As in the rest of the book, it is the pattern and its consequences I am after.

That said, the only way to discern the pattern is to identify its elements: to zoom in to be able to zoom out. The empirical study is primarily based on quotidian details available in the diaries of Margaret van Kleffens. She often listed these occasions, in contrast to her husband who, in his diaries, noted only the occasions he felt a need to say something about. Even if her notes are often brief – many comments are limited to 'lunch with X' or 'to a cocktail at Y' or 'Z to tea' – and although they do not provide an entirely complete overview, they are uncommonly comprehensive, occasionally extensive and have been meticulously kept over a period of many years. That makes it possible to form a pretty good idea of the prevalence and range of diplomatic events built around eating and/or drinking in different diplomatic settings and positions. Moreover, her more detailed and candid diary reviews of the guests, hosts and settings of certain diplomatic dinners (or cocktails, receptions, or tea parties) offer revealing insights into the etiquette and *faux pas* of dinner diplomacy. Other people's life writings, as well as newspaper articles, photographs and foreign office personality reports complement this view.

Chapter 8 highlights the general characteristics of dinner diplomacy as a daily practice. It surveys the diversity of diplomatic occasions involving the sharing of food and/or drink, making an inventory of their frequency and different kinds of guests and discusses the purposes and organization of dinner diplomacy events. Chapter 9 deals with one of three ingredients central to dinner diplomacy: food. The other two, dressing (in the widest sense of the word, ie both table and people) and discourse, say so much about the division of tasks in everyday diplomatic work and the (tacit) norms of diplomatic culture that they are discussed in a part of their own under the heading diplomatic aptitude. In both parts, the relationship between political and personal is at the core of the analysis, with special attention for the roles played by class, gender, ethnicity and/or nationality. The aim is to identify any common denominators of dinner diplomacy as well as to gauge and illuminate the bandwidth of the phenomenon.

The elements of the chapters come together in an analysis of the patterns of dinner diplomacy as an overarching phenomenon, with a discussion of its implications for postwar diplomatic relations.

8 Dinner diplomacy as an everyday practice

From the very beginning, dinner diplomacy played a big role in the personal relationship between Eelco van Kleffens and Margaret Horstmann. The first empirical part already told the story of how she turned down his initial marriage proposal, but said she would be glad to get to know him better if their acquaintance came with no strings attached.[10] This was not as simple as it might seem: in The Hague in 1934, a man and a woman from their social circles could not freely go out together without risking a lot of gossip, which could have harmed their (her) reputation. So, while in his next letter, Eelco van Kleffens eagerly clutched at the straw offered, he worried that with the social season of The Hague at its end, there would be 'so miserably few opportunities in front of us to meet'.[11] Besides leading the couple to write letters *in lieu* of having face-to-face conversations, the problem was partly solved by Margaret Horstmann inviting Eelco van Kleffens to tea at her parents' house and by arranging to play games of golf (sometimes followed by tea).[12] Another solution, which Eelco van Kleffens proposed in the letter cited above, was that he could ask her 'to a small dinner I am in the habit of giving from time to time if there are any of our own diplomats (mostly the younger ones) here on leave, or if there are foreigners I feel I should entertain'.[13] Later letters confirm that Margaret Horstmann attended a diplomatic lunch at her suitor's apartment only two weeks later. Besides a Miss Nixon and Miss Horstmann herself, the invited guests were all diplomats with wives, save the Dutch Chargé d'Affaires of the Oslo Embassy, GA Scheltus, temporarily in The Hague, who came alone. The other guests were the Dutch diplomatic couple the Bosch van Rosenthal's (home from London) and the two Dutch diplomats' counterparts in The Hague with wives, British Chargé

---

[10] Letter from Margaret Horstmann to Eelco van Kleffens 20 March 1934, inv nr 434, 2.05.86, NL-HaNA.
[11] Letter from Eelco van Kleffens to Margaret Horstmann 23 March 1934, inv nr 434, 2.05.86, NL-HaNA. As in London and other European capitals, it was customary for the social and political elite of The Hague primarily to organize big dinner parties, dances, and other social events during a few months of the year. This was known as the social season.
[12] See the couple's 1934 correspondence, inv nr 434, 2.05.86, NL-HaNA.
[13] Letter from Eelco van Kleffens to Margaret Horstmann 23 March 1934, inv nr 434, 2.05.86, NL-HaNA.

d'Affaires Christopher and Catherine Steel, and Norwegian Chargé d'Affairs Jack and Cecilie Raeder.[14]

This snippet of history from the very early stages of the relationship between Eelco and Margaret van Kleffens already gives rise to at least three observations about mid-twentieth century dinner diplomacy. One is that a diplomatic lunch seamlessly fitted into general upper-class socializing in The Hague. Margaret Horstmann's tea invitation belonged to the same culture of acceptable socializing for an uncommitted couple as Eelco van Kleffens's lunch invitation. A second and overlapping observation is that the most personal and emotional of affairs were, without hesitation, mixed with diplomatic ones. Eelco van Kleffens seems to have had no qualms about using the performance of his diplomatic duties as an excuse to see the object of his affection. The third observation is too isolated for drawing any general conclusions at this point, but worth keeping in mind as the story unfolds: the only people to join the luncheon mentioned above who were not (married to) diplomats were two unmarried women, one of whom we know for sure did not hold a diplomatic position to merit her inclusion.[15] Apparently, this was neither a breach of protocol nor a violation of diplomatic norms.

The first observation about dinner diplomacy is no surprise. Diplomatic culture in the mid-twentieth century in many ways remained an extension of a more general Western European elite culture.[16] Yet, it might be worth emphasizing that the overlap was not only one of rules and habits, but also a literal overlap of participating individuals and daily practices. The possibility that the overlap observed here was a chance feature of this particular courtship is easily ruled out by moving back in time a little. Letters from the late 1920s and early 1930s by Margaret Horstmann's younger sister Aileen Emilie Horstmann (Dicky to family and friends) show that Eelco van Kleffens and Margaret Horstmann were already part of the same social circle before they met. In fact, they are likely to have attended at least some of the same parties before they became aware of each other and, although they did not share the same inner circle of close friends (easily explained by their age difference, places of birth and schooling) they

---

[14] Letters from Eelco van Kleffens to Margaret Horstmann 8 and 9 April 1934, inv nr 434, 2.05.86, NL-HaNA. See also ch 2, where that lunch is described.

[15] I have not been able to ascertain the identity of Miss Nixon, but if I were to make an educated guess, I would put my money on her being Eelco van Kleffens's secretary, knowing that he sometimes invited subsequent secretaries of his along with diplomat colleagues to this kind of smaller lunches or dinners. His war-time secretary, Elly van Alphen, is mentioned as one of the lunch guests in MvK diary 13 December 1943, inv nr 393, 2.05.86, NL-HaNA.

[16] See their introduction and several of the contributions in Markus Mösslang and Torsten Riotte, eds., *The Diplomats' World: A Cultural History of Diplomacy, 1815-1914* (New York; Oxford: Oxford University Press, 2008).

certainly shared a great number of acquaintances. The letters that Dicky Horstmann sent to her mother and/or father are full of descriptions of society lunches, dinners and dances that the two sisters attended during their parents' absences from The Hague. They prove that, long before the connection to Eelco van Kleffens, many of their friends and acquaintances belonged to well-known Dutch nobility and diplomatic families (two categories that often overlapped) and included foreign diplomats and their families stationed in The Hague as well as royalty. Royal appearances were rare enough to prompt a special mention in the letters but, even on more ordinary occasions, Dicky Horstmann reported to her parents who had attended. Usually, she named at least some of the other guests, though she might rush through her list by saying that 'so-and-so' and 'the whole crème de la crème' had been there.[17]

Though the social circles of diplomats and local elites overlapped, they did not entirely coincide. While there was no obstacle to inviting diplomats to high society parties, there was no obligation to do so and, in practice, it seems not every diplomat was invited. Notably, the letters of Dicky Horstmann only mention Western European diplomats (or their young adult children). Conversely, not every diplomatic party was open to socialites who did not have an official diplomatic position. Moreover, diplomats were sometimes required to socialize with people with diplomatic positions who might not have made it into the local high society circles. The correspondence between Eelco van Kleffens and Margaret Horstmann not only mentions diplomatic meals that she attended, but also those she did not, and could not, attend. In one letter, for example, Eelco van Kleffens asked if he could come a little later than originally arranged because he had been 'upbraided by the wife of the Portuguese Minister for neglecting that Legation ... So I had to accept her invitation for lunch on Saturday, on condition that I'll be free to depart at 2.15'.[18] He was invited in his capacity as Head of Diplomatic Affairs at the Ministry of Foreign Affairs by a woman in her capacity as wife of a Head of Mission. Only after the couple were married did Margaret van Kleffens become part of these kinds of diplomatic social obligations.

Spectrum and quantity

After they were married, dinner diplomacy for the diplomatic couple included a whole range of more or less obligatory social events involving food and/or drink.

---

[17] Letters from Aileen Emilie (Dicky) Horstmann to her parents 1928–1937, UK-Wilson.
[18] Letter from Eelco van Kleffens to Margaret Horstmann 30 August 1934, inv nr 437, 2.05.86, NL-HaNA.

To form a general idea of the span, one might consider the rather personal and intimate practice of having house guests – sharing meals with people who also stayed the night – at one end of the dinner diplomacy spectrum and the tea-drinking coupled to (semi-)formal calls at the other. Both have already been described in Chapter 7 as parts of the diplomatic work done in homes. In between, ranging from more intimate and targeted to more impersonal dinner diplomacy of a more general importance, there were dinners, lunches, cocktail parties and receptions. The order is rough rather than absolute and the variations were considerable within the different categories. Obviously, an informal cup of tea with friends or close colleagues at someone's home was quite different from having tea at formal and obligatory calls made when one was the new ambassador ('s wife) in town and expected to make the rounds. Aspects like location, occasion and (type of) guests would matter, besides the type of meal. While receptions and cocktail parties were generally less intimate than dinners and lunches by virtue of their mingling character, a big, formal dinner did not necessarily make for more personal conversations.

Dinners and lunches had a wide variety of formats and functions. As with weekend guests, sincere personal feelings of friendship sometimes arose and could become a reason to invite certain people in diplomatic functions more often than others, regardless of specific political purposes. This, for example, seems to have been the case with the friendship between the Van Kleffenses and the Greek diplomat Thanassis Aghnides, who was a frequent dinner guest both during the war, when he was ambassador to the United Kingdom and afterwards, when he represented Greece at the United Nations in New York. Personal friends or family members without an official diplomatic function were often added to the mix, as described in connection with house guests in the previous chapter. Other people were unmistakably treated as friends for political reasons, such as the war-time adviser to the Belgian government in exile Georges Kaeckenbeeck and his wife. 'Fed lunch to the Kaeckenbeeck's', Margaret van Kleffens wrote in her diary in 1944, 'this is a chore and a bore, but it has to be done about once every two months for good relationship's sake'.[19]

Meals could be exclusive and intimate, particularly when hosted at private homes, like the Vanbenberg party mentioned in connection to the diplomatic functions of homes. When hosted at restaurants, the sense of intimacy could vary considerably depending on the number of guests and the occasion, from

---

[19] MvK diary 3 January 1944, inv nr 393, 2.05.86, NL-HaNA.

small and informal to large and formal. In her war-time diary, Margaret van Kleffens noted that she usually went into London once a week to do voluntary work, and once so that she and her husband could have guests for lunch.[20] Those lunches were usually with a few Dutch colleagues or foreign counterparts, but they also attended huge lunches, like the 250-person luncheon offered by Imperial Chemical Industries in honour of a Holland–Belgium football match.[21] Both dinners and lunches were occasionally all-male, for example when Eelco van Kleffens had lunch with his allied colleagues at the Foreign Office or when he gave or went to a stag party.[22] Similarly, Margaret van Kleffens would occasionally have lunch at the Red Cross in North Row, where she made clothes for refugees together with other Dutch exile ladies during the war, or – more frequently after she became ambassadress in Washington – give or go to all-ladies tea parties or luncheons.[23]

As an everyday diplomatic practice, then, dinner diplomacy took on many shapes. The frequency of the different forms of dinner diplomacy depended on the post, with Washington, DC (where the van Kleffenses were posted from July 1947 to June 1950) being particularly busy. The materials used for this study do not allow for a reliable approximation of how many social events involving food and drink an average ambassadorial couple – if such a thing exists – might have attended yearly in postwar Washington. The number probably varied between different countries' representatives, depending on national status, customs, expectations and – not in the least – finances. Personal preferences and aptitude no doubt also played a role. Nevertheless, a superficial survey of the mentions of dinners, lunches, teas, receptions and cocktails in Margaret van Kleffens's diaries from the couple's first year in Washington – 25 July 1947–24 July 1948 – can serve to form at least an impression of the quantitative importance of dinner diplomacy. Even accounting for the possibility that she might occasionally have mentioned the same dinner twice, such a count should yield an approximate minimum, considering that she likely also omitted a number of events: on some days she devoted her diary notes to other matters, such as contemplations about life, politics, family, or personal problems. In those 366 days (1948 was a leap year), there are 230 mentions of dinners, 162 lunches, 31 receptions, 108 teas,

---

[20] MvK January 1941 account, inv nr 391, 2.05.86, NL-HaNA.
[21] MvK diary 14 January 1944, inv nr 393, 2.05.86, NL-HaNA. Imperial Chemical Industries (ICI) was involved with the United Kingdom's top-secret nuclear weapons programme (codename Tube Alloys). The Tube Alloys project was subsumed into the American Manhattan Project in 1943.
[22] See, eg, MvK diary 18 January and 22 April 1943, inv nr 392; 18 July 1946, inv nr 396, 19 Feb. 1948, inv nr 397, 2.05.86, NL-HaNA.
[23] MvK diary 16 April 1943, inv nr 392; in the Washington diaries inv nrs 397–400, 2.05.86, NL-HaNA.

and 31 cocktail parties. That means that the couple had, or were, guests for dinner more than four times a week on average. The total number of occasions during which food or drinks were shared in a diplomatic context by far exceeded the number of days in a year.[24] Considering that these events, by definition, involved a lot of other people and, judging by the company they kept, their habits do not seem to have deviated significantly from the habits of many other Western ambassadorial couples.

Official foreign office documents, too, testify to the importance of dinner diplomacy. In the United Kingdom, personality reports were systematically collected by the Foreign Office. Envoys serving abroad were supposed to write annual reports on the heads of foreign missions as well as on the leading personalities in the country where they served. These mini biographies, of different lengths, readily available in the Foreign Office's so-called Confidential Print, sometimes contain a description of the educational or professional background of individuals, in line with what one would expect in a very brief curriculum vitae. However, they also (and sometimes only) include information of a personal and social character. In Sir Hughe Montgomery Knatchbull-Hugessen's 1945 Annual Report on Heads of Foreign Missions at Brussels, for example, he noted that he knew the Netherlands Ambassador Baron B Ph van Harinxma thoe Slooten from when he was posted in Angora and was 'able to exchange views and information with but little reserve' with him. He also reported that the Dutch envoy's wife was half-British and that she did work for the Dutch Red Cross. The note about the Swiss Maxime de Stoutz confirms the perceived relevance of social relations: 'Serious, hardworking and conscientious, but without social gifts', Knatchbull-Hugessen wrote. 'I think he must be the dullest man in the world.' His report on the Turkish minister, Basri Lostar, included not only information on the language skills of the envoy's wife and daughter, but also that his secretary was married to the niece of the Turkish ambassador in Paris.[25] The inclusion of facts like these in very short, obligatory reports to the Foreign Office shows that information about personal relational ties and the people surrounding a diplomat was treated as being politically relevant.

Many details mentioned in the personality reports are of the kind that testify to the importance ascribed to social relations. Matters that few people would spontaneously define as a foreign relations concern appear: 'His full-dress

---

[24] MvK diary 25 July 1947–24 July 1948, inv nrs 397 & 398, 2.05.86, NL-HaNA.
[25] Denis Smyth, ed., *Part III, From 1940 through 1945. Series F, Europe*, British Documents on Foreign Affairs: Reports and Papers from the Foreign Office Confidential Print, vol 19 (Bethesda, MD: University Publications of America, 1997), 7.

uniform is the high-light of official diplomatic receptions' Oliver Hardy wrote about the Nepalese head of mission in Paris, for example. Information about envoys' marriages seems to have been considered particularly relevant. In most cases, British mid-twentieth century personality reports mentioned the wife, or the fact that the head of mission was a bachelor. The charms, language and social skills of both husband and wife were often mentioned; marital status was frequently coupled to remarks on entertaining. In Oliver Hardy's 1950 report on the foreign heads of mission in France, you can read that the Belgian envoy and his wife were a 'very friendly and hospitable couple who entertain lavishly and rather indiscriminately' and that the Portuguese envoy, 'an excellent colleague with a pleasant Greek wife', entertained 'with dignity in his fine embassy'. The Cuban minister had 'a particularly attractive wife and they go about a good deal in society', while the Finnish envoy was 'somewhat outshone by his really extraordinary wife'. The new Swedish envoy, however, was 'very friendly when I meet him, but he is not a very interesting personality and by no means of the same calibre as his predecessor. He is unmarried and entertains little'.[26]

Purposes and organization

The amount of attention given to envoys' entertaining and social skills and the quantity of meals attended by diplomatic couples in daily life all testify to the significance of dinner diplomacy. But what was it for? The frequent entertaining of compatriots points to the fact that dinner diplomacy was not only about relations with foreigners but also about strengthening national coherence. I have argued elsewhere that it was of crucial importance in international negotiations to keep the national story straight. Displaying national unity and widespread support for the country's foreign policy position helped to gain other countries' trust in the government's capability as well as its intention to keep its promises. It was especially important to keep all ministers and diplomats (and the monarch, in some cases) in line, but in a democracy, a high degree of general consensus

---

[26] Denis Smyth, ed., *Part IV From 1946 through 1950, Series F, Europe 1950*, British Documents on Foreign Affairs: Reports and Papers from the Foreign Office Confidential Print, Vol. 23 (Bethesda, MD.: University Publications of America, 2003). The heads of mission referenced here were General Shanker Shamser Jang Bahadur Ranathe of Nepal, Belgian Baron Jules Guillaume, Portuguese Dr Marcello Mathias, Cuban Dr Hector de Ayala y Saaverio, Finland's Johan Helo, and the Swede Karl Westman. The latter's predecessor, incidentally, was married to, in the words of Swedish historian Nevra Biltekin, the 'femininely attentive' Margaret Boheman. Biltekin describes her as an important asset to her husband, Erik Boheman. N Biltekin, *Servants of Diplomacy: The Making of Swedish Diplomats, 1905-1995* (Stockholm: Department of History, Stockholm University, 2016) 183–85.

regarding foreign policy was also important, to maintain international stability beyond the next elections.[27]

The part of dinner diplomacy of Eelco and Margaret van Kleffens that was aimed at compatriots fits this pattern. It was often about strengthening the sense of unity and loyalty among important colleagues and staff. The context could be markedly personal. On her first birthday in Washington, DC, for example, Margaret van Kleffens and her husband had the top ten people at their new embassy to a dinner, to eat, get to know each other and bond.[28] Margaret van Kleffens also gave periodic teas all through the Washington years 'for our "blue book" Embassy wives, plus a few prominent Dutchwomen not belonging to "us"'. If we are to believe her diary, these teas 'afforded little amusement' to her personally. 'However,' she wrote in 1949, 'Aimée [Reuchlin, wife of one of the embassy employees] reports that it is considered a social uplift so I must continue the tradition.'[29]

Compatriot dinner diplomacy could also be about encouraging patriotic loyalty and a more close-knit Dutch community of expats. In the United States, descendants of Dutch settlers as well as more recent expats were important, both as a support system for Dutch diplomats and for public diplomacy, as they often promoted their homeland culture by celebrating national traditions and holidays.[30] In practice, expats could become unofficial diplomatic representatives of their country of origin.[31] Dinner diplomacy for this group was often a large-scale, not-so-intimate affair. Queen Wilhelmina's birthday, for example, was celebrated every year at the Washington embassy with a reception for the wider Dutch 'colony', as Margaret van Kleffens called it. On the Queen's birthday in 1947, there were about 200 guests whom she identified as consisting 'largely of Embassy staff, Int. bank and monetary fund people, with a sprinkling of professors, scholarship people from Holland; and Surinamers'.[32]

A third type of compatriot dinner diplomacy aimed to create and maintain close personal relationships with individually important people like politicians,

---

[27] S Erlandsson, *Window of Opportunity: Dutch and Swedish Security Ideas and Strategies 1942–1948*. Uppsala: Acta Universitatis Upsaliensis, 2015, 56–67.

[28] MvK diary 6 September 1947, 2.05.86, NL-HaNA. She summarized the evening as 'makan-kennismaking-toenadering'. 'Makan' is Indonesian for 'eat' or 'meal'; 'kennismaking' and 'toenadering' are Dutch words for 'acquaintance' and 'rapprochement'.

[29] MvK diary 21 October 1949, inv nr 400, 2.05.86, NL-HaNA.

[30] On this wider phenomenon in an American-Swedish context, see Adam Hjorthén, *Cross-Border Commemorations: Celebrating Swedish Settlement in America* (Amherst: University of Massachusetts Press, 2018).

[31] See Nevra Biltekin, 'Unofficial Ambassadors: Swedish Women in the United States and the Making of Non-State Cultural Diplomacy', *International Journal of Cultural Policy: CP* 26, no 7 (2020): 959–72.

[32] MvK diary 31 August 1947, inv nr 397, 2.05.86, NL-HaNA. Surinam was a Dutch colony.

high-ranking diplomats, royalty, businessmen, artists, journalists, scientists, or (in this period) resistance heroes – people whose work and/or status in Dutch society made them welcome guests. Often, these were people visiting from the home country, but they could be individuals of the guest country as well. 'E. flew to New York for the annual dinner of the Holland Society of New York,' Margaret van Kleffens wrote in November 1948. Although seemingly a Dutch expat organization like those mentioned above, she added that this was 'a group of self-glorifying, pompous, rich and rather idiotic men who do absolutely nothing for Holland, so that we look upon them with a minimum of favour'. Yet, 'poor E.' had to 'don white tie, tails – and decorations' and 'address them once yearly, much to his irritation' because '[a]las, they seem to be important individually'.[33]

Part of the couple's irritation about this representation might well be that it seemed comparatively pointless: it was just a formality which had to be done so as not to insult important people. As discussed above, the more personal and informal the dinner diplomacy with influential guests, the better. Eelco and Margaret van Kleffens clearly considered it a success when a higher-ranking guest, such as Prince Bernhard, acted in a relaxed and casual manner. Conversely, they could use relaxed and casual behaviour to gain goodwill themselves. An ambassadorship was a high-ranking position in any country and conferred something of a celebrity status in the postwar United States. Another example of dinner diplomacy aimed at the Dutch colony shows that the strategies for gaining the goodwill of different sorts of groups had similarities, despite different contexts. In November 1947, the couple travelled to a commemoration of the centenary of Dutch settlement in Michigan. After what Margaret van Kleffens described as an inadequate dinner eaten on their laps, Eelco van Kleffens took the chance to speak to a large number of students of a Dutch fraternity about Indonesia, sitting on the floor, smoking a pipe, the attentively listening students sitting around him.[34] Not all dinner diplomacy was equally glamourous, but in all its shapes, making relationships personal and informal seems to have been a winning game if goodwill and loyalty was what you were after.

When it comes to transnational contacts, one of the most obvious reasons for all the dinner diplomacy was that it helped to extend and maintain diplomatic networks, that is, networks that might one day come in handy for the sake of national interests. Describing her life as a Dutch diplomat's wife from 1932–1971, Dé Buma makes a point of stressing that those networks were of central

---

[33] MvK diary 18 November 1948, inv nr 398, 2.05.86, NL-HaNA.
[34] MvK diary 2 and 3 November 1947, inv nr 397, 2.05.86, NL-HaNA.

importance to the job. It is completely unjustified, she says, that the 'the outside world' sometimes adopts a scornful attitude towards 'all those cocktails and dinners'. She explains that you never knew in advance what background information the Foreign Office would suddenly require. All the same, when a request came, you were expected to know exactly who to contact in the country where you were stationed – not the second best in the field, but (as she phrases it) 'the top man'. And that, she adds, had to be someone you knew well. Therefore, you had to make sure you got to know everyone 'who meant anything' as quickly as possible, and the only way to do that was to accept every invitation you received and to entertain a lot yourself. Dinner diplomacy was simply the most effective way to improve your diplomatic network. 'Everyone likes a good dinner and good wine.'[35]

Another benefit of socializing was visibility, which was good both for building networks – more people would know who you were – and for status. The papers kept tabs of which embassy had housed which guests. Repeated mentions in the press make it clear that dinners and other social events had a public diplomacy function. In the early twenty-first century, the female Israeli Ambassador to South Africa, Tova Herzl, wrote that she was often not invited to social events during her posting. 'In a trade in which being seen is an indication of status – both of the diplomat and of the country she represents – this matters', she wrote.[36] This was equally true in the mid-twentieth century. A big difference, however, was that while Tova Herzl had to do all the chores involved in dinner diplomacy herself, almost all mid-twentieth century ambassadors were supported by their wives.[37] The previous chapter mentioned how the *Saturday Evening Post* called it 'a social-diplomatic triumph' that the Dutch ambassador had the foreign ministers of all the Benelux countries as well as Secretary of State Dean Acheson for dinner. The article ascribed that achievement to Margaret van Kleffens.[38] Her diaries confirm that the magazine was right to credit her, not because she was unusually successful – she herself thought the French ambassador's wife the most efficient of her Washington counterparts[39] – but because they showed that she did what ambassadresses were supposed to do: work hard to get the right people to attend dinners and other events hosted by the embassy.

---

[35] Buma, *Donderdag Komt de Koerier*, 120–24. My translation from Dutch.
[36] Tova Herzl, *Madame Ambassador: Behind the Scenes with a Candid Israeli Diplomat* (Lanham MD: Rowman & Littlefield, 2015), 74.
[37] Herzl, *Madame Ambassador*, 71–76.
[38] Morrow and Thayer, 'We Toured the Embassy Kitchens', 32 'Mme. Eelco van Kleffens … had just achieved a social-diplomatic triumph …'.
[39] MvK diary 24 February 1949, inv nr 400, 2.05.86, NL-HaNA.

After a few months in Washington, Margaret van Kleffens wrote in her diary that her 'desk-work is increasing so much that I am beginning to wonder whether a secretary will not be the only solution on the long run'.[40] A few days later, she specified what that work entailed: 'Ye Gods! all this desk-work. Paying bills, returning cards ... writing notes of invitation, acceptance, regret and thanks. I know it all belongs; but I seem to find no time for a walk even.'[41] The available evidence testifies to the significance of this work, not only in terms of amount of labour, but also in terms of political significance. 'All my mornings recently have to be spent at my desk or at the telephone; the social season is at its height', Margaret van Kleffens wrote in February 1949.

> Even three weeks in advance it is quite hard to find the more attractive and/or prominent people free for dinner. As for those in high office: Dean Acheson is unable to go out for pressure of work, and Sen. Conally and Representative Sol Bloom, heads of the Senate and House Foreign Relations bodies respectively, have declined our invitations so long in advance that we know it must be for political reasons: we Dutch stink, because of Indonesia.[42]

Even if she could have been wrong about their motives in this particular case, the fact that Margaret van Kleffens interpreted the dinner rejections of Conally and Bloom as political at the very least tells us that such an interpretation appeared feasible.

The example is also particularly illuminating because she went on to share more of her reasoning with the reader: 'It is all the more remarkable as E. has had the friendliest of personal relationships with these two men over a period of years.'[43] Whether sincere or not, the pre-existence of a friendly relationship rules out that these two men would have repeatedly turned down invitations either because of personal dislike or unwittingly. Moreover, the additional sentence shows that the amicable networks built by dinner diplomacy were expected to yield diplomatic benefits. Since Margaret van Kleffens (a) interpreted the dinner rejections as political and (b) qualified the behaviour of Conally and Bloom as 'remarkable' because of pre-existing friendship, means that (c) friendly personal relations led to expectations with political implications. Unfavourable political treatment from long-standing personal friends was not what Margaret van Kleffens felt entitled to expect.

---

[40] MvK diary 17 October 1947, inv nr 397, 2.05.86, NL-HaNA.
[41] MvK diary 21 October 1947, inv nr 397, 2.05.86, NL-HaNA.
[42] MvK diary 23 February 1949, inv nr 399, 2.05.86, NL-HaNA.
[43] MvK diary 23 February 1949, inv nr 399, 2.05.86, NL-HaNA.

The logical inference of this reasoning is that to achieve and extend these 'friendliest of personal relationships' was a daily diplomatic task that should not be underestimated. It re-emphasizes how much a male diplomat benefitted from the assistance of a female spouse. Some twentieth-century diplomats' wives, like American Evangeline Bruce, became quite famous for their socializing. Scholars writing about her and her husband have emphasized how well the couple worked together.[44] Little attention has been paid to the fact that diplomatic couples worked together as a rule, even if they were not all as successful as the Bruce's. By working together, a diplomatic couple could enhance their visibility and their diplomatic network more than could a single diplomat. The most obvious advantage was that there were two of them, which meant that they were able to speak to more people at events they hosted or attended together than one of them could have managed alone. When two events coincided, they could go to one each.[45] An ideal diplomatic couple also complemented each other, giving the spouses an even wider reach since their personalities might appeal to different people or be suitable for different tasks.

Regardless of compatible or complementary personalities, dinner diplomacy in the mid-twentieth century had a distinct division of tasks based on gender. This gave diplomatic couples a significant advantage over single diplomats. Crucial aspects like invitations and seating could not be left to lower-ranking staff. Even in the twenty-first century, Tova Herzl, an ambassador without a wife, still had to do these dinner diplomacy chores herself.[46] For Eelco van Kleffens and his married contemporaries, their wives were responsible for invitations, seating plans and dinner decorations, not to mention their job as hostess. A diplomat without a wife generally had to find another woman, often a relative, whom he could trust with these tasks.[47] Besides the gendered preparations, the gendered norms for appropriate social behaviour at the event itself gave women other ways than their husbands to charm important men (more on which in subsequent sections). At mixed-sex luncheons and dinners, a male guest of honour always sat next to the hostess and his wife always next to the host. Diplomatic protocol thus

---

[44] See John Young, *David Bruce and Diplomatic Practice: An American Ambassador in London, 1961–69* (New York: Bloomsbury Publishing, 2014), 34–35; Kenneth Weisbrode, 'Vangie Bruce's Diplomatic Salon. A Mid-Twentieth-Century Portrait', in *Women, Diplomacy and International Politics since 1500*, edited by Glenda Sluga and Carolyn James (Abingdon & New York: Routledge, 2015) 240–53.
[45] Eg, MvK diary 5 March 1947, inv nr 396; 10 June 1948, inv nr 398, 2.05.86, NL-HaNA.
[46] Herzl, *Madame Ambassador*, 71–76.
[47] After becoming a widower, Swedish Foreign Minister Östen Undén had a daughter function as his hostess, for example. See also the story of Thanassis Aghnides in Chapter 4, 'The diplomatic couple as template'.

gave wives close access to many politically important people. Moreover, because gendered norms also, to some extent, separated the spheres occupied by women and men, a wife gave her diplomat husband indirect access to women's networks. Birgitta Niklasson has shown how this gendered access to networks still plays a role for present-day diplomats. She debunks the notion that exclusion from all-male social networks would make female diplomats less efficient. Male diplomats are excluded from all-female social networks too, she points out. Though male and female diplomats may, to a degree, have access to different contacts, she shows that the contacts of male diplomats are neither less numerous nor less diplomatically relevant than those of female diplomats.[48]

In the mid-twentieth century, a diplomatic couple could achieve a more complete network than tendencies towards homosociality would allow any single diplomat, male or female. There were lunches and dinners that were for men only, and there were lunches and dinners especially for ladies, who also had tea parties and made social calls on one another. Margaret van Kleffens often complained about these all-female gatherings, making denigrating comments like 'the company of my sex, unless friends, means little to me as such, being largely lacking in grey matter!'[49] Still she kept going to 'these female get-togethers ... because it gets me into the circulation, because I meet many people I would not meet otherwise – in fine, because it is good for our position here.'[50] On another occasion, Margaret van Kleffens noted in her diary having had to tea 'some fifteen or twenty press-, radio-, and clubwomen who have (either they or their husbands) spoken up, written, or been active on behalf [of] our interests. A tea which went with a swing, and...... bored the hostess to tears'.[51] There can be little doubt that her entertaining of groups of women and participation in female networks was motivated by political expediency rather than personal preference.[52]

A 1948 *Hartford Times* piece on the tea parties hosted by Madame van Kleffens at the Dutch embassy testifies to their success and her ability to appear personally interested, whatever her true feelings. According to journalist Robbie

---

[48] B Niklasson, 'The Gendered Networking of Diplomats'. *The Hague Journal of Diplomacy* 15, no 1–2 (2020): 13–42
[49] MvK diary 15 August 1947, inv nr 397, 2.05.86, NL-HaNA. In fine = Latin for 'to sum up' or 'in short'.
[50] MvK diary 16 April 1948, inv nr 397, 2.05.86, NL-HaNA.
[51] MvK diary 20 February 1948, inv nr 397, 2.05.86, NL-HaNA.
[52] For a discussion of how gendered assumptions have skewed historical research on Margaret van Kleffens, see S Erlandsson, 'Off the Record: Margaret van Kleffens and the Gendered History of Dutch World War II Diplomacy'. *International Feminist Journal of Politics* 21, no 1 (2019): 29–46 ; S Erlandsson and R van der Maar, 'Trouw aan Buitenlandse Zaken. Margaret van Kleffens, Anne van Roijen, de ambassade in Washington en de betekenis van het diplomatiek partnerschap voor de naoorlogse Nederlandse buitenlandse betrekkingen'. *Tijdschrift voor Geschiedenis* 134, no 3 (2021).

Johnson, the Dutch ambassadress had a desire 'to become better acquainted with more interesting women of the capital' beyond the 'necessarily casual encounters at receptions'. It was 'a rare and delightful experience to drink a quiet cup of tea with a gracious, diplomatic hostess and a mere dozen soft-spoken, charming women' at the Dutch embassy as compared to the 'sardine-can crushes of usual embassy functions'. The success of the tea party was coupled to characteristics that conveyed a sense of an intimate gathering in the private home of the hostess. Johnson stressed that Margaret van Kleffens had decorated the embassy herself with the utmost taste and care and mentioned a clock that had 'been in her family for generations'. The outspoken and sometimes condescending comments that Margaret van Kleffens made in her diaries are in sharp contrast to the way Johnson described her: 'Quiet almost to the point of self-effacement, she is one of the most gracious and popular hostesses in the diplomatic corps.' According to Johnson, '[e]ach of her guests leaves with a warm feeling of having made an interested friend'.[53]

It is worth noting that, when it came to specific women, Margaret van Kleffens often spoke admiringly of their intelligence or how successful they were and I have found no record of her having any reservations about women (like Pandit or Roosevelt for example) holding positions of power. That Margaret van Kleffens still evidently felt a need on the (private) record to distance herself from women in general testifies to her susceptibility to a structural rather than personal misogyny. Her behaviour seems to have been more to do with distancing herself from a certain stereotype rather than actually believing women to be less intelligent than men. Her concrete descriptions of men and women did not depict women as less witty or interesting than their husbands. Sometimes it was quite the opposite: in April 1946 she talked about 'that formidable little live-wire Mrs. Ogden Reid of the New York Herald Tribune' but defined Mr Ogden Reid as 'her apparently balmy husband'.[54]

While women's networks were often informal, some postwar ambassadors' wives in Washington developed a more instrumental approach to female networking in support of their husbands. In February 1949, Margaret van Kleffens described a tea party for ladies at the embassy of France:

> Hellé Bonnet, who in calculating efficiency outstrips any ambassadress I have known, is giving a series of these affairs in order to bring Congressmen's wives

---

[53] Robbie Johnson, 'Tea Happy at Dutch Embassy', *Hartford Times*, 20 March 1948.
[54] MvK diary 6 April 1946, inv nr 395, 2.05.86, NL-HaNA.

together with diplomats' spouses. We are all neatly labelled with name and state, or country, upon entering the house, and told to introduce ourselves and 'meet the folks'. Very tiring, very uninteresting, but very worth while, in this country where personal contacts mean so much and where women influence their husbands much more than with us.[55]

Beyond what it reveals about wives' networking structures in postwar Washington, the quotation is interesting because it points to a change in diplomatic culture with the move of the major Western diplomatic hub from London to Washington. Margaret van Kleffens seems to have perceived personal contacts to be particularly important in the United States and American wives as being more influential than Dutch, or possibly European ones. At the same time, Julia Eichenberg shows in her study of the so called 'London Moment' that a change towards more personalized diplomatic relations had already taken place in the United Kingdom during the war. Because of the physical proximity of so many exiled governments, academics, journalists, etc., it became easy to meet and discuss things in person in London.[56]

The increased diplomatic focus on Washington, which meant a merger of European with American high society culture, probably strengthened this trend after the war. It was not only the French ambassador's wife who picked up on the possibilities: Margaret van Kleffens's successor at the Washington embassy, Anne van Roijen (1950–1964), created a semi-official and (according to several testimonies) very efficient women's network together with Betty Fulbright, wife of the well-known American senator of the same name. Together, they initiated the exclusive so called 'Neighbors Club' to bring together the wives of ambassadors, politicians, businessmen and reputable journalists. Should one of their husbands need a favour, the wives would arrange it. The club still exists and, for a long time, remained exclusively female. The first male spouse joined in 2008.[57]

While the purpose of most dinner diplomacy was general networking and visibility, specific visits or invitations could sometimes serve more specific political purposes. During the war, Margaret van Kleffens once made a call on

---

[55] MvK diary 24 February 1949, inv nr 399, 2.05.86, NL-HaNA.
[56] Julia Eichenberg, 'Informal Encounters and Transnational Networks. European Diplomacy in British Exile during the Second World War' (New Diplomatic History Conference: Diplomacy between Crisis and Cooperation, Aarhus, Denmark, 2021). See also J Eichenberg, 'London Calling. Adressbücher des britischen Exils im Zweiten Weltkrieg', in: *Zeithistorische Forschungen* 16, no 2 (2019): 363–74; J Eichenberg, 'Legal Legwork: How Exiled Jurists Negotiated Recognition and Legitimacy in Wartime London', in: *Crafting the International Order. Practitioners and Practices of International Law since c. 1800*, edited by Marcus M. Payk and Kim Christian Priemel (Oxford: Oxford University Press, 2021) 162–90.
[57] Erlandsson and Maar, 'Trouw aan Buitenlandse Zaken'.

Clementine Churchill at the express request of the Dutch queen, who asked her to 'let Mrs Churchill know that in spite of ours being an agricultural country, our food problem is far from being over (as she thinks) as soon as the war ends'. Margaret van Kleffens's diary description of the occasion shows how important it was for women to keep their ostensibly apolitical profile: even though her visit had an explicitly political goal, she could not come right out and say that the British should count on the Netherlands needing postwar aid. Instead, she set out to change the British prime minister's wife's perceptions – presumably on the assumption that her views would influence her husband's – by casually, 'with as much tact and nonchalance as I could muster' bringing the matter up as part of a personal chat. Her struggle to 'work this ... fact into the conversation with the unsuspecting Mrs. C.' kept her from properly enjoying 'a (non-austerity) tea, with cake, cheese-puffs and currant-bread, to which I did but little justice owing to my concentration on trying to turn the discourse the way *I* wished it to go'. Ultimately, she 'fulfilled [her] mission'.[58]

On several occasions between 1947 and 1949, the Washington dinner diplomacy of the Netherlands' ambassador and his wife also had an immediate political connection to the controversy surrounding the Dutch political and military actions in Indonesia. Lunches and dinners were among the available diplomatic tools to handle the international crisis that the Netherlands faced. Back in 1942, as Foreign Minister, Eelco van Kleffens had been central to formulating the Dutch policy regarding Indonesia. He had argued that the Atlantic Charter principle that established the right of a people to choose its own government – which the Dutch had signed – was not applicable to an Indonesian Republic because there were so many different peoples in Indonesia. Surely, it was no progress (as compared to a benevolent Dutch rule of a federalized Indonesia) to allow one of the Indonesian peoples to suppress the others?[59]

In line with this argument, it was politically opportune for the Netherlands to highlight and pamper those Indonesians who supported the Dutch attempt to establish a federal United States of Indonesia. A 1947 intimate dinner at the Netherlands' Washington residence for the presidents of East Indonesia and West Kalimantan (the latter consistently called West Borneo by Margaret van

---

[58] MvK diary 20 and 26 October 1943, inv nr 393, 2.05.86, NL-HaNA. See also Erlandsson, 'Off the Record', 37.

[59] Typed copy of the Dutch cabinet protocol 13 October 1942, inv nr 246, 2.02.05.02, NL-HaNA. Van Kleffens kept arguing that the Republic was merely one of several Indonesian regions, see Jennifer L Foray, 'The Republic at the Table, with Decolonisation on the Agenda: The United Nations Security Council and the Question of Indonesian Representation, 1946–1947', *Itinerario* 45, no 1 (2021): 124–51.

Kleffens in her notes) and their entourage was clearly motivated by a political need that was at the time acute. Less than a month earlier, a Dutch military intervention in Indonesia had ignominiously ended through pressure from the United States and the UN Security Council. The international rebuke was a severe blow to the image of the Netherlands as the country of The Hague, symbol of peace and international law. At this stage, it was crucial to the government of the Netherlands to frame the conflict, not between Dutch and Indonesians, but between legitimate and benevolent governors and malicious insurgents. To show that the Dutch entertained friendly relations with those parts of Indonesia that in 1947 did not (yet) belong to the new Indonesian Republic was, in this light, highly opportune from a political point of view.

The diary notes of Margaret van Kleffens confirm the dinner's character of political performance. In part, the performance might have been put on for the guests themselves – to convince them that supporting the Dutch was a rewarding strategy – but it was, in all likelihood, also meant to send a signal to onlookers. In any case there seem to have been no sincere attempts to build friendly relations behind this staged intimacy. Her description shows that she went to great lengths to arrange the evening to perfection and she portrayed the setting as superb, but the atmosphere as 'so tense you could cut it with a knife'.[60] On other occasions too, guests were invited because of the Indonesian question, regardless of whether the couple enjoyed their company. 'To lunch came the American judge in the Int. Court – with whom we now wish to stand well! – and his slightly less inarticulate lady' wrote Margaret van Kleffens on 3 September 1948.[61] Political interests trumped the preference for guests with good conversation skills. On another occasion, the maintenance of the Dutch colony of Surinam was the cause of an invitation. Margaret van Kleffens complained about having the 'less inspiring' Ambassador de Thomen of the Dominican Republic on her right, as one of the guests of honour, 'whom we had to award in this manner for bringing some wild plot to seize Surinam to our Govt.'s attention, at the behest of his own'.[62]

Both specific political goals and more general aims such as visibility and public diplomacy were served by including journalists and media magnates in dinner diplomacy. A week after the note on the congressmen's dinner rejections, Eelco van Kleffens had an especially successful lunch date, public relations-wise. His wife, who was not present because she had an operation on her varicose

---

[60] MvK diary 27 August 1947, inv nr 397, 2.05.86.
[61] MvK diary 3 September 1948, inv nr 398, 2.05.86, NL-HaNA.
[62] MvK diary 15 March 1949, inv nr 399, 2.05.86, NL-HaNA.

veins that day, noted from her hospital bed that 'E. had Mr. Henry Luce, (of "Life", "Time" + "Fortune"), … to lunch; and converted Luce to our viewpoint re Indonesia – good work!'[63] She did her part too, taking care of the female press people. 'Another tea party', she noted about six months after her arrival in Washington, DC, 'this time for press women, radio women and society editors'.[64] She often had either lunch, tea, or dinner with influential journalist and society column writer Mary van Rensselaer Thayer. A comment from an occasion when she was cross with Thayer for printing that the Dutch embassy cook had once burned a steak – the cook was very upset – shows that Margaret van Kleffens was well aware of the power of the press. 'I rang up Molly Thayer', she wrote in her diary, 'and gave her a careful (press-relations – beware!) piece of my mind'.[65]

9 Diplomatic food

Anyone who doubts the relevance of food and drink to personal and power relations should read Virginia Woolf's *A Room of One's Own*, published in 1928. 'It is a curious fact that novelists have a way of making us believe that luncheon parties are invariably memorable for something very witty that was being said, or for something very wise that was done', she writes. 'But they seldom spare a word for what is eaten.' There is an unwritten rule not to mention 'soup and salmon and ducklings', she notes. Breaking that rule with a vengeance, she goes on to describe exquisite courses and how 'the wineglasses had flushed yellow and had flushed crimson; had been emptied; had been filled'. She pinpoints the impact of a good meal:

> And thus by degrees was lit, half-way down the spine, which is the seat of the soul, not that hard little electric light which we call brilliance, as it pops in and out upon our lips, but the more profound, subtle, and subterranean glow which is the rich yellow flame of rational intercourse. No need to hurry. No need to sparkle. No need to be anybody but oneself. We are all going to heaven and Vandyck is of the company – in other words, how good life seemed, how sweet its rewards, how trivial this grudge or that grievance, how admirable friendship and the society of one's kind, as, lighting a good cigarette, one sank among the cushions in the window-seat.[66]

[63] MvK diary 3 March 1949, inv nr 399, 2.05.86, NL-HaNA.
[64] MvK diary 13 November 1947, inv nr 397, 2.05.86, NL-HaNA.
[65] MvK diary 26 October 1949, inv nr 400, 2.05.86, NL-HaNA.
[66] V Woolf, *A Room of One's Own*. (London: Penguin Books, 2004).

Virginia Woolf describes emotions by evoking them in her reader, which is why her account is so efficient and possibly more convincing than an elaborate theoretical explanation of why emotions matter: even our most rational beliefs are, after all, emotional.[67] The state of body and mind described by Woolf is conducive to the kind of emotions that can tip the scale towards taking the leap of faith that is necessary to trust someone, whether in private life or in diplomatic relations. A wartime description of a meal by Margaret van Kleffens conveys her idea of a perfect evening as similar to that described by Woolf:

> Last evening turned out one of those exceptionally perfect, rare evenings, when everyone enjoys himself, and all m*igh*ty merrie! How we laughed, and how delicious was the dinner: green asparagus 'à la hollandaise', grilled salmon with peas + potato purée, and fresh strawberry flan, with some Portuguese wine to give added sparkle. Before dinner Floris [van Pallandt] put my precious, expensive lemon to the best of uses in a super-cocktail concoction. Not for a long time have I enjoyed myself so much and been so gay.[68]

Unlike the novelists to whom Woolf refers, Margaret van Kleffens evidently thought this dinner party memorable for what was eaten and drunk – in fact, she did not spare a word for what was said, even if a fair guess would be that it was something witty, since everybody laughed.

So, what does this mean for our understanding of daily diplomacy? In literature on culinary diplomacy, commensality as a tool to create a sense of communality and to improve diplomatic discussions is one of two things usually emphasized. The other is the use of a national cuisine in public diplomacy, as a sort of nation branding. In both cases, food tends to be viewed as something that is useful and beneficial to diplomatic relations.[69] It is indeed easy to see how creating an atmosphere like the one described above would help the networking mentioned earlier and be conducive to goodwill. The opening example of this part of the book even points to an impact of shared meals on the outcome of direct political negotiations between heads of state. However, one should not be too quick to conclude that food had a generalized positive influence on diplomatic relations. Another 'perfect' dinner, the one described towards the

---

[67] J Mercer, 'Emotional Beliefs'. *International Organization* 64, no 1 (2010): 1–31.
[68] MvK diary 13 June 1943, inv nr 392, 2.05.86, NL-HaNA. Floris van Pallandt, second man at the Dutch legation in London when war broke out, had recently been appointed Head of Diplomatic Affairs. Some may know him as the father of Frederik van Pallandt of the 1960s Danish–Dutch singing duo Nina & Frederik.
[69] Chapple-Sokol, 'Culinary Diplomacy'; Séverine Boué, 'Les Réceptions à la Résidence de France à Washington: Vitrine Gastronomique de la France et Outil Diplomatique des Ambassadeurs (de 1893 à Aujourd'hui)', *Bulletin de l'Institut Pierre Renouvin* 50, no 2 (2019): 33–45.

end of Chapter 8 that Eelco and Margaret van Kleffens gave for the East-Indonesian party seems to have done nothing at all to 'strengthen ties and reduce antagonism' which, according to Chapple-Sokol, is what a shared meal serves to do 'with either friends or enemies'.[70] And the *Saturday Evening Times* story about Western as opposed to Soviet food that was mentioned in Chapter 6 is an example of how food was used symbolically to create feelings not only of communality, but also of enmity in public diplomacy.

Other historians' accounts confirm how shared food or drink have played equally powerful but diverse diplomatic roles in different twentieth-century contexts. Describing the 1993 Washington talks between Israelis and Jordanians, Barbara Keys recounts how the antagonistic delegates were brought together by their shared dislike of American coffee, finding common ground in a sense of 'the superiority of the Middle Eastern version of the drink'.[71] Though far from the good dinner conducive to good talks that might serve as the ideal of diplomatic commensality, the shared bad coffee experience achieved what days of hard diplomatic work had failed to accomplish: to get the delegates to talk at all. In a different time and setting, Naoko Shimazu highlights the more conscious use of food to forge bonds by marking distance to someone else. She describes the 1955 Bandung conference, which put newly independent African and Asian states on the diplomatic map while (and by) excluding Western states. The conference cuisine displayed and performed post-colonial independence by serving Indonesian food and food from the national cuisines of the delegates rather than the standard so-called world – that is, French – cuisine. Shimazu also points out the symbolic unifying role of commensality by showing how eating together was an important part of a sociability that was emphasized at Bandung and 'worked like a social glue that brought people together and generated a semblance of a collective identity'.[72]

Shimazu's study confirms the symbolic use of cuisine as a kind of nation-branding, in this case setting it off against a Western diplomatic cuisine heavily influenced by the French. It also exposes the bias of the existing diplomatic culture. Transnational norms that were heavily modelled on the norms of an Early Modern Western European aristocracy meant that different countries' diplomats had unequal opportunities to succeed at dinner diplomacy. Unsurprisingly, the French cuisine is often a model for the success of culinary

---

[70] Chapple-Sokol, 'Culinary Diplomacy', 166.
[71] Keys, 'The Diplomat's Two Minds', 1.
[72] Shimazu, 'What Is Sociability in Diplomacy?', quote on p 59.

diplomacy. Séverine Boué has shown how French postwar ambassadors gave exquisite dinners to relax the atmosphere in times of tension between France and the United States. When people went to eat at the French embassy, they expected excellent food and the best wines. She has also highlighted the importance of food to nation branding and called the receptions at the French residence in Washington a 'gastronomic showcase of France'.[73] But not all countries could use their national cuisine as successfully. As Boué points out, France had a special position in postwar Washington, world famous French gastronomy being especially popular among the American elite.[74] If anything is to be said in general about how food played a role in daily diplomacy, the different preconditions of different countries need to be taken into account. Serving food from one's national cuisine was one thing for the French ambassador, but quite another for his non-Western colleagues, for example.

Elise Morrow's and Mary van Rensselaer Thayer's article 'We Toured the Embassy Kitchens', published in the *Saturday Evening Post* on 29 October 1949, is revealing in this regard, because they make explicit references to the diplomatic aspect of cooking. 'Although plainly a diplomat', they write about the French embassy chef, 'M. Ducluzeau does not wear striped pants, nor does he wear a tweed jacket like his boss, Ambassador Henri Bonnet. He is not even a military attaché; he is the chef.' What, then, made him a diplomat in their eyes? In Morrow's and Thayer's description of his cooking, they highlight two things: his elaborate and time-consuming French cooking and his use of American ice cream for dessert. Henri Ducluzeau is quoted as saying about the first: 'Frankly, I don't think any American would have the patience', so that his cooking comes across as typically French and/or as foreign to Americans. The remark might seem on the verge of derogatory but, according to the two journalists, 'he diplomatically made amends' by saying about his choice of dessert: 'Who am I to be telling you about ices? ... You Americans make the best ice cream in the world.'[75]

While this example features a French chef, it is not necessarily the French food that comes across as diplomatic, but the balance between offering something exotic while putting one's own national character in a favourable light and paying homage to the host country. It is too simple to say that culinary diplomacy was about using national food to promote the country. The rest of the article shows that while some countries did, others did not. The Italian ambassador's wife,

---

[73] Boué, 'Les Réceptions à la Résidence de France à Washington', 40, 43. My translation.
[74] Boué, 'Les Réceptions à la Résidence de France à Washington', 34.
[75] Morrow and Thayer, 'We Toured the Embassy Kitchens', 33.

Signora Tarchiani, is quoted as saying that her guests expect Italian food and she never serves anything else. However, the Greek Madame Dendramis 'says she is afraid to serve an entirely Greek menu to Americans for fear their taste would reject it as too unfamiliar'. The Dutch, as already mentioned, had a Guatemalan cook who served food 'native style' – which certainly did not allude to Dutch natives. The typical Swedish menu, the authors shared, 'might have one Swedish specialty … but everything else would be a specialty of some other country'. And the British, well, they were 'resigned to a hopelessly negative culinary heritage of their own' so that they had simply surrendered to the pre-eminence of the French cuisine as the diplomatic food par excellence and hired a French cook.[76] It would not have been good culinary diplomacy to serve diplomatic guests a national cuisine at all costs, without any consideration for their tastes. Moreover, as in the Dutch and Swedish examples, food could be used to exhibit international as well as national values.

What all the descriptions in the *Saturday Evening Post* do have in common is the emphasis on the skills of the various chefs and cooks and how much effort they made. At the only non-Western embassy visited, that of recently independent Burma (Myanmar), the authors described how the third secretary served them exotic Burmese food at his home because the chef was sick. The Burmese curry was described as 'eye-watering and alien to the American taste' but the overall tone was positive, focusing on the hospitality and massive effort of the secretary who cooked himself and explained all the dishes. It is telling that the only food that was described as downright bad, the food at the Soviet embassy, was described in terms of negligence and general inhospitality towards the guests. Based on hearsay, since they had not visited the Soviet embassy themselves, the authors claimed that the guests there had been served soup that was cold and meat that was burnt. Moreover, 'all the Americans present were glum and wary, but the Russians were gay and full of vodka'. A reference to the Soviets even withholding the best that their national cuisine had to offer was the last drop: 'No caviar either.'[77] This story, however made-up it may have been, places the use of national cuisine in a somewhat different light than as pure nation branding. It tells us that good diplomats offered their guests their best (and that those who did not were bad hosts). Food should make a lavish impression and help to expose the guests to beauty, generosity and good taste. Particular national foods could (and should) be served if it meant displaying that generosity by including someone in your

[76] Morrow and Thayer, 'We Toured the Embassy Kitchens', 32–33, 130.
[77] Morrow and Thayer, 'We Toured the Embassy Kitchens', 32.

Figure 3.1 Swedish minister Erik Sjöborg and the Van Kleffenses eat 'beschuit met muisjes' in London, 28 January 1943, at a reception to celebrate the birth of Dutch Princess Margriet. Photo: Sport & General Press Agency. Courtesy of Rijksmuseum, Amsterdam, Netherlands.

community. The story of the Soviets portrays them as not including their guests, not only because they did not feed them caviar, but because they got drunk and happy among themselves, while excluding the Americans.

National cuisine, then, could be used both as nation branding and as a way to demonstrate hospitality. When, in 1943, Princess Margriet of the Netherlands was born, the Dutch ambassador and his wife in London (Edgar and Henriette Michiels van Verduynen) held a large reception for both compatriots and foreign colleagues which featured the biscuits with sweet aniseed sprinkles that are typically served when the birth of a child is celebrated in the Netherlands (see Image 3.1). Normally, the sprinkles would be pink and white but, on this day, they were orange since the Dutch royal family was from the House of Orange.[78] While the culinary excellence of these biscuits is arguably debatable, they served to make their foreign colleagues feel included in a typically Dutch celebration. On the other hand, serving national dishes was no guarantee of a feeling of inclusion. 'Two w*hole* roast lambs were paraded around the luncheon table', Margaret van

[78] MvK diary 28 January 1943, inv nr 392, 2.05.86, NL-HaNA.

Kleffens wrote in her diary when at a lunch given by that month's president of the United Nations Security Council Hafez Afifi Pasha. 'I suppose this is an Egyptian custom', she wrote. Rather than strengthening a sense of goodwill and communality however, she claimed it made the wife of the British Security Council delegate, Lady Theo Cadogan, wail: 'Oh, the poor little things, how *can* we eat them?'[79]

In practical terms, making sure that there was good food to serve all the guests they were supposed to entertain was a never-ending task for the diplomatic couple. Food took a lot of preparation and planning. Like so many other of the crucial dinner diplomacy tasks, decisions regarding menus were the responsibility of the wives.[80] The authors of the *Saturday Evening Post* article confirm this as female territory, even if they noted that the Italian ambassador liked to cook as a 'hobby' and explained that the third secretary of the Burmese embassy had learned how to cook 'because his mother died when he was young and he had no female relatives'. Male diplomats taking an interest in the preparation of food were presented as an exception. About the wives, however, Morrow and Thayer said that 'many can cook, and all are at least competent critics of food'.[81] Throughout the article, besides describing the cooking of the cooks and chefs, the focus is on what embassy wives served *their* embassy guests.

The cooking itself was otherwise not straightforwardly gendered, in the sense that both men and women cooked and were hired in the highest embassy kitchen position. However, in the materials I have studied, women are consistently called cooks – which usually refers to someone who does all-round cooking but is not highly trained – while men are referred to as chefs, a title that implies special skills (and a higher salary). Yet in practice, there are no indications that there was any difference in the type of cooking or level of skills. The wording of the *Saturday Evening Times* article – which featured five cooks who were all female and four chefs who were all male – seems to indicate that a woman was never a chef while a man was never a cook. The authors even commented on the discrepancy. 'It is a common notion that a male chef is a greater artist than a woman cook', they wrote. 'This prejudice', they continued, 'is not supported in Washington.'[82] Nevertheless, they continued to consistently refer to women as cooks and men as chefs.

---

[79] MvK diary 14 May 1946, inv nr 395, 2.05.86, NL-HaNA.
[80] Not only diplomats' but also politicians' and other elite wives; the archive of Clementine Churchill, for example, includes boxes with notebooks with page after page of menus. Menu Books, 1936–1975, inv nrs 9/3/1–9/3/17, The Papers of Clementine Ogilvy Spencer-Churchill, Baroness Spencer-Churchill of Chartwell, CSCT, UK-CAC.
[81] Morrow and Thayer, 'We Toured the Embassy Kitchens', 126.
[82] Morrow and Thayer, 'We Toured the Embassy Kitchens', 32.

Whether male or female, it was an immense advantage to have a cook or chef who could be trusted to do a lot of the work independently, like Rosa de Zepeda or Henri Ducluzeau. Their skills were highly valued. The dedication of the French chef was extensively described by Morrow and Thayer who even called him a diplomat. Their description of Rosa de Zepeda similarly showed her great commitment, albeit in a way that the Dutch cook perceived as disastrous. 'Understandable consternation below stairs about an article in this week's issue of the Sat. Evening Post', Margaret van Kleffens wrote in her diary. 'It really is mean to write such "sensationalized" stories about defenceless, simple people like Rosa, who possess only their skill.'[83] The problem was the following passage:

> Such a mishap as a burned steak is rare, indeed, at any well-run embassy, but it did happen, also, last spring in the Dutch kitchen. Mme. Eelco van Kleffens ... had just achieved a social-diplomatic triumph by lining up for dinner the foreign ministers of the Benelux countries, plus Secretary of State Dean Acheson. Normally, the cook never knows whom she is cooking for, but Mme. van Kleffens, this time, told her. Rosa went to pieces. She was so nervous that she not only produced fillets which were burnt black instead of the usual lovely pink but she also botched the *crème brulée*, a fancy custard. It separated disastrously. 'Madame,' the cook said, weeping, 'you should not have told me who was coming for dinner.'[84]

Margaret van Kleffens must have told the journalists this story herself, though she might have assumed they would not print it. Her diary entry from the evening in question confirms the facts: 'Rosa, seized with the jitters, rate'd more than one of the dishes, to my infinite discomfiture and humiliation. Moral: *never tell the cook what's cookin'*.'[85]

Both her tears in April and her consternation when the article was published in October show that Rosa de Zepeda was deeply committed to her work and aware of what was at stake when there were important diplomatic guests. The diplomatic interests of her employers overlapped with her personal career interests. It is easy to imagine what a disaster it would be for an embassy cook in Washington, DC, to become known as someone who spoiled several dishes at an important diplomatic dinner. It was probably true that her skill and reputation were all she had. Still, Rosa de Zepeda need not have worried. Morrow and Thayer immediately added: 'This was, of course, the only disaster in Rosa's

---

[83] MvK diary 26 October 1949, inv nr 400, 2.05.86, NL-HaNA.
[84] Morrow and Thayer, 'We Toured the Embassy Kitchens', 32–33.
[85] MvK diary 2 April 1949, inv nr 399, 2.05.86, NL-HaNA.

professional career' and went on to describe her Guatemalan delicacies. Moreover, finding a good cook was not at all easy, as the chapters in Part II showed and Margaret van Kleffens was well aware of her cook's worth. There was never any question of firing her because of that one failed dinner, even if it did reflect badly on the hostess herself. Rosa de Zepeda stayed with the van Kleffenses until they left for Lisbon in 1950 and was gratefully employed by their successors Anne and Herman van Roijen, so that she remained the Netherlands Embassy cook for years to come.[86]

Although its national origin and ways in which food was used in twentieth-century diplomatic relations defy schematic generalizations, there is no doubt that food was considered of great value as a diplomatic tool in both symbolic and practical ways. Food and drink clearly had an impact on personal emotions and feelings of good- or ill-will and, if one general thing can be said about its role in daily diplomatic work, it is that providing food and eating it was a sensitive issue coupled with a lot of effort. What that effort looked like and which aspects were emphasized depended on the circumstances. During the war, a lot of time and effort went into   obtaining enough suitable food and drink to begin with, and 'a super, peace-time sort of lunch' was high praise.[87] Margaret van Kleffens's war-time diaries are full of notes on shopping, rations, keeping chicken for extra eggs and meat, picking berries to make up for the unavailability of fruit, etc. When the Greek ambassador brought as a gift 'a piece of ham, a thing we haven't seen for years', the cook Mrs Wiltshire was 'in raptures' and she and Margaret van Kleffens 'spent quite a while debating how to eat it'.[88] And already at midsummer 1943, the cook 'broached the subject of currants and sultanas for the Christmas cakes and puddings, which we shall have to lay in bit by bit on our "points".'[89]

In postwar Washington, DC, where food was plenty and Margaret van Kleffens did not have to do the shopping herself, those kinds of concerns were absent and notes-to-self were instead made of menus to remember, or improvements in choices regarding food and drink. After their first celebration of the Dutch Queen's birthday in Washington, DC, for example, she wrote: 'authoress please note: serve white wine punch next year!' The heat and humidity of the American

---

[86] Rosa de Zepeda is pictured with Anne van Roijen in a brochure published by the Netherlands embassy in 1952, Lonore Kent, *First Lady of the Embassy* (Washington, DC: Netherlands Embassy, 1952) The brochure is a recent addition to the archive of dr J.H. van Roijen, 2.21.183.70, NL-HaNA.
[87] MvK diary 26 March 1943, inv nr 392, 2.05.86, NL-HaNA.
[88] MvK diary 8/9 May 1943, inv nr 392, 2.05.86, NL-HaNA.
[89] MvK diary 22 June 1943, inv nr 393, 2.05.86, NL-HaNA. See also MvK diary 5 November 1943, inv nr 393 on being fortunate to have extra diplomatic rations, chickens and Mrs Wiltshire's honest preparation of food.

capital, to which she was not yet accustomed, had meant that 'the hard liquor lagged in popularity behind the saft, so that we were sadly short of the latter'. She also noted that 'Rosa's sandwiches looked perfectly delicious and so did the cookies' while the caterer's sandwiches had been 'a waste of money'.[90] At a successful musical evening hosted for about 100 high-flying American guests (including Under Secretary of State Robert and Adele Lovett) however, their lovely sandwich and cookies buffet 'went almost untouched', which was duly noted as a 'lesson for next time'.[91] When next year's celebration for the birthday of Queen Wilhelmina came around, Margaret van Kleffens noted that, this time, the drinks served – white wine punch, Manhattan's, Martini's, and fruit juice – had been perfect, but the food insufficient. 'Note to hostess: with the voracious Dutch colony, count on 3½–4 sandwiches each instead of the customary three. Have a table with food in the drawing room as well as in the dining room, instead of only a bar.'[92] Specific dishes or combinations of courses were noted. 'It was an exceptionally successful menu and one to be remembered by me', she wrote after naming each course of their 1948 Christmas dinner, to which they had 16 guests.[93] The matter of what food and drinks to serve, in what quantities and manner was a constant concern, with never-ending attempts at improvement.

It is interesting to think about what this centrality of food at so many diplomatic gatherings says about how diplomacy functioned. When Iver Neumann speaks of international relations as necessarily embodied, he refers primarily to the significance of diplomats' gendered appearances.[94] However, few things are as embodied as eating. The food may have a symbolic value, it might be served for political reasons, but eating and drinking is inescapably personal in the most literal sense: what we eat becomes part of our body. That not only makes for a physical and emotional impact of food that might strengthen bonds, it also turns the ability to eat all kinds of food into a matter of diplomatic suitability. Usually, Margaret van Kleffens worried more about what to serve than about what she and her husband had to eat in the line of duty, though it certainly mattered to her: she often commented that the food had been bad, or good, or so perfect that it made up for the company being 'the town's most crashing bores'.[95]

---

[90] MvK diary 31 August 1947, inv nr 397, 2.05.86, NL-HaNA.
[91] MvK diary 18 February 1948, inv nr 397, 2.05.86, NL-HaNA.
[92] MvK diary 31 August 1948, inv nr 398, 2.05.86, NL-HaNA.
[93] For example, MvK diary 24 December 1948, inv nr 398, 2.05.86, NL-HaNA.
[94] I Neumann, 'The Body of the Diplomat'. *European Journal of International Relations* 14, no 4 (2008): 671–95.
[95] MvK diary 26 March 1943, inv nr 392, 2.05.86, NL-HaNA. The boring people were the Van Lynden's, the Dutch-born minister of the Liberian legation and his wife.

However, the importance of dinner diplomacy made personal diets or medical issues a diplomatic disadvantage that could hamper the ability to entertain diplomatic networks. According to Maurice Bloch, the refusal to share food is 'one of the clearest marks of distance and enmity' in any society.[96] Reality is not that black-and-white, of course – a refusal to share food will be interpreted very differently in different contexts and depending on the reason for it. However, in mid-twentieth century everyday diplomatic socializing, even with good reasons, a diet was a handicap. About a British couple who were 'vegetarians by predilection *and* on doctors orders', Margaret van Kleffens wrote that 'their gruesome diet is a current nightmare to Washington hostesses'.[97] Presumably, such troublesome guests were only invited when protocol demanded it.

Eating became a diplomatic problem for Margaret van Kleffens herself. In 1946, a physician in New York City had diagnosed her with essential hypertension and, after her arrival in Washington, DC in 1947 her blood pressure rose alarmingly (the climate and the stress of the post were mentioned as possible causes). There was no cure for hypertension, but one of the treatments often attempted in those days was a strict diet. After a visit to the doctor in July 1948, she noted in her diary that she had been given 'bad news indeed': she was 'to try the rice diet, to try and get pressure down. This is rice, fruit, a small amount of vegetable, sugar and corn syrup; voilà tout. No meat, eggs, milk, fats of any sort'.[98] Besides the personal agony of such a diet (and the side-effect of a person as thin as she was quickly becoming undernourished), it hampered her daily diplomatic work. Her 'accursed diet' prevented her from accepting some invitations altogether and, when she did attend, but did not eat everything on the menu, it caused comments which were 'much unwelcome', however 'well intended'.[99] After a Dominican Embassy dinner, Margaret van Kleffens lamented that she had been 'forced to explain' her medical condition because her 'host got quite offended, in typical Latin American style, about my not partaking of wines etc'.[100] Pointing out a guest's inappropriate behaviour was a diplomatic *faux pas* that made the matter doubly embarrassing for Margaret van Kleffens. It drew attention to her failure to show appreciation for the food and drink she was served and left her with no choice but to violate another diplomatic rule: that of appropriate conversation (to be explained in Chapter 11).

---

[96] Bloch, 'Commensality and Poisoning', 133.
[97] MvK diary 30 September 1948, inv nr 398, 2.05.86, NL-HaNA.
[98] MvK diary 9 July 1948, inv nr 398, 2.05.86, NL-HaNA.
[99] MvK diary 1 and 4 September 1948, inv nr 398, 2.05.86, NL-HaNA.
[100] MvK diary 7 April 1949, inv nr 399, 2.05.86, NL-HaNA.

The incident can be used to revisit the idea of food as a helpful tool of diplomatic relations. Based on the evidence examined here, there is no doubt that the sharing of food and drink played an important role in the building and maintaining of mid-twentieth century diplomatic relations which made personal emotions, strengths, vulnerabilities and preferences even more relevant. Food was no impersonal device with indiscriminate and universally unifying qualities. As the example of the Dominican embassy dinner shows, food made an entirely personal matter that intrinsically had nothing to do with diplomacy – the hypertension suffered by the Dutch ambassador's wife – a threat to the diplomatic goodwill between the Dutch and the Dominican ambassador. Moreover, Margaret van Kleffens's explanation of her host's reaction as 'typical Latin American', together with the above stories about the Soviet and the Egyptian hosts, shows that food and drink could serve to strengthen prejudice and emphasize distance as well as to make relations closer. Part of understanding its significance for the development of twentieth-century international relations lies in understanding that food as a diplomatic tool could function differently for different people and be more useful to some than to others.

Concluding remarks on dinner diplomacy

Entertaining – as host or guest – was an everyday matter for diplomatic couples in the mid-twentieth century. Hardly a day went by without a social obligation involving eating and drinking in some form. The wining and dining diplomat is a common trope, but few people are aware of all the different shapes and implications of dinner diplomacy. This part has shown that dinner diplomacy served several purposes. It could be used to strengthen national coherence as well as to strengthen transnational bonds, to uphold existing networks and to build new ones. It could also be used as show, for publicity purposes and to enhance status. A reputation as a host of good dinners increased the likelihood that important diplomatic guests would accept a future invitation and created an air of glamour and popularity conducive to public diplomacy.

Certain parts of dinner diplomacy, like making calls and participating in formal dinners, were overtly obligatory tasks for both a diplomat and his wife. As the irritation about the annual Holland Society dinner shows, participation was sometimes perceived as necessary simply not to offend powerful people, even if some of these rather impersonal events were not perceived as particularly useful. These events had a very different character from more personal, informal dinners and entertaining house guests. The latter were often perceived as much more useful and, although they had a more personal character and might not be formally required, diplomatic couples could certainly not opt out of them. Most of this work was aimed at building and maintaining networks, getting to know people one might come to need to know in the future. These aspects of dinner diplomacy are very similar to how Naoko Shimazu has described sociability in diplomacy as seemingly without any content other than associating for associating's sake. Even if 'sociability in diplomacy does have an implicit underlying objective of creating a congenial association in order to exchange information', oftentimes 'the association engineered operates as if it exists for the sake of association alone'. And since the association is often seen by others, it also has a performative character.[101]

Specific meals could have specific political purposes, too. Margaret van Kleffens went to tea with Clementine Churchill in the hope that she would influence her husband Winston Churchill's perception of the Netherlands in a way that would increase the chance for British postwar aid. Members of the press core in Washington, DC were courted in the hope that they would convey the Netherlands' point of view in their papers. The East Indonesians were given the highest honour of being invited to an intimate dinner at the residence as a part of the Dutch strategy to emphasize that the Republic of Indonesia was just one of several Indonesian states and that the Dutch had excellent relations with the others. In this particular case, networking or building genuinely close relations had little to do with the invitation.

Whether the individual occasion was directly motivated by a certain political situation or was more generally aimed at networking and making a good impression, it clearly had political motivations and implications. At the same time, dinner diplomacy relied on the work of a lot of people who were ostensibly apolitical, such as servants and wives. Moreover, personal and political preferences and guests were mixed. In fact, they were linked: the higher the political status, the higher the honour of being treated as a personal friend rather than as a political contact. That means that a lot of unacknowledged work was, in fact, central to the success of 'greasing the wheels of diplomacy'. Wives were crucial diplomatic actors in this context, partly because they organized so much of the dinner diplomacy and partly because their presence made the setting more personal. The fact that British annual personality reports refer to particularly

---

[101] Shimazu, 'What Is Sociability in Diplomacy?', 57.

attractive wives or to envoys who were either hospitable or boring shows that these were considered important attributes in daily diplomatic work.

This also demonstrates that characteristics such as ethnicity, health, gender were crucial. While good food and drink could make for a convivial, intimate atmosphere conducive to friendly relations and good talk, it could also exclude people, not on the basis of their political standpoints, but on the basis of their ability to eat and drink what was served. Even culinary background had implications for the chances of dinner diplomacy success. One might be able to adapt and serve good food of a different national origin to please guests (provided one could find and afford a suitable chef or cook), however, the playing field was uneven to say the least. The connection between the transnational diplomatic culture of the mid-twentieth century and a Western European elite culture and general upper-class socializing meant that some countries had a considerable head start when it came to gaining personal and culinary popularity. It was often easier for a Western European aristocratic woman who was not a diplomat to be accepted as a suitable guest at a Western diplomat's dinner than a mediocre non-Western male colleague. If the interaction at these dinners was diplomatically relevant and if diplomatic influence has anything to do with what we call power, this should have consequences for our perception of the power of diplomatic actors.

This part has touched on some of the success factors of dinner diplomacy: the right guests and the right food. The discussions of both have demonstrated how, in dinner diplomacy, political proficiency was intrinsically connected to personal, bodily assets. However, is it possible to say anything specific about what personal assets made diplomatic actors successful? If there were systemic patterns to dinner diplomacy, basic (unwritten) rules about how things should be and if these had a bearing on who was considered a trustworthy diplomatic actor, they are relevant to the understanding of how diplomatic power developed in the postwar world. Finding the common denominators of a phenomenon that took on so many different shapes and purposes might seem impracticable. However, the sheer number of events mentioned in Margaret van Kleffens's diaries actually help to identify some constants. Whenever she assessed the success or failure of a diplomatic dinner, lunch, reception, tea or cocktails, she almost invariably mentioned at least two things besides food: dress and discourse. Food has already been discussed. Part IV will scrutinize the norms of diplomatic dress and discourse.

Part Four

Diplomatic Aptitude

Anne has become a first rate ambassadress, genuinely interested in people and conditions and eager to work hard and take endless trouble. Her sense of humour and of fun are an ideal foil to Herman's gentleness and seriousness.[1]
Diary of Margaret van Kleffens, 25 May 1964

A person looking to become a diplomat today will learn that in many (Western) countries, 'the first step to qualifying for a diplomatic career is passing a general aptitude test'. But what is diplomatic aptitude? The cited article is sweeping: Foreign Services need a diversity of skills and qualifications 'because each position is unique'; therefore diverse personal aptitudes are required. The qualities mentioned are not very specific: overall knowledge, flexibility, creativity and the ability 'to adapt quickly and assess the priorities of a situation or project'.[2]

In reality, no single diplomat can possess all the diverse skills that successful diplomacy requires. As anyone who has read this book from the beginning knows by now, a diplomat has always needed access to capable assistance. Part I of the book told the story of how, despite all Eelco van Kleffens's leadership skills and legal expertise, the ratification of a treaty (achieved by a whole team of negotiators) depended on his ability to find a competent secretary on short notice. The part on the diplomatic home featured servants as essential to running a diplomatic household and showed how a whole network of diplomatic contacts was activated to replace a '*super*-excellent' butler. As Part III showed, the successful entertaining that was so important to diplomats' daily work relied on the highly skilled work of cooks and other personnel, the benevolent attention of journalists and the assistance of family and friends. In all these tasks, a married

---

[1] MvK diary 25 May 25 1964, inv nr 416, 2.05.86, NL-HaNA.
[2] Elizabeth Koprowski, 'Four Steps to Becoming a Diplomat', 14 July 2016 on the Keystone Masterstudies website. Available at: www.masterstudies.com/article/Four-Steps-to-Becoming-a-Diplomat/ (accessed 29 June 2021).

male mid-twentieth century diplomat was assisted by his wife acting as a trusted head secretary, housekeeper and hostess.

With a lingering focus on dinner diplomacy, this final empirical part will take a closer look at what personal diplomatic aptitude looked like in the everyday work of the diplomatic couple. When Margaret van Kleffens looked back on her own diplomatic qualities in 1954, she was self-critical. 'I would have liked more of a sense of humour,' she wrote, 'and a less wry one, and a lighter touch in general, and a more optimistic outlook on life'.[3] Margaret van Kleffens had qualities that, in many ways, resembled those of her husband. Both were intellectual, conscientious and critical. However, while these were excellent qualities for a diplomat, they were less ideal for his wife. Ten years later, after her husband had left the Diplomatic Service and they had come to London to work for the High Authority of the European Coal and Steel Community, Margaret van Kleffens praised the new Dutch ambassador's wife to the United Kingdom, Anne van Roijen. The introductory quotation shows that, her unruly childhood friend, successor to her position in Washington and now the London embassy's new chatelaine, had become 'a first rate ambassadress'. Among her assets were her hard work and dedication, but also a personality that complemented her husband's. That Van Roijen had inferior language skills and was less well-read than Margaret van Kleffens was less important than natural charm and easy-going manners that made people like her.[4]

To bring into view how the norm for diplomatic aptitude differed according to a diplomatic actor's gender and position, the chapters in this part will take a closer look at two factors that, besides food, determined the success or failure of dinner diplomacy: dress and discourse. The goal is not to arrive at a definite definition of diplomatic aptitude, but to reveal patterns in how diplomatic aptitude was assessed. Though the focus on the diplomatic couple places gendered patterns in the spotlight, judgements based on racialized, classed and national presumptions are noted. This part brings to light not only the systemic sexism of twentieth-century Western diplomatic practices but also how perceptions of race and class coloured diplomatic interactions and assessments.

Part III has already shown a clear gendered separation in the organization and networks of dinner diplomacy. It has also discussed the conditions for

---

[3] MvK diary 4 March 1954, inv nr 404, 2.05.86, NL-HaNA.
[4] S Erlandsson and R van de Maar, 'Trouw aan Buitenlandse Zaken. Margaret van Kleffens, Anne van Roijen, de ambassade in Washington en de betekenis van het diplomatiek partnerschap voor de naoorlogse Nederlandse buitenlandse betrekkingen'. *Tijdschrift voor Geschiedenis* 134, no 3 (2021).

utilizing national culinary traditions and the role of good food and hospitality. This part will focus on how diplomatic actors and places were supposed to look and behave to make a favourable impression. Chapter 10 focuses on physical appearances. Chapter 11 takes a closer look at daily diplomatic discourse: what made for good diplomatic dinner conversation and who could speak about what where? A few concluding remarks ponder what the identified patterns say about diplomatic aptitude in the mid-twentieth century.

10 Diplomatic appearances

Recent research on present-day ambassadors speaks of a gendered *appearance management labour*, focusing on personal appearances. It emphasizes the importance of good looks and shows that matters of style and taste are not only gendered and classed but also a result of conscious and concrete work. Iver Neumann speaks of international relations as being necessarily embodied and discusses the hierarchies of different types of appearances available to male and female diplomats respectively.[5] Ann Towns adds to his observations by studying the practices behind the presentation: the management of personal appearances. She argues that this daily task for ambassadors requires time, effort and skill and should be understood as labour.[6] That labour is gendered in at least two ways. First, what is considered an appropriate diplomatic look differs considerably depending on whether you are (perceived as) a man or a woman. Second, appearance management is more costly and time consuming for women than for men because of these gendered expectations (eg regarding dress, hair, and make-up).[7]

In the mid-twentieth century, diplomatic appearance management was gendered very specifically. There were few female diplomats, but a diplomat's wife who prepared for dinner diplomacy did a considerable amount of appearance management. This included dressing herself, if she was a guest and, if she was the hostess, both herself and the table, partly in the shape of overseeing the work of domestic staff. Men also dressed up for dinner, but their choices were more limited and they were rarely involved in dinner decorations. This chapter

---

[5] IB Neumann, 'The Body of the Diplomat'. *European Journal of International Relations* 14, no 4 (2008): 671–95.
[6] Ann Towns (2020) 'Gendered Appearance as Diplomatic Labor'. Paper presented to the GenDip-Diploface Workshop, 19 November 2020.
[7] Ann Towns, 'Gendered Appearance as Diplomatic Labor', 2020.

highlights both the importance of looks and the scope for manoeuvre of different diplomatic actors.

Physical appearances were one of the success (or failure) factors of dinner diplomacy. When Margaret van Kleffens described dinner diplomacy events, she generally saved a few remarks for the table and/or room as well as for what people wore. When reading these, one must keep in mind the interplay between prejudice and actual impressions, which can be used to indicate the socially shared beliefs of the time. In an individual case, it can be difficult to say with certainty whether a judgement is based on actual appearance or governed by preconceptions. However, comparing a large number of cases, such as in this chapter, makes it possible to discover patterns. Part II on the diplomatic home already compared two descriptions of calling on someone for tea: one visit to the prime minister's wife in the United Kingdom during the war and one to the Soviet ambassador's wife in The Hague shortly after. The quoted passages show how the tone is entirely different, despite describing what, on the surface, seem like fairly similar circumstances. To convey her opinion, Margaret van Kleffens on both occasions described both interior decoration and personal clothes. The following provides a closer look at the norms, practices and perceptions of how mid-twentieth century diplomatic actors dressed themselves and their tables for dinner, focusing on early postwar Washington, DC, the new hub for Western diplomacy, with occasional descriptions from other places and periods for comparison's sake.

Dressing for dinner

Dressing up and dressing well was important for both men and women. However, it is enough to scroll through a few pages of images from diplomatic dinners from the 1940s and 1950s to see that the conditions for that dressing differed considerably between the sexes: while you will see lots of men in almost identical dark suits with short, brushed back hair, the women wear dresses of different colours, patterns, fabrics and cuts, distinctive jewellery, boas, capes or wraps and a variety of elaborate hairdos, sometimes – but not always – finished off with just-as-elaborate hats. While men's dress almost comes across as a uniform, women clearly had more choices.

Men did dress differently for different diplomatic occasions though and were not entirely without options. In 1943, Margaret van Kleffens noted how her husband had thought of a way to use his appearance to make an impression on the Soviets:

E. came in very pleased with himself just now, having decided to wear a morning coat to the Soviets' reception tomorrow, the reason for this decision being a rather astonishing remark to him once by Bogomolov (former Soviet ambassador to the "exiled" governments in London) that "you are so obviously a government of the right, and that is why I respect you."[8]

The note shows that men could choose a more formal style of dress than required to send a particular message. In this case, Eelco van Kleffens seems to have enjoyed the idea that he could command respect from the representatives of a numerically and militarily much more powerful country by emphasizing a class system that he knew his hosts officially rejected, but might privately still be sensitive to. Showing off his class and refinement in this context comes across as competitive rather than a way to make friends. This can be contrasted by his behaviour when an American who carried out public relations for the Netherlands seemed intimidated by Margaret van Kleffens's British accent and stood 'in awe of my supposed refinement'. On this occasion, Eelco van Kleffens compensated by toning down any upper-class manners. 'E. "Goddam's" along with him,' his wife wrote in her diary, 'to get him going'.[9] Establishing jovial friendliness and making people relax was clearly not the effect he was after with the Soviets.

While formal dress could be used to emphasize status, casual dress could signal trust and intimacy. That could be taken as a compliment, provided the person dressing down was perceived as being high(er) in rank. On another wartime occasion, Eelco van Kleffens evidently interpreted the fact that United States President Franklin Delano Roosevelt received him and a group of his compatriots wearing neat but informal summer clothes as a friendly gesture. The mention of the president's dress in his diary stands out because these were work-related notes that contained far fewer personal details than those of his wife. In all likelihood, it would not have been included had he not ascribed it political significance. The context confirms that reading:

> We stayed a full hour with the President, whose views on the programme of the visit of the Queen proved to run almost parallel to ours. He received us dressed in a white shirt and white trousers.[10]

---

[8] MvK diary 6/7 Nov (Sat./Sunday) 1943, inv nr 393, 2.05.86, NL-HaNA.
[9] MvK diary 22 October 1949, inv nr 400, 2.05.86, NL-HaNA.
[10] Diary of Eelco van Kleffens (EvK diary) 24 June 1942. Diary kept during three work trips (10 January–7 March 1942, 17 June–16 August 1942, 24 May–5 July 1943), inv nr 98, Collection Netherlands government in London 233b, Netherlands Institute of War Documentation in Amsterdam, the Netherlands (NL-NIOD). In the published diary (Riemens 2019), part of the quote used here is underlined, but there is no underlining on the original manuscript. Riemens seems to have adopted the underlining in red ink done by someone else, or possibly by Van Kleffens himself at a later stage, on the photocopy of the diary that is kept in inv nr 206, 2.05.86, NL-HaNA.

As Eelco van Kleffens noted with satisfaction that the president had been generous to him and his colleagues with both his time and agreement (not always the case, other notes reveal), the added remark about the dress reads as another sign of the president's goodwill. At the very least, the inclusion of this observation in a work diary shows that ascribing significance to the way people were dressed cannot be dismissed as a female pastime, even if women were supposed to put more effort than men into dressing. Also, as with other aspects of everyday diplomatic relations, it seems that the chillier the political relationships, the more formal dress was used to emphasize status and distance, while more informal and personal dress implied more friendly relations.

There were more ways to use dress for women, who could make a wider variety of choices not only about clothes, shoes and headwear, but with their style of hair, jewellery and make-up. In her research on contemporary diplomats, Birgitta Niklasson has pointed out that this gives female diplomats a visibility advantage over their male counterparts.[11] Women could also enhance the status of their country by what they wore, for example by choosing national designers, as Molly Wood has discussed when it comes to early twentieth-century American diplomats' wives and other women in diplomacy and Nevra Biltekin when it comes to Swedish diplomats' wives in the 1960s–1980s.[12] However, most individual women could not dress down as a sign of diplomatic friendship, so in that sense, any room for manoeuvre was narrower. According to a book by Beryl Smedley, the wife of a British postwar diplomat, the demands became less strict after the Second World War. However, the diaries of Margaret van Kleffens show that she still adhered to – and judged others by – many of the pre-war standards that Smedley mentions. When making courtesy calls, a wife should wear hat and gloves; as a hostess and as a dinner guest, she should not only wear a high fashion dress, but also real jewels or pearls.[13] Although buying ready-made became increasingly common after the war, diplomats' wives were still very much judged by what they wore. Few women in diplomatic circles could get away with dressing

---

[11] B Niklasson, 'The Gendered Networking of Diplomats', 26; See also Towns, 'Gendered Appearance as Diplomatic Labor'.

[12] M M Wood, 'Diplomatic Wives: The Politics of Domesticity and the "Social Game" in the U.S. Foreign Service, 1905–1941'. *Journal of Women's History* 17, no 2 (2005): 142–65 ; M M Wood, '"Commanding Beauty" and "Gentle Charm": American Women and Gender in the Early Twentieth-Century Foreign Service'. *Diplomatic History* 31, no 3 (2007): 505–30; N Biltekin, 'The Diplomatic Partnership: Gender, Materiality and Performance in the Case of Sweden c. 1960s–1980s'. *Genesis* XI, no 1–2 (2012): 159–65; For a discussion of the relationship between fashion and nation, see Marie Riegels Melchior, 'Catwalking the Nation: Challenges and Possibilities in the Case of the Danish Fashion Industry', *Culture Unbound* 3 (2011): 55–70.

[13] Smedley, *Partners in Diplomacy* (Ferring: The Harley Press, 1990), 73, 77–82.

down or dressing badly; those who did – a salient example is Queen Wilhelmina of the Netherlands – indeed got away with it, as opposed to being able use it as a way to create a sense of intimacy.[14]

To be clear, it is worth noting here that the norms were neither absolute nor the same for everyone. American gossip columnist and professional hostess Elsa Maxwell, for example, displayed looks and behaviour that were generally considered inappropriate in diplomatic circles. Yet she entertained diplomats and, if one measures power by networks, was one of the most powerful people in Washington after the Second World War. Everyone knew Elsa Maxwell.[15] Almost any rules could be broken by exceptional people and, for those few, their ability to break the rules could even become their strongest asset. Maxwell seems to have been able to make people laugh by making jokes at her own expense, turning perceptions of herself as fat and ugly to her advantage.[16] Another factor that explains her ability to break the rules is that Elsa Maxwell did not have a diplomatic background or position: she represented only herself. Diplomats' wives had less leeway.

The general significance of dress as part of national representation becomes visible in comments about diplomatic actors being dressed improperly. In 1944, Margaret van Kleffens described the clothes of Madame Massigli, wife of the Free France ambassador, as hideous. 'Instead of representing and doing credit to Paris by putting everyone else sartorially in the shade,' she wrote, 'she was the worst-dressed woman in the room besides looking exaggerated and rather bad class.'[17] Whether Margaret van Kleffens's judgement was fair, it tells us what a woman should do through her dress: represent and do credit to the place she represented, with class. In the United States after the war, where diplomatic culture was increasingly influenced by American celebrity culture, dress became perhaps even more important because of media attention. Even if wearing ready-made became more common, some ambassadors' wives clearly considered it substandard. One of the most successful diplomatic hostesses in Washington, DC, Greek-born Hellé Zervoudaki, wife of the French ambassador Henri Bonnet, certainly wore designer dresses. She even made hats using her own

---

[14] Margaret van Kleffens noted the queen's bad taste in clothes in her diary as a matter of fact. See MvK diary 28 January and 31 March 1943, inv nr 392, 2.05.86, NL-HaNA.

[15] Eve Goldberg, 'Elsa Was Best Known for Her Parties', *The Gay & Lesbian Review Worldwide* 20, no 5 (2013); See also Sam Staggs, *Inventing Elsa Maxwell: How an Irrepressible Nobody Conquered High Society, Hollywood, the Press, and the World* (New York: St Martin's Press, 2013).

[16] EvK diary 22 May 1945, as reproduced in E N van Kleffens, *Majesteit, U Kent Het Werkelijke Leven Niet: De Oorlogsdagboeken van Minister van Buitenlandse Zaken Mr. E.N. van Kleffens*. Edited by MJ Riemens. (Nijmegen: Vantilt, 2019, 372).

[17] MvK diary 22 November 1944, inv nr 394, 2.05.86, NL-HaNA.

designs, causing Margaret van Kleffens and her Greek colleague Madame Dendramis to forge the plan 'to order some hats from Paris together (from sketches) and thereby dumbfound Mme. Bonnet'.[18]

No number of ready-made dresses could beat the attraction of being original. New designer dresses were expensive, however, which put those who did not possess a fortune at a disadvantage. Margaret van Kleffens occasionally re-used dresses, with minor alterations, rather than succumb to *prêt-à-porter*. 'As a special note', she wrote in a description of an embassy reception she had hosted,

> I want to add that I wore my 8-year old lilac crepe and satin dinner dress, the sleeves shortened for this hot occasion, and the set of amethysts (necklace, earring and brooch) which match it exactly. In this outfit I felt – and was! – better dressed than in anything under $400 I could have bought new in this country.[19]

The note shows that the norms for dress were indeed changing, as Smedley claims, but also that there were wives who resisted those changes and perhaps even used an air of Old World-class to stand out in the American media. Washington journalist Robbie Johnson's description of Margaret van Kleffens's classy tea party mentioned in Chapter 8 conveys an admiration for the European version of a female get-together that fits in with a more general American fascination for age-old European traditions.

Descriptions of diplomats' wives' dresses and photographs of them were featured in countless society columns and gave well-dressed women a chance to stand out. Men's dress was occasionally mentioned, but it was harder for them to stand out in a positive way. In line with the observation above, the exception was if their dress was viewed as part of a venerable tradition. 'For once the men peacocked instead of women', famous society columnist Mary van Rensselaer Thayer wrote in December 1947 in the *Washington Post*. 'Ambassador Martins' diplomatic uniform was thick with gold embroidered leaves, his grand chest sprinkled with decorations, splashed with the fuchsia ribbon of Belgium's highest decoration.' The extravagant diplomatic uniforms were increasingly a thing of the past, which seems to have given them a nostalgic appeal to the columnist.

---

[18] MvK diary 8 September 1947, inv nr 397, 2.05.86, NL-HaNA. Hellé Bonnet had gained fame as a milliner in New York City during the war. For research on Hellé Bonnet's 'fashion diplomacy' and her role in Marshall Plan efforts to tie the United States and Europe together through consumer goods, see Stephanie M Amerian, 'Buying European: The Marshall Plan and American Department Stores', *Diplomatic History* 39, no 1 (2015): 45–69; See also the unpublished paper by Haakon Ikonomou, 'Hellé Bonnet, the Washington Scene and Cold War Couture' (New Diplomatic History conference Diplomacy between Crisis and Cooperation, Aarhus, Denmark, 2021).

[19] MvK diary 31 August 1947, inv nr 397, 2.05.86, NL-HaNA.

'Uniforms of many other Ambassadors were wartime casualties', Thayer lamented, mentioning how 'three beauties' of the Netherlands Ambassador had been 'burned down by the Nazis'. She went on to describe only one more man's dress – the 'native dress' of Indian Ambassador Asaf Ali – while she gave detailed descriptions of no less than eight of the 'lovely dresses' worn by 'the feminine element'. Among them was Hellé Bonnet's 'Christian Dior numero'. While the extravagant colours and styles of the women were described as inducing 'ohs and ahs', Thayer deemed the 'most outstanding piece of frippery' of the evening a man's hat: Senator Arthur Capper's 'bright green fedora' – the only other colourful male accessory mentioned.[20]

While it was important for men in diplomatic relationships to look good, frippery or all too perceptible beautification was a male *faux pas*. Nevra Biltekin has described how diplomats in their memoirs often judged each other on posture and presentation. She identifies some common notions: a diplomat should appear intelligent and charming, and his looks give an impression of power and elegance.[21] Occasionally, men might dress extravagantly by donning a national costume or uniform, or as part of traditional upper-class male bonding games. At a stag party luncheon near Bar Harbour in Maine in 1946, Eelco van Kleffens and the other male guests all had to 'don white chef's caps and aprons'.[22] Beyond those very specific contexts however, men's variations were limited. It was not necessarily a compliment that Eelco and Margaret van Kleffens in private referred to British wartime Foreign Minister Anthony Eden as 'de mooie-mooie' – the pretty-pretty. Luckily for Eden, he was not only 'devastating', but 'cheerful, boyish and very pleasant' too, so that their reference to him being 'mooi' (beautiful) does not seem to have connoted to anything but natural good looks.[23]

Otherwise, anything that reeked of (feminine) vanity risked evoking reactions of bemusement or ridicule. Ambassador Henrik de Kauffmann of Denmark was, according to Margaret van Kleffens in her first year in Washington, 'superlatively good looking'.[24] A year later she declared that she could 'never keep my eyes off him, he is so handsome!'[25] However when, a few months later, the sunshine revealed to her 'incredulous eyes' that 'the melancholy Dane's thatch of

---

[20] Mary van Rensselaer Thayer, '... And President's Smile Flashed, The Marine Band Played, And Chandeliers Sparkled As the "Dips" Lined Up', *Washington Post*, 3 December 1947.
[21] N Biltekin, *Servants of Diplomacy: The Making of Swedish Diplomats, 1905–1995*. (Stockholm: Department of History, Stockholm University, 2016) 175–79.
[22] MvK diary 18 July 1946, inv nr 396, 2.05.86, NL-HaNA.
[23] MvK 1941 account, inv nr 391; MvK diary 6 January 1943, inv nr 392; MvK diary 24 July 1944, inv nr 394, 2.05.86, NL-HaNA.
[24] MvK diary 26 December 1947, inv nr 397, 2.05.86, NL-HaNA.
[25] MvK diary, 5 November 1948, inv nr 398, 2.05.86, NL-HaNA.

Figure 4.1 Anglo-Netherlands Society luncheon, London 24 July 1944. UK Foreign Minister Anthony Eden – to whom the Van Kleffenses in private referred in Dutch as 'de mooie-mooie', 'the pretty-pretty' – next to Margaret van Kleffens, who wrote in her diary: 'The Anglo-Netherlands Society gave a luncheon today (at the Connaught Rooms) at which E. and I were the guests of honour ... E. gave the principal speech ... He had taken a lot of trouble over it, as he wanted parts of it quoted by the papers. Eden, who was my cheerful, boyish and very pleasant neighbour, also spoke, and very well. He was kind and complimentary about our country. Excellent food, and no bombs during the meal.' Photo: unknown, unmarked photograph from MvK diary, inv nr 394, 2.05.86, NL-HaNA. Courtesy of the Netherlands National Archives, The Hague, with permission of the Van Kleffens family.

aristocratically silvered hair had been expertly, but unmistakably, blue-rinsed', she called the discovery '[s]hattering' and commented that 'he posed himself to show his beauty to good advantage, purring the while like six cats'.[26]

Women, on the other hand, were always expected to make an effort to make themselves pleasing to the eye, in particular to men. 'Both without our husbands, Betty T. and I lunched at the Ritz with Dick Karnebeek and one Major Cayzer,' Margaret van Kleffens wrote in June 1945. 'For their delectation we both wore

---

[26] MvK diary 30 March 1949, inv nr 399, 2.05.86, NL-HaNA.

our newest bonnets (I my frothy black tulle), which was highly appreciated by our not very highflying but pleasant host.'[27] It is only one of numerous references to wearing things to please men or to men appreciating what she wore. Modest flirting was the norm for socializing between men and women: men were supposed to be gallant and gentlemanly and women beautiful and attentive. The latter should not display characteristics that were perceived as masculine. 'E. says I am very critical', Margaret van Kleffens wrote in 1949, 'but also of myself. We both are', she added. 'Is there harm in that, I wonder, so long as you are careful not to hurt others?' The problem, she concluded, was not in the quality itself, but in appearances. 'E. also says I frighten people by *looking* critical. That is bad, and I must watch it.'[28] In addition to wearing the right dresses, jewels, hats and gloves, women had to wear the right expression on their faces.

Good diplomatic looks and manners were so important and so fundamentally gendered that they were the very reason that Eelco van Kleffens opposed female diplomats. His 1943 diary recounts a meeting with a man whose daughter wanted to join the diplomatic service, 'to which I object', Eelco van Kleffens wrote, 'because the pretty girls get married and the ugly get nothing done anyway'.[29] His comment shows that he assumed that the way women got things done was by looking good and charming men. His conclusion that women were therefore undesirable as diplomats required the further assumption that this charming of men would inevitably lead to marriage for any woman who was any good at the job, and that marriage would be irreconcilable with a woman's work as a diplomat. Not all male diplomats of the time came to that same conclusion. In 1948, Swedish Foreign Minister Östen Undén wrote in his diary, after an 'unusually nice' dinner for Indian Ambassador to Moscow Vijaya Lakshmi Pandit and her daughters, that he found Mrs Pandit (who was a widow) an 'alert observer and handsome lady'. He added: 'Women as diplomats is probably not a bad idea.'[30] This need not be to do with any fundamentally different perception on Undén's part of how women got things done, but was more likely a recognition of diplomacy as an art that benefitted from so-called feminine qualities.[31]

---

[27] MvK diary 19 June 1945, inv nr 395, 2.05.86, NL-HaNA. Betty T. = Betty Teixeira de Mattos.
[28] MvK diary 12 May 1949, inv nr 399, 2.05.86, NL-HaNA.
[29] EvK diary 1 September 1943, inv nr 207, 2.05.86, NL-HaNA. My translation from Dutch 'waartegen ik bezwaar heb want de mooie meisjes huwen en de leelijken krijgen toch niets gedaan'.
[30] Diary of Östen Undén 12 May 1948, Östen Undén and Karl Molin, *Anteckningar: 1918–1952*, vol 24 (Uppsala: Stockholm), Kungl. Samf. för utgivande av handskrifter rörande Skandinaviens historia, 2002), 241–42. My translation. The Swedish word that I have translated as handsome is 'stilig'.
[31] See Ann Towns, '"Diplomacy Is a Feminine Art": Feminised Figurations of the Diplomat', *Review of International Studies* 46, no 5 (2020): 573–93.

Diplomatic decorations

Whether they thought women should be diplomats in their own right, mid-twentieth century male diplomats already interacted with women as part of everyday diplomacy and relied on them to contribute essential elements of dinner diplomacy, such as adding beauty to its setting. Even at events that excluded women, such as all-male diplomatic lunches and dinners, wives were often responsible for their embellishment. Margaret van Kleffens's London diary shows that she made a habit of taking care of the decorations not only when Eelco van Kleffens gave a party at home, but even when the meal was hosted at a restaurant and she herself did not participate: 'E. gave a stag lunch for twelve at Claridge's, for which I did the table decoration as is my wont.'[32] On the same day, her husband wrote in his diary that he had given a successful lunch 'with beautiful flower decoration by M'.[33] Though the staff tended to do the actual table setting, it was done according to her instructions, and she did some of the decorations personally. Ordering and arranging the flowers was one of her recurring tasks, evidenced by more diary mentions than can be listed here. Sometimes other women, such as her sister, helped her. 'Dick, who looked highly decorative, helped me with a new flower-arrangement', Margaret van Kleffens wrote about another luncheon that she and her husband had given at Claridges, which had been the 'bright spot of the day'.[34] Women made, and were part of, the decoration.

The exact design varied according to degree of formality and types of tables and occasion. Similar to food though, if one thing can be pointed out as the general goal of dinner table decorations, it would be to make a lavish impression. The meals Margaret van Kleffens described as perfect always featured classy beauty and generosity. In early 1949, she described the dinner of a Mrs Hitchcock, the widow of a United States Senator, as 'absolute perfection, from the food to the lace-over-gold-lamé tablecloth to the gilt epergnes filled with luscious, overhanging fruits and flowers. Pleasant company of 18.'[35] Food has been discussed in the previous chapter and what made company pleasant will be a topic of the next, but as far as appearances go, 'absolute perfection' comes across as a manifestation of upper-class wealth and luxurious abundance. A description from one of her own Washington, DC dinner parties a little more than a year earlier paints a similar picture. With evident pleasure, Margaret van Kleffens noted that 'the table always

---

[32] MvK diary 22 April 1943, inv nr 392, 2.05.86, NL-HaNA.
[33] EvK diary 22 April 1943, inv nr 207, 2.05.86, NL-HaNA. My translation of 'met mooie bloemenversiering door M'.
[34] MvK diary 5 February 1943, inv nr 392, 2.05.86, NL-HaNA.
[35] MvK diary 17 January 1949, inv nr 398, 2.05.86, NL-HaNA.

makes the women give a slight gasp, so lovely it looks with its 4 big candelabra, deep red dahlia's, and silver and crystal sparkling on dark mahogany.'[36] Making people gasp seems to have been the aim. The wording recurs:

> We gave a highly successful and decorative dinner party of 22 (see clipping next page). Our table with the beautiful cut crystal on its gleaming surface and the sparkling silver, really looked a sight of which we may be proud. People always gasp a little when entering the dining room.[37]

The mention of a clipping points to another aim already mentioned: media coverage. Entertaining important guests was not only a matter of network building but also of public diplomacy. Moreover, a reputation for enjoyable dinners and hosting important people could help get important people to accept invitations in the future. That does not mean that all lavish dinners were extensively covered in the media. The one mentioned here, from the *Times-Herald*, read in its entirety:

> Eisenhowers Are Guests of Van Kleffens
> Dinners on embassy row always make news and last evening the retiring Chief of Staff of the Army, Gen. Dwight D. Eisenhower, and Mrs. Eisenhower were honoured at a dinner by the Ambassador of the Netherlands, E. N. van Kleffens, and Mme. van Kleffens at the recently redecorated embassy on S street.
> The Ambassador of Denmark and Mme. De Kauffmann were present as were the new ambassador for Portugal, Pedro Theotonio Pereira, and Australian Minister Alfred Stirling and his sister, Miss Dorothy Stirling.
> Gen. and Mrs. Hoyt Vandenberg were also at the gathering as were Mrs. Woodrow Wilson, Mr. and Mrs. Charles Carroll Glover jr., Mr. and Mrs. Harold Jefferson Coolidge, Mrs. Truxtun Beale, Clarence B. Hewes, the Minister of the Netherlands embassy and Mme. Daubanton, Cornelis Kolff and Mr. and Mrs. James B. Reston.[38]

Short newspaper stories like these were common as this notice itself remarks: embassy dinners made the news. They often did little more than list the guests, which in this case makes the mentioning of the recent redecoration all the more eye-catching. Appearances mattered.

---

[36] MvK diary 8 November 1947, inv nr 397, 2.05.86, NL-HaNA.
[37] MvK diary 4 December 1947, inv nr 397, 2.05.86, NL-HaNA.
[38] News clipping pasted in the diary of MvK after the entry on 4 December 1947, inv nr 397, 2.05.86, NL-HaNA. The name of the paper and the date do not show on the clipping, but 'Times-Herald' is handwritten and the date is presumably 5 December 1947.

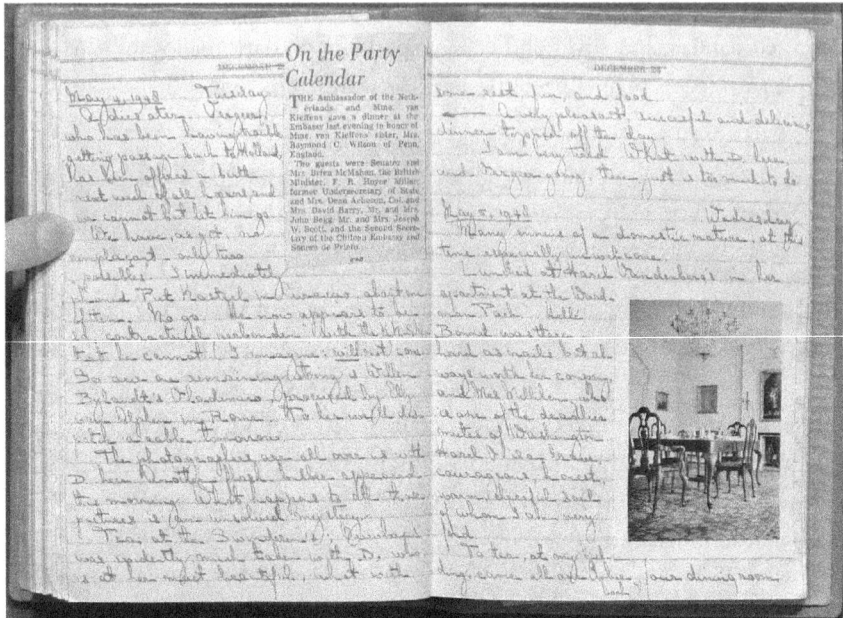

Figure 4.2 Spread from Margaret van Kleffens's diary 4 and 5 May 1948, MvK diary inv nr 397, 2.05.86, NL-HaNA. Origin of newspaper clipping unknown. Photographer of dining room photo unknown, but possibly Margaret van Kleffens herself. Courtesy of the Netherlands National Archives, The Hague, with permission of the Van Kleffens family.

Considering that making a favourable impression could gain a country both better networks and favourable media coverage, it is relevant to note how perceptions of good looks had distinctly Western features. The 1947 dinner with the Indonesian guests already mentioned in Chapter 8 will serve as an example, not only because it is a very telling one, but also because records of any occasions with guests of honour who were not Westerners are rare. Describing the evening in her diary, Margaret van Kleffens began with the setting she herself had created.

> Our table was laid with our best, 100-year old damask ('roos met harp' [rose with harp]) and our cut crystal dishes, mingled with old silver and filled with fruit, nuts and chocolates made a superb sight!

So far, the description is similar to those of other successful dinner parties. The appearances of the guests, however, failed to meet with her approval. She ascribed Sultan Syarif Hamid II, first (and last) President of West Kalimantan (which she called West Borneo), uncivilized manners through the portrayal of his wife as his sad-looking, shy Dutch wife, who wore an emerald as bit as a pigeon's egg and whom he address [sic] as 'van Delden' (which is her maiden name) and speaks of as 'de baas' [the boss].

And while she had just proudly described the extravagance of her own table, the tone was unmistakably condescending when she wrote that '[t]hese people … adore everything showy and incidentally, go round getting themselves photographed in colour at $150 a throw!' The high-born lineage of the Indonesian leaders was not enough to impress her. 'For all their mile-long names, these men are singularly unimpressive in every way: they have neither looks nor bearing,' she wrote.[39]

Besides adding to the above examples of dressing as a political activity, the diary entry reveals how norms about appearances were gendered, classed, and racialized. Describing how the dinner table was laid, Margaret van Kleffens made clear that she had spared no effort – using 'our best' – and that the table was not only dressed to display riches and abundance, but class, as expressed by her stressing the age of tablecloth and silver. This is in marked contrast to her portrayal of the riches and extravagance of her counterpart. While her own display of beautiful things was classy and a sign of good taste and generosity, theirs was vulgar, indiscriminate and a sign of conceit: they liked 'everything showy' and did not understand the value of things but spent money on overpriced photographs of themselves. The discourse is reminiscent of that used to describe lower classes. To illustrate, her criticism of British munition workers during the war has a remarkably similar ring to it:

> London shops are empty beyond description; all they've got left is trash at sky-high prices. I saw a perfectly simple crepe de chine nightie – the price tag said 17 gns! It is impossible even to think of buying things at such prices – but it seems that the munition workers, finding themselves suddenly 'in the money' of the value of which they have no conception, actually pay them. So up and up they go![40]

In this case, Margaret van Kleffens blamed rising prices on the lack of moderation and financial insights of overpaid workers. At the dinner party, a similar lack of moderation and financial insight was ascribed to guests who came from the very highest echelons of society. Ethnicity, it seems, trumped pedigree. The colonial relationship allowed Margaret van Kleffens to invoke another common trope

---

[39] MvK diary 27 August 1947, inv nr 397, 2.05.86, NL-HaNA.
[40] MvK diary 25 January 1943, inv nr 392, 2.05.86, NL-HaNA.

linked to an imperial discourse which described coloured people in general and colonial subjects in particular as primitive, uneducated and unable to take care of themselves, often comparing them to children (with the imperial state as the responsible parent).[41] The rest of the diary entry confirms that reading. 'These boys has been naughty again on their own hook,' she wrote, the grammatical error no doubt intentional. Her husband apparently not only shared this opinion, but expressed it, because she added that 'E. let them have it!' The result, she claimed, was that they apologized and blamed each other. 'These people are about as competent in looking after themselves and their own interests as six-year olds', she wrote, consistent with the trope mentioned.[42] It is hard to imagine Eelco van Kleffens making candid reproaches during dinner to any other countries' heads of state.

In this case, the judgemental attitude was obviously connected to the specific political history of the Netherlands and Indonesia. The fact remains that the criticism was, at least in part, cast as a disapproval of racialized appearances, intersecting with gendered ones. The conveyed sense of inappropriateness of the (presumably too showy) giant emerald was enhanced by describing the woman wearing it as lacking feminine charm. That her husband referred to her by her last name and called her 'the boss' could signal either her or his inappropriate conduct (or both), but it was decidedly a female *faux pas* to look both sad and shy. Compare it to another judgmental description; that of the wife of Swedish envoy Gunnar Hägglöf, Italian-born Countess Anna Folchi-Vici, in London in 1944:

> Mme Hägglöf, wife of the new Swedish Minster, paid me her first visit and we had tea together at the Ritz. 'Young, gay, and beautiful' were how I had heard her described, but I was hardly prepared for quite such a glamour girl as entered the hall through the revolving door opposite where I sat waiting, with mannequin figure and steps, enormous black halo hat, and most unsuitably dressed on this cold day, in a flowered silk frock that would have looked right at a hot-weather garden party. I could hardly believe it were really she, thinking rather that this apparition had come for the benefit of the many Yankee officers present ...

---

[41] See Wood, 'A Diplomat's Wife in Mexico', *Frontiers* 25, no 3 (2004): 113; for more background on the trope of the colonial subject as a child, see ch 3 of Bill Ashcroft, *On Post-Colonial Futures: Transformations of Colonial Culture* (London, New York: Continuum, 2001); for a longer history of the Hierarchy of Race in US diplomatic relations, see Michael H Hunt, *Ideology and U.S. Foreign Policy* (New Haven, CT: Yale University Press, 2009), 46–91; on long-term influence of imperial discourse, see Branwen Gruffydd Jones, '"Good Governance" and "State Failure": Genealogies of Imperial Discourse', *Cambridge Review of International Affairs* 26, no 1 (2013): 49–70.
[42] MvK diary 27 August 1947, inv nr 397, 2.05.86, NL-HaNA.

So far, there is a similarity: both women were perceived as not dressing modestly enough, wearing something inappropriate, whether the word for it was 'showy' or 'glamour girl'. While Margaret van Kleffens found no redeeming qualities in the sad-looking and shy sultana, however, the gay countess managed to get on her good side after all. Just after insinuating that her appearance gave the impression of promiscuity, Margaret van Kleffens continued

> ... but let me not be catty; she really is all she was described as being, and a quite lovely creature, of about my own height and colouring, (the first time I see an authentic 'beauty' with my non-descript colour of hair). She is 26 and looks younger, has been married for eight years to the shining hope of the Swedish Foreign Office, whose first post abroad this is ... and has a great deal to learn as a diplomat's wife! She failed to say every single thing she should have said on this occasion; her husband who makes (I hear) no such mistakes having apparently forgotten to prompt her. Her English is good and her charm considerable.[43]

Not just inappropriate looks but inappropriate behaviour could also be forgiven, which points to an important observation: you cannot become part of a culture simply by learning and conforming to its rules. At least as important is knowing when they can be broken and by whom.[44] Anna Hägglöf, a European countess, simply had things left to learn. Her husband, a Swedish upper-middle-class diplomatic talent, must have 'forgotten to prompt her'. In comparison, there was little goodwill towards either Dutch Didie van Delden or her Indonesian high-born husband. Van Delden's marriage to an Indonesian probably made Margaret van Kleffens suspicious of her to begin with and her inability to hide her shyness and look happy surely did not help.

In this case, it is hard to know whether the dissatisfaction with the sultana's lack of female charm was due to a lack of effort on her part, or a result of the racial prejudices on display in the notes. Besides the aforementioned slurs, Margaret van Kleffens described President Soekawati of East Indonesia as 'incoherent, monkey-like' and Prime Minister Nadjamoeddin as 'his wickedly-leering prime minister'.[45] As a comparison, she called the American diplomat Adolph Berle a 'pompous ass'.[46] Though Margaret van Kleffens was brazenly candid in her diary and called people she disliked things she would never have said to their faces, the condescending remarks she made about people of other ethnicities than her own

---

[43] MvK diary 22 May 1944, inv nr 393, 2.05.86, NL-HaNA.
[44] I owe this insight to Professor Johanna Gehmacher, who pointed it out to me when we were both trying to figure out the rules of British academia.
[45] MvK diary 27 August 1947, inv nr 397, 2.05.86, NL-HaNA.
[46] MvK diary 27 May 1946, inv nr 395, 2.05.86, NL-HaNA.

Figure 4.3 Delegation East Indonesia received by Queen Wilhelmina at Huis ten Bosch palace, 17 September 1947. Wives were not included in this official photograph of the same delegation that visited the United States in August 1947. Tjokorda Gde Raka Soekawati, President of the State of East Indonesia, is on the queen's right, and Sultan Hamid II of Pontianak, President of the State of West Kalimantan, on her left. On his left: Nadjamoeddin Daeng Malewa, Prime Minister of East Indonesia. Photo: Anefo. Courtesy of the Netherlands National Archives, The Hague.

diverged from her usual repertoire. While Dutch businessman Frits Philips did not escape remarks such as 'unprincipled', 'wishy-washy', and 'nincompoop', for example, his alleged cruelty was described only in relation to his actions ('cruel in business'). By contrast, the 'wickedly-leering' used to describe Nadjamoeddin connotes to an inherent characteristic more reminiscent of her 1944 description of the Chinese-Indonesian international socialite Oei Hui-lan, wife of Chinese Ambassador Wellington Koo: 'clever as a snake, harder than nails, ghost-like and cruel in appearance'.[47] While she compared President Soekawati to a monkey and on another occasion again referred to Madame Koo as a 'snake-like lady', Margaret van Kleffens usually did not come closer to comparing white people to animals than calling the director of the National Symphony Orchestra Hans Kindler

---

[47] MvK diary 28 June 1944, inv nr 393, 2.05.86, NL-HaNA.

'asinine'.⁴⁸ Similarly, although she described Hellé Bonnet as 'hard as nails' and 'calculating' in her efficiency, there are no references to the French ambassador's wife being snake-like or looking cruel.⁴⁹

The point I am trying to make is not that Margaret van Kleffens always had more negative opinions of people of other ethnicities but that, when she had them, she used a different language to express them. There are examples of positive comments about people of other ethnicities too: for one, she called Oei Hui-lan's husband Wellington Koo 'highly intelligent and quite likable'.⁵⁰ She approvingly described a Dutch diplomat's South American wife as 'Chilean-born, dark, and a real beauty, though on the small side; what's more, sweet and well-mannered and "easy"'.⁵¹ However, when she did mention less attractive qualities of persons of a different ethnical background, she tended towards a terminology that fits a racist discourse that in that time was normal for a person of her standing. She often used racial or ethnic slurs indiscriminately, even for people she liked (or at least did not dislike), which indicates that she did not reflect much on her use of them. As it happens, the day before she expressed such dislike for her Indonesian dinner guests, she expressed her like of (the Chinese–Indonesian) Oei Hui-lan while describing her in similar racist terms. Her notes say that she had tea with 'the vaguely hypnotic, slinkily wicked-looking Chinese Ambassadress whom I have known for years and rather like'.⁵²

Only in a system that normalizes racism can racial and ethnic slurs be used not only to express personal dislike but also simply to describe people. Dr Oscar Ibarra García, like Eelco van Kleffens a former delegate of the 1945 San Francisco conference, casually appears in one of Margaret van Kleffens's lists of esteemed lunch guests as 'an Argentinean dago named Ibarra Garcia'.⁵³ To mention a case from an entirely different type of relationship and hierarchy, she referred to their African American New York cleaner both as 'Robert the coloured man' and 'Robert the coon' without any evident personal antipathy.⁵⁴ This is an important point to make since, as with misogyny, there is a tendency to ascribe racism to racist individuals rather than to a racist culture.⁵⁵ The racism expressed by

---

⁴⁸ Reference to Koo from MvK diary 22 November 1944, inv nr 394, 2.05.86, NL-HaNA; reference to Kindler in MvK diary 13 March 1949, inv nr 399, 2.05.86, NL-HaNA.
⁴⁹ MvK diary 5 May 1948, inv nr 397 and 24 February 1949, inv nr 400, 2.05.86, NL-HaNA.
⁵⁰ MvK diary 28 June 1944, inv nr 393, 2.05.86, NL-HaNA.
⁵¹ MvK diary 15 November 1949, inv nr 400, 2.05.86, NL-HaNA.
⁵² MvK diary 26 August 1947, inv nr 397, 2.05.86, NL-HaNA.
⁵³ MvK diary 3 September 1948, inv nr 398, 2.05.86, NL-HaNA.
⁵⁴ MvK diary 17 June, 1 July, 10 July, 14 August 1946, inv nr 396, 2.05.86, NL-HaNA.
⁵⁵ Compare Kate Manne, *Down Girl: The Logic of Misogyny* (New York: Oxford University Press, 2018).

Margaret van Kleffens may seem flagrant to a twenty-first century reader but it was, in fact, mild in comparison to the racism of some of her contemporaries. Moreover, it was not to do with any conscious conviction on her part that coloured people should not have equal rights. After a 1946 New York party, Margaret van Kleffens wrote in her diary that she had been seated next to 'an ex-diplomat southerner called Hewes … who shocked me profoundly with his views about the negroes. He thought they should be treated as "inferior beings" and have neither equal rights nor opportunities'.[56] For all her own prejudice, she emphatically distanced herself from such a view. 'This goes very much against my grain' she wrote, since 'every human being has, I think, a right to equality.' And yet, although it is evident that she thought his views abhorrent, when she noted that she feared that Mr Hewes' claim that 'most people in the south share his views' was true, it led her to conclude that the coloured population – rather than Hewes and his like – was 'becoming a sore problem in the U.S.'.[57]

The definition of who was the problem as well as the racist language used by Margaret van Kleffens testify to racist beliefs and prejudices, but it does not give us reason to assume that she had an uncommonly racist personality. Rather, it points to a diplomatic culture steeped in racial prejudice. While openly expressed beliefs in the inferiority of other human beings shocked Margaret van Kleffens, the racist epithets mentioned above did not. They were used as if they were merely descriptive and stereotypical ridicule was a matter of course. The examples from her diary echo countless upper-class contemporaries: Prince Bernhard of the Netherlands, in a 1949 letter to the former British ambassador to the Netherlands Sir Nevile Bland, mentioned the presentation of a Chinese award to him and his wife (Crown Princess Juliana), which he implied was showy but cheap much in the way Margaret van Kleffens dismissed the long names of Indonesian nobility as meaningless frills. The letter has an informal, jovial tone, indicating that Prince Bernhard expected Bland to enjoy his description that 'my wife got the Propitious Cloud and I the Cloud Banner. Wonderful names, but I am afraid that if sold they won't bring very much'.[58]

---

[56] Clarence Bussey Hewes, 1890–1962, retired from the Foreign Service in 1933 but was active in Washington society and in diplomatic circles, 'appeared regularly in the society columns of newspapers – many articles attest to his prowess as a desired guest and an excellent host'. He was also politically active in the Republican Party. See DC History Center, archive containing Hewes' scrapbook collection. Available at: https://dchistory.pastperfectonline.com/archive/575E0022-3184-42C3-B57D-832301142300 (last accessed 26 April 2021).

[57] MvK diary 26 July 1946, inv nr 396, 2.05.86, NL-HaNA.

[58] Letter from Prince Bernhard of the Netherlands to Sir Nevile Bland, dated Soestdijk Palace, 5 January 1949, The Papers of Sir (George) Nevile (Maltby) Bland, BLND 6/23, UK-CAC.

Making airily condescending remarks about people of other ethnicities and cultures was part of Western diplomatic culture.

There is much work left to be done on the ways in which differently racialized discourses for different groups influenced diplomatic relations. In the context of the diplomatic aptitude of appearances, it must suffice for now to point out that the management of decorations and dressing for dinner was not an equal task that demanded the same type of labour of all who engaged in it. To make a favourable impression was important for all who took part in dinner diplomacy, but the scope for manoeuvre of those dressing for dinner depended on how they were gendered, classed, and racialized. Beauty cannot be determined outside of the eye of the beholder.

11 Diplomatic discourse

When Margaret van Kleffens was 'forced to explain' her medical condition to the Dominican ambassador, as mentioned in the context of food in Chapter 9, she clearly thought it quite embarrassing. Her unease was not only to do with the attention to her failure to show appropriate appreciation for what was served, but with the ensuing need to break a rule of conversation. Fortunately, the circumstance was 'slightly mitigated by his being a dr. by profession'.[59] That she was glad in this situation that the Dominican ambassador, Dr Luis Francisco Thomen, was a medical doctor – he later became a representative to the World Health Organization – says more about the rules of dinner conversation than may be obvious at first glance. Without contextual knowledge, the reference to his profession as a mitigating circumstance may seem insignificant: it seems natural, perhaps, for a person to feel more at ease talking about an ailment to someone with professional knowledge about health issues. However, it was hardly her own comfort Margaret van Kleffens was worried about. She was not dining with friends but present in her capacity as a representative of the Netherlands. Her task was to help entertain good diplomatic relations. In all likelihood, she viewed his profession as a mitigating circumstance because a conversation about a medical condition could be framed as an appropriately interesting topic for a medical doctor. It made it possible for her to turn her explanation into something that was to do with him and his skills, rather than

---

[59] MvK diary 7 April 1949, inv nr 399, 2.05.86, NL-HaNA.

with herself and her problems. Margaret van Kleffens was well-versed in the art of diplomatic dinner discourse.

This final empirical chapter will submit that art to closer scrutiny. For all the attention to the taste of the food and the beauty of people and settings, good discourse – as Margaret van Kleffens often called it – was a *sine qua non* for a successful social event. It was the most prominent feature of her notes as a measure of a diplomatic dinner's success or failure. Appropriate conversation was an essential part of informal diplomacy and it had its own (unwritten) rules – rules that were inseparably intertwined with the dinner diplomacy aspects already discussed.

To experts on Foucault, my use of the term discourse for this chapter might seem somewhat offhanded, so to clarify, it should not be taken to imply the use of a different approach than in previous chapters. The analysis of how looks were gendered and racialized, for instance, was also based on the way people spoke about them. I use discourse in this chapter as an empirical as much as a theoretical term. Margaret van Kleffens herself spoke of the discourse when she generalized about an evening's talk. In my use, the term is more consciously a tool to point to the general patterns of diplomatic interaction based on the speaking of persons in diplomatic positions. However, my aim is not to make a full-blown, formal discourse analysis counting the use of individual words, for example. The questions I pose are aimed at revealing who was trusted to do (in this case say) what, when, where and how. How were informal (table)talks conducted in practice and what roles did diplomats, their wives, and other guests play in these talks? What characterized good (and bad) mid-twentieth century dinner discourse? What was its purpose? What determined which topics were appropriate? The chapter ends with some reflections on what the norms of mid-twentieth century diplomatic discourse can tell us about how the diplomatic relations of the postwar world were shaped in practice.

The rules and demands of diplomatic conversation

From the early days of their relationship, her talent for conversation was one of the qualities that made Eelco van Kleffens see Margaret Horstmann as a suitable diplomat's wife. 'Having you so near is heaven', he wrote in one of his early love letters after an evening they spent together in company.

> I love watching your 'brown delightful head' as our friend Rupert Brooke says, and the continuous change of expression on your face which is the most

exquisitely carved thing I know in the whole world ... and I greatly admire that when talking to people you don't know, you find, in an astonishing effortless manner, words they like to hear or are interested in.[60]

Already in 1934, he described what Margaret van Kleffens herself would later define as an indispensable quality in her line of work:

> I sometimes inwardly laugh at myself for being, in conversation, such a Jack-of-all-trades and master of none; a necessary asset, however, for an envoy's wife, and one which I will surely include in my handbook for such as we, if ever it is written.[61]

Unfortunately, she never got around to writing a handbook for 'such as we', that is, diplomats' wives, though she toyed with the idea during the Washington years. Nevertheless, her diaries convey plenty of information about the art of dinner discourse. Comparing a large number of comments about different kinds of dinner diplomacy occasions, a pattern emerges: positive mentions of 'good talk' or 'excellent discourse' were usually coupled with descriptions of the event using words such as 'pleasant', 'civilized', 'cultured', 'interesting' and sometimes 'gay' or 'merry'. As the two quotes above show, a good conversationalist was able to talk about things that interested others and a common compliment was that someone was easy to talk to. Things should be kept interesting, but light. When she called Sir Alexander and Lady Theodosia Cadogan 'perfect hosts', Margaret van Kleffens specified that they were 'full of small talk at meals'.[62] Having had the new British Ambassador and Lady Franks to dinner in Washington, DC, she noted that he was 'boyish and charming, easy to talk to, and as unassuming as she is'.[63]

Negative comments often included people being incapable of small talk or difficult to talk to. In one of her war-time complaints about having to take the Belgian Kaeckenbeeck's to lunch again since they were 'continually expecting such marks of friendship', Margaret van Kleffens hinted at an explanation to why she tended to describe lunch with these people as 'a chore', while she quite often enjoyed entertaining guests. The reason seems to have been that she found Georges Kaeckenbeeck 'an insufferable shop-talker and bore'.[64] Similarly, she

---

[60] Letter from Eelco van Kleffens to Margaret Horstmann 17 April 1934, inv nr 434, 2.05.86, NL-HaNA. The reference is to English poet Rupert Brooke's 1909 sonnet 'Oh! Death Will Find Me, Long Before I Tire'.
[61] MvK diary 20 November 1948, inv nr 398, 2.05.86, NL-HaNA.
[62] MvK diary 27/28 September 1947, inv nr 397, 2.05.86, NL-HaNA.
[63] MvK diary 3 July 1948, inv nr 398, 2.05.86, NL-HaNA.
[64] MvK diary 15 October 1943, inv nr 393, 2.05.86, NL-HaNA.

complained of Acting Governor-General of the Dutch East Indies Hubertus van Mook that he was only interested in business, and that 'small talk or graces he has none'.[65] This was not to do with a lack of personal interest of someone not involved in that business: her husband similarly emphasized small talk as an important diplomatic skill. At the 1945 San Francisco Conference, after a Soviet reception held to celebrate the victory over Germany, Eelco van Kleffens wrote in his diary: 'The ambassador Gromyko speaks fairly good English; for the rest they were speechless people who were not very sympathetic. They have still not understood that it is good diplomacy to make nice to people.'[66]

Sometimes, defective discourse was ascribed to the way an event was organized. After hosting a small dinner in New York City in 1946, Margaret van Kleffens regretted the combination of Eelco van Kleffens's Brazilian colleague in the UN Security Council Dr Pedro Leão Veloso and 'his amusing wife', Virgínia de Castro Leão Veloso, with two Dutch ministers whose 'French was of the high school variety, so they kept mum'. She concluded that she did not 'believe in such small, intimate parties with mixed languages, everyone feels uncomfortable and nobody really enjoys it'.[67] In Washington, DC, two years later, she complained about being 'badly placed' at a Belgian Embassy dinner. To her left sat Prince-Regent Charles of Belgium, the host, who was 'vamped' by his left-hand neighbour Gladys Rose Vandenberg (wife of US General Hoyt Vandenberg, not to be confused with Hazel Vandenberg, wife of Senator Arthur Vandenberg). Her neighbour to the right, Belgian Foreign Minister Paul-Henri Spaak, in turn had on his right US Under Secretary of State Dean Acheson, so that '[n]ot unnaturally these two talked politics leaving me on an island'. Her husband, 'E., as ranking man, was not even spoken to by H.R.H. [His Royal Highness]'. That dinner was labelled a 'bad show; poor management'. Though she condemned Mrs Hoyt Vandenberg's bad manners and called the prince 'as maladroit a man as ever we did see', the primary blame befell Belgian Ambassador Robert Silvercruys who 'stood along the sidelines instead of taking royalty firmly in hand'.[68]

Her comments reveal a few things about the rules of dinner diplomacy discourse. First, it clarifies that to talk about politics was not the same thing as to

[65] MvK diary 8 September 1947, inv nr 397, 2.05.86, NL-HaNA.
[66] EvK diary 25 May 1945, inv nr 208, 2.05.86, NL-HaNA. My translation. In Dutch: 'De ambassadeur Gromyko spreekt vrij goed Engelsch; voor de rest waren het sprakelooze lieden die weinig sympathiek aan deden. Zij zijn er nog altijd niet achter dat het goede diplomatie is, zich bij de menschen aangenaam te maken.'
[67] MvK diary 14 June 1946, inv nr 396, 2.05.86, NL-HaNA.
[68] MvK diary 11 April 1948, inv nr 397, 2.05.86, NL-HaNA.

talk shop or talk about business (even if, in this case, politics was the business of both Spaak and Acheson). As a comparison, when Margaret van Kleffens complained that their friend Thanassis Aghnides, at the time Greek representative to the United Nations, had been boring at dinner, she mentioned too much 'talk about motions, amendments and dockets'.[69] There was a difference between speaking about specific work issues and talking politics more generally. Even if Spaak and Acheson talked politics in that sense though, it was rude to ignore one of two neighbours at the table. And yet, although Margaret van Kleffens liked to talk politics herself, she did not hold Spaak and Acheson accountable for their negligence. She accepted as 'natural' that two political men would be more interested in discussing politics with each other than with her. Her other two neighbours, however, did not have a valid excuse for leaving her 'on an island'. The prince should not have allowed his attention to be claimed so totally by the lady on his left, especially since he was the host and therefore had a special obligation to speak to all the guests. Yet she thought him merely the inept victim of that lady's 'tasteless, ill-bred determination: – patting him on the shoulder, reading his hand, and butting into what conversation he could have with me'. Although the visiting prince acted as host, she blamed the ambassador for bad seating, poor overall organization of the event and even the oversights of His Royal Highness.[70]

Appropriate dinner discourse depended on rank, gender, nationality, political interests, previous relationships and the way these and other factors intersected in particular settings. What is clear is that more was expected of professional diplomats and their female spouses than of other actors. A disproportionate amount of responsibility for good discourse rested on the diplomat arranging the event, whether or not officially its host. A salient detail in the above example is that Baron Silvercruys was a bachelor. Had he been married, chances are that the primary blame would have befallen his wife, since a female spouse, if there was one, did the lion's share of diplomatic dinner organization.[71]

---

[69] MvK diary 5 April 1948, inv nr 397, 2.05.86, NL-HaNA.
[70] MvK diary 11 April 1948, inv nr 397, 2.05.86, NL-HaNA.
[71] Five years later, in September 1953, Ambassador Silvercruys married the widow of US Senator Brian McMahon, Rosemary (née Turner). Margaret van Kleffens, by then in Portugal, noted in her diary that McMahon's widow had married 'our Belgian colleague in Washington, the dance-masterish Robert Silvercruys. He was generally thought to be a pansy on account of his uncommonly exquisite taste and his long bachelorhood. I suppose Rosemary has just decided she wants to be an ambassadress, as I can see no other reason for this step. She is still young, beautiful, and was left comfortably off.' Van Kleffens's silence on the groom's reasons for 'this step' implies that the advantage to him was obvious to her. MvK diary 25 September 1953, inv nr 404, 2.05.86, NL-HaNA.

Margaret van Kleffens herself always made attempts to organize her dinner diplomacy to avoid bad combinations or compensate for one bad conversationalist by inviting another. 'To ease the situation', she wrote about a 1945 London visit by the 'fairly speechless' Chinese Ambassador's wife Madame Tung, 'I had invited Lady Theo Cadogan, who came bustling in chattering as a magpie as is her wont.'[72] It was a good trick to combine guests so that they entertained one another. 'Gave a luncheon for fourteen of Washington's more prominent old battle-axes to whom I was indebted' Margaret van Kleffens noted in June 1948; 'as they were sure to relish each other's company, this was a splendid way to get rid of them.'[73] In the course of their career, she and her husband also developed another solution to the problem of bad but mandatory guests. 'Tonight we assembled here for a bang-up dinner all the horrors, impossibles and speechless duds on our "owed dinner-party" list,' Margaret van Kleffens noted in her diary some two years after they had left the United States embassy for the Portuguese. 'This is a good thing to do once in a while, we've found, to get the whole thing over with – rather than spread them out over 3 or 4 dinners, and ruin them all!'[74]

Of course, such an approach was not always possible. Particular people had to be invited to particular dinners, even if they were terrible at small talk. And no matter how good the management, bad seating could be unavoidable because of diplomatic protocol. Even in preparation for relatively intimate dinners, Margaret van Kleffens consulted her husband to make sure that the best seating, from a conversational point of view, would not upset anyone based on rules of rank.[75] Foreign Office archives also testify to the significance of these kinds of formalities. They contain numerous files on questions of protocol, such as the rules of precedence in different countries and advice on preferable seating in specific contexts. Special officials in charge of protocol matters spent quite a lot of time answering questions and writing extensive explanations and clarifications about correct procedures.[76] The many questions show that even diplomatic protocol was not set in stone. In spite of the transnational character of the

---

[72] MvK diary 3 July 1945, inv nr 395, 2.05.86, NL-HaNA.
[73] MvK diary 10 June 1948, inv nr 398, 2.05.86, NL-HaNA.
[74] MvK diary 15 November 1952, inv nr 403, 2.05.86, NL-HaNA.
[75] MvK diary 25 December 1947, inv nr 397, 2.05.86, NL-HaNA. Her note reveals that she consulted her husband in cases of doubt, because on this occasion, one of the guests – Ambassador Silvercruys, incidentally – became angry about being placed second after the UK representative to the United Nations Alexander Cadogan. Margaret van Kleffens, in turn, noted how much this upset her because her husband had affirmed that Silvercruys was 'more or less justified in this' even though she had consulted him in advance and he had said it was alright.
[76] For the period 1945 to 1954, there are 1,056 folders on protocol matters in the Code archive of the Netherlands Ministry of Foreign Affairs, access nr 2.05.117, inv nrs 1840–2895, NL-HaNA.

diplomatic corps, there were national variations depending on where diplomats were posted.

How strict the rules were also varied according to the size and formality of the situation. The more official the event, the more potential sensitivities about the visual hierarchy and less leeway for shuffling with the seating. At a big, formal dinner hosted by US President and Mrs Truman to celebrate the signing of the North Atlantic Treaty, Margaret van Kleffens 'spied disastrous combinations, protocol-engendered', mentioning as an example the seating of the famously stylish French ambassador's wife Hellé Bonnet next to the 'Lombroso type' Icelandic foreign minister Bjarni Benediktsson. She could also see Bess Truman 'finding Spaak, whose English is virtually nil, heavy going'. Talking about the remarks that all the present foreign ministers had made when they had signed the treaty earlier that day, Margaret van Kleffens called Spaak a 'born orator' and 'the most eloquent by far'.[77] The problem in this case, then, was not his social or speaking skills, but the lack of language skills, whether his or Mrs Truman's. The combination made for bad conversation.

Protocol-engendered or not, a hostess (or host) could not be held responsible for forestalling or ending all awkward situations. Sometimes, bad conversation was simply blamed on individual people. Margaret van Kleffens praised American socialite and diplomat Florence Harriman for arranging a dinner with 'interesting company', for example, but noted that General Carl 'Spaatz is hard to converse with, save on fishing and on air force, and of both subjects my knowledge is scanty'. The comment illustrates why a diplomat's wife had to be a 'Jack-of-all-trades' to keep conversation going. She contrasted General Spaatz with her other neighbour. 'The Justice [Robert H. Jackson] thereagainst is a bright boy!'[78] The fact that she put the tedious talk of one man in contrast to how smart another man was reveals that she coupled conversational skills to intelligence. This is in line with her disdain for female gatherings on the grounds that these women were 'largely lacking in grey matter'.[79] She also tended to couple a lack of intelligence in women to their talking too much, mentioning 'vapid garrulous females' for example.[80] 'Vapid women's talk: How boring', she noted on another occasion.[81]

---

[77] MvK diary 4 April 1949, inv nr 399, 2.05.86, NL-HaNA. 'Lombroso type' refers to the nineteenth-century claim of Italian criminologist Cesare Lombroso that physical characteristics could reveal an inherited predisposition to crime.
[78] MvK diary 30 March 1948, inv nr 397, 2.05.86, NL-HaNA.
[79] MvK diary 15 August 1947, inv nr 397, 2.05.86, NL-HaNA.
[80] MvK diary 11 April 1947, inv nr 396, 2.05.86, NL-HaNA.
[81] MvK diary 31 October 1949, inv nr 400, 2.05.86, NL-HaNA.

Interestingly, though her general comments about the capabilities of men and women suggest a discrepancy, the difference disappears when the comments become concrete. On average, Margaret van Kleffens seems not to have met a larger number of unintelligent women than unintelligent men, even by her own account. On the contrary, her diary often praises individual women for their intelligence and singles men out for their stupidity. To give just a few examples, she named New York Times columnist Anne O'Hare McCormick's presence at a dinner the reason that 'the conversation was at times quite worth listening to', proceeding to quote Mrs McCormick's opinions on the Palestine question. She added that 'her husband makes a singularly stupid impression; perhaps his clever wife has made him take refuge in the bottle, like Mr. Ogden Reid'.[82] This was a month after the incident mentioned in Chapter 8, when she had called American newspaper publisher Helen Rogers Reid a 'formidable little live-wire' and Mr Reid 'her apparently balmy husband'.[83]

The comment reveals the underlying assumption that men should rank higher than women. Evidently, being outshone by his wife would depress a husband enough to drive him to drink. That perception of the nature of things persisted in spite of women outshining men often enough. Even at one of the female gatherings she so loathed, a Women's City Club meeting that she attended solely because of 'the desirability of meeting Americans other than those we meet socially or officially', Margaret van Kleffens had been pleasantly surprised. Two of the speakers, American writers Willie Snow Ethridge and Margaret Widdemer, made quite an impression on her by their ability to speak without notes and be 'so amusing that they had the whole room in stitches with laughter'. She 'felt almost sorry for Jim Farley', the male American politician who had to follow their act and 'fell quite flat'.[84]

In line with the gender norms and perceptions to which this testifies, Margaret van Kleffens never talked about men as a group as stupid (let alone 'vapid' or 'garrulous'). As already shown however, she did express negative opinions about the aptitude of individual men. 'Sad to think that such nincompoops can through wealth wield such power', she said about Dutch businessman Frits Philips, for instance, after concluding that 'he uttered not one worthwhile word' at the dinner she had arranged.[85] And about Cornelius Vanderbilt "Sonny" Whitney, US Under Secretary of Commerce at the time, she said after they had talked: 'I am afraid he

---

[82] MvK diary 4/5 May 1946, inv nr 395, 2.05.86, NL-HaNA.
[83] MvK diary 6 April 1946, inv nr 395, 2.05.86, NL-HaNA.
[84] MvK diary 7 April 1948, inv nr 397, 2.05.86, NL-HaNA.
[85] MvK diary 23 February 1949, inv nr 399, 2.05.86, NL-HaNA.

has rather a bird-brain.'[86] In practice, then, intelligence was a prized asset for both men and women and one that was generally coupled to good speaking and social skills. However, though some measure of intelligence was a necessary condition for good diplomatic conversation, it was not sufficient – at least not for women. When Margaret van Kleffens first met Lady Barbara Franks, for example, she wrote about the British ambassador's wife that she was 'painfully shy and ill at ease and unattractive'. That did not mean she placed her in the ranks of vapid women or did not like her. 'I pity her heartily,' she wrote instead, 'as she is obviously intelligent, over-sensitive, and disgruntled about being here instead of in the English provinces where she so obviously hails from and belongs.'[87]

Perhaps she recognized something of herself in Barbara Franks. Margaret van Kleffens, too, was evidently intelligent and she had a conscientious and critical character in common with her husband. However, she knew that those qualities were not enough to make a good diplomat's wife. They could even be a disadvantage, particularly in combination with a tendency toward anxiety and brooding. Such depressing traits were no great advantage to a man either, but when Margaret van Kleffens reflected on the pros and cons of her own character, she put them in relation to her (female) looks:

> I do so wish I had a) charm; b) a considerable sense of humour; c) no nerves. All three such infinitely more effective and more lasting assets than my moderately creditable face and figure.[88]

This ideal seems to have remained over the years. Pondering in 1954, a decade later, her own qualities as a diplomat's wife, she wrote: 'I would have liked more of a sense of humour, and a less wry one, and a lighter touch in general, and a more optimistic outlook on life.'[89] And in a sombre mood in 1957, she described her brooding nature as a social handicap. 'My nature is a curse' she wrote, '– and not only to me, which is the worst of it.' The toll on her was considerable though, the rest of the note shows.

> Certainly I am abnormally nervous; to be obliged to take a glass of sherry, a nip of brandy, and two Miltown tablets in order to relax enough to enter a dinner-party without making everyone tense through one's own extreme and visible tension is abnormal.[90]

---

[86] MvK diary 1 May 1949, inv nr 399, 2.05.86, NL-HaNA.
[87] MvK diary 17 June 1948, inv nr 398, 2.05.86, NL-HaNA.
[88] MvK diary, 7 December 1943, inv nr 393, 2.05.86, NL-HaNA.
[89] MvK diary 4 March 1954, inv nr 404, 2.05.86, NL-HaNA.
[90] MvK diary 20 January 1957, inv nr 408, 2.05.86, NL-HaNA.

The description of her effect on others should be taken with a grain of salt: she wrote it on a bad day. Even if she was not as easy-going as her successor as ambassadress in Washington, Anne van Roijen, the evidence shows that Margaret van Kleffens was well-liked and that she managed her tasks as a diplomat's wife excellently.[91] And on good days, her notes testify to her taking considerable pleasure in dinner diplomacy. It does show that none of it was effortless. Though acting according to mid-twentieth century diplomatic norms of appropriate femininity no doubt came easier to some than to others, it was no exception that she had to work for it. Barbara Franks, too, had that quality which was perhaps more important than any other: she was prepared to make an effort. Only six months after their first meeting, Margaret van Kleffens noted that Lady Franks was 'improving by leaps and bounds in both appearance and manner: she now does her best to talk and smiles frequently which she never used to do'.[92] Diplomatic dinner discourse was an art to master. It took practice.

Margaret van Kleffens practiced too. Although she had quite a bit of experience with entertaining after seven years as a foreign minister's wife, the post in Washington, DC brought new demands. One was that ambassadors' wives, like the ambassadors themselves, were not only expected to converse one-on-one with numerous strangers, but also to make speeches: at dinners, to groups of people, on the radio. Her husband was used to this. Admiringly, Margaret van Kleffens commented how her husband talked 'with such ease and conviction, simplicity and sincerity in addition to holding himself well and having a pleasant voice'.[93] While she loved listening to her husband, she herself was so terrified of speaking in public that after their arrival in Washington, DC, she told the public relations person at the Dutch chancery of her 'regrettable inability to speak in public so that she shall not sell me to groups of well-doing clubwoman (sic)'.[94] Less than a month later however, she overcame her fear.

> Today I gained the greatest victory over myself ever; I did, so help me, get up at a women's luncheon and made a speech! 'Making a few remarks' is one of the less pleasant things an ambassadress may quite frequently be called upon to do in this country, and being excessively self-conscious and full of stage-fright I have dreaded this part of my duties – although not an inescapable part – like the

---

[91] S Erlandsson and R van der Maar, 'Trouw aan Buitenlandse Zaken. Margaret van Kleffens, Anne van Roijen, de ambassade in Washington en de betekenis van het diplomatiek partnerschap voor de naoorlogse Nederlandse buitenlandse betrekkingen'. *Tijdschrift voor Geschiedenis* 134, no 3 (2021).
[92] MvK diary 13 January 1949, inv nr 398, 2.05.86, NL-HaNA.
[93] MvK diary 19 August 1946, inv nr 396, 2.05.86, NL-HaNA.
[94] MvK diary 25 August 1947, inv nr 397, 2.05.86, NL-HaNA.

plague; more than that, I have let it be known I was regretfully unavailable! However, I felt it was going to be increasingly awkward to keep on refusing.

To get herself over the threshold, she picked a small and good-natured group of 22 doctors' wives and took an Abasin tablet[95] – her doctor, who was ex-German and Jewish, called them 'Schwatzpillen': chatting pills. Fortified by this, the encouragement of others, and

> a prepared speech, composed and typed out by me, I launched myself on my maiden venture in this line and glad to tell, came through not only alive, but proud, relieved, with flying colours and a sense of having enjoyed hearing myself. Can you beat it?[96]

The sense of relief is palpable. Although the note conveys that it was possible for an ambassador's wife to refuse to speak in public, a conscientious person and loyal wife such as Margaret van Kleffens saw it as part of her duties and felt that she had to try. She even felt it was so important that after this 'maiden venture', she decided to take speaking lessons to become better at it and less nervous. Between October 1947 and January 1948, she attended both private and group lessons in public speaking given by a Mrs Harold Butler.[97] She did so well that on the last occasion, she was voted 'the best speaker among us' by her five classmates.[98] Moreover, in December, she wrote and made a speech 'Woman's eye-view of Holland' together with one of her classmates, a Mrs Luther. Elinor Lee from the radio station WTOP (Columbia Broadcasting System) who happened to be visiting class 'to hear us do our stuff and give us hints for improvement' liked their speech so much that she offered to broadcast it, to Eelco van Kleffens's delight.[99] Margaret van Kleffens lengthened the speech from 8½ to 13 minutes, practised it together with Mrs Luther and, on 13 January 1948, elatedly reported in her diary that 'Columbia (CBS) likes it so much that they are sending it out over their *network*; in other words coast-to-coast! Are we proud, or are we?'[100]

---

[95] Brand name for Acecarbromal, a hypnotic and sedative drug discovered by Bayer in 1917 that was formerly marketed in the United States and Europe, 'Acecarbromal', in *DBpedia*. Available at: https://dbpedia.org/page/Acecarbromal (accessed 28 June 2021); The pills were popular because they could be administered to nervous patients without them becoming drowsy, according to the United States. Congress. Senate. Committee on Agriculture and Forestry, 'Administration of Federal Food and Drugs Act: Hearings before the Committee on Agriculture and Forestry, United States Senate, Seventy-First Congress, Second Session, on Administration of Federal Food and Drugs Act. February 12 to June 30, 1930' (Washington, District of Columbia: U.S. Govt. Print. Off., 1930), 1647.
[96] MvK diary 23 September 1947, inv nr 397, 2.05.86, NL-HaNA.
[97] Possibly the wife of the head of the British Information Service in Washington, DC from 1942, Sir Harold Beresford Butler. In that case, born Olive Augusta Newenham Walker Waters (1890–1989).
[98] MvK diary 16 January 1948, inv nr 397, 2.05.86, NL-HaNA.
[99] MvK diary 17 December 1947, inv nr 397, 2.05.86, NL-HaNA.
[100] MvK diary 2 and 13 January 1948, inv nr 397, 2.05.86, NL-HaNA.

The radio speech went well – she even received fan mail.[101] It became only the first of several radio speeches that spring, targeting an audience of housewives with topics such as 'a homemaker's day in Holland'; the origin of tulips and how they are cultivated; and 'Washington wives'.[102] Both the radio shows and the newspaper items that featured her focused on topics that were supposed to be of special interest to women: pets, looks, clothes, children, interior decoration, flowers, gardening, but also personal-political stories. She spoke of how the Germans had stolen all their silver and furniture during the war, of social-economic political issues like how difficult it was for Dutch people to purchase anything American due to the lack of foreign exchange, and commented on the material conditions in Europe and food supply in the Netherlands after the war.[103] Her interest in politics, dogs, flowers and gardening was genuine, but the choice of topic was usually less to do with Margaret van Kleffens's own personal interests than with her target audience. To a New York radio show on the 'First Ladies of the UN', in which she participated, she somewhat condescendingly referred as 'a kitchen-maid-chat for the housewife'.[104]

Her ability to target a different audience than her husband when speaking in public about politics and about the Netherlands made her a valuable asset. Considering how she had initially declined to speak in public out of sheer terror, her progress was amazing. 'How I love broadcasting' she wrote in her diary in March 1948. 'When the announcer says "One minute – ten seconds – stand by" – it's as thrilling to this strange and silly creature as taking off in an aeroplane.'[105] On 12 May 1948, the column by Molly Thayer in the *Washington Post* even carried the notice: 'Radio notes: Mme. van Kleffens, the youthful, Netherlands Ambassadress, broadcasts several times a week. She's good. Listen in...'[106] Next

---

[101] A letter from Dutch expat L Herbert Loeb in Massachusetts dated 15 January 1948, praising both the content of her speech and her beautiful voice with its slight Oxford accent, is kept in her diary next to the entry MvK diary 20 January 1948, inv nr 397, 2.05.86, NL-HaNA.

[102] MvK diary 10 March, 17 April, and 8 May 1948, inv nr 397, 2.05.86, NL-HaNA.

[103] A small selection of interviews and newspaper clippings featuring Margaret van Kleffens include Elizabeth Maguire, 'Dutch Embassy's New Chatelaine is Charming Mme. van Kleffens', *Washington Post*, 27 August 1947; 'The Netherlands Ambassador's Wife Visits Patients', *Washington Post*, October 1947; Margaret Hart Canby, 'Dutch Hostess Serves Tea; Brilliant Party at Union', *Washington Evening Star*, 14 November 1947; Evelyn Peyton Gordon, 'Mme. van Kleffens', *Washington Daily News*, 18 November 1947; Mary van Rensselaer Thayer, 'Gifts to Green Thumbers', *Washington Post*, 26 November 1947; Maguire, 'Mme. van Kleffens Entertains for Children' All of these are included as clippings in MvK diary inv nr 397, 2.05.86, NL-HaNA.

[104] MvK diary 4 March 1947, inv nr 396, 2.05.86, NL-HaNA. My translation – she wrote this in Dutch: 'een keukenmeidenpraatje voor de huisvrouw'.

[105] MvK diary 2 March 1948, inv nr 397, 2.05.86, NL-HaNA.

[106] Mary van Rensselaer Thayer, 'Tom Clarks Entertain – Hush Hush Party Honors President; Needed – A Class for Dancing Diplomats', *Washington Post*, 12 May 1948.

to the clipping, which Margaret van Kleffens glued in her diary, she has written 'strictly inaccurate I'm afraid; but good publicity!'[107] There is no doubt that she became quite a successful speaker, an asset to the public relations of her country. She also appeared on the television show 'Meet Mrs. Markel' (together with Jansen the dog), and continued to speak frequently at dinners and women's clubs between 1947 and 1950.[108] On the last day of her speaking class in 1948, two days after her CBS radio performance, she wrote in her diary:

> Seldom has anything I undertook given me more pleasure or profit than this course, which has opened up a field for me so far undreamt of and given me some priceless self-confidence instead of the terror which used to grip at the mere thought of a public utterance.[109]

Nevertheless, she never quite got over her nerves. 'With much inward trembling and fortified by a glass of sherry and one of Dresel's pills,' she wrote three months after the end of her classes, 'I made my speech this evening at the Alpha Xi Delta annual banquet. As usual, it went off very well, and as usual, I blamed myself for a silly ass, when it was over, to have had any qualms'.[110]

Whether for speeches or for dinner conversation, considerable efforts were made for the sake of successful informal diplomatic discourse. Aside from those made by individual people such as Margaret van Kleffens and Barbara Franks to overcome what were viewed as undesirable personal traits in order to become more entertaining and likeable, diplomats and their wives often prepared for conversations by trying to learn personal facts about their guests or hosts. How much of that preparation was the responsibility of the individual diplomat seems to have depended on which country they represented. Overall, the United Kingdom Foreign Office was well-organized when it came to dinner diplomacy. In preparation for dinner parties and teas in the early 1950s, Foreign Secretary Anthony and Clarissa Eden sometimes received rather extensive descriptions of their guests and the countries they came from in advance.[111] The Dutch were not quite so formally organized in this respect. I have found an occasional list of descriptions of the guests he was supposed to meet when serving as foreign minister in Eelco van Kleffens's archive too, but there seems to have been less of

---

[107] MvK diary 12 May 1948, inv nr 397, 2.05.86, NL-HaNA.
[108] A reference to and clipping about the televised appearance respectively can be found in MvK diary 6 and 12 July 1948, inv nr 398, 2.05.86, NL-HaNA.
[109] MvK diary 16 January 1948, inv nr 397, 2.05.86, NL-HaNA.
[110] MvK diary 12 April 1948, inv nr 397, 2.05.86, NL-HaNA.
[111] Lady Avon: Correspondence, etc., relating to entertainments, 1952–1956, AP/3/2/3, Avon papers, UK-CRL.

a systematic and consistent supply of that sort of information.[112] Although it left less of a paper trail, it is nevertheless evident that both Eelco and Margaret van Kleffens too did prepare by collecting information about the people they were about to meet. 'Armed with the relevant information', Margaret van Kleffens wrote about a reception given by Bess Truman for diplomatic newcomers, 'I was able to tell Mrs. Truman ... that we had distant relatives in common.... This interested her greatly.'[113] Personal information was valuable in a culture where few efforts were spared to create an informal atmosphere and to display feelings of friendship (even if insincere). It was all part of greasing the wheels of diplomatic relations.

Dinner discourse as a gendered, heterosexual practice

In a 2017 interview, former American diplomat Barbara Bodine claimed the diplomatic advantage of having feminine-coded skills because 'diplomacy is the art of building relationships to deal with issues that you don't even know you're going to have. There's a lot of time spent talking with people, not necessarily on what the issue is.... "Tell me about your wife, your kids, the dog", kind of conversation'.[114] Ann Towns, who interviewed Bodine, uses the example to highlight that for all its association with masculinity, having long been an all-male profession, there are also figurations of the diplomat depicting diplomatic skills as typically feminine, and therefore diplomats as feminized. Comparing mid-twentieth century diplomatic discourse ideals for men and women respectively brings some nuance to the idea of diplomacy as either a masculine or a feminine art. In practice, it was both.

Regardless of the male prerogative when it came to the title of diplomat, both men and women served diplomatic purposes by playing a part in the game of diplomatic dinner discourse, albeit on different terms. Men were present because of their position, while most women were present because of the position of a man they were related to. In that sense, Barbara Bodine was right to describe the art of building relationships as a feminine power tool. Irrespective of any natural inclinations, in a setting where only men were entitled to compete for formal power, many women created their power base by building relationships. As

---

[112] Personal description of guests to lunch with Van Kleffens, 16 June 1943, kept in EvK diary next to entry 16 June 1943, inv nr 98, 233b, NL-NIOD.
[113] MvK diary 25 November 1947, inv nr 397, 2.05.86, NL-HaNA.
[114] As cited by Ann Towns, '"Diplomacy Is a Feminine Art": Feminised Figurations of the Diplomat', *Review of International Studies* 46, no 5 (2020): 573–93 at 592.

Figure 4.4 Eelco van Kleffens seated next to actress Sylvia Regis de Oliveira, whose father had been a Brazilian ambassador, at a dinner party given by Elsa Maxwell in 1945. Photo: Peter Stackpole/The LIFE Picture Collection, Getty Images.

discussed in Part I, for a woman, marriage to a diplomat meant joining the Foreign Service, but aside from marriage, women such as Elsa Maxwell or other unmarried or widowed hostesses participated by virtue of their ability to build attractive networks. There was really no equivalent position for men. Considering how their options and routes to power differed, to be perceived as successful, women needed to make more of a social effort than men. Although ideally, men in diplomacy too should make a social effort, it was less central to their survival as respected diplomatic actors and they were not judged for failing to make an effort as often as women were.

To illustrate, Margaret van Kleffens noted in her diary that she had tried to talk to the Italian foreign minister, Count Carlo Sforza, after the luncheon preceding the signing of the North Atlantic Treaty. His social performance was weak, not because of a lack of skill, but due to a lack of effort.

His English and French are fluent; not without trouble I found out he liked Oriental art and knew it well; but even the last-resort stratagem of trying to make him talk about himself met with so little response that I found him heavy going and ungenerously abandoned him to E., who could make a granite rock talk, if anyone could.[115]

While their lack of social effort had made Margaret van Kleffens write about the wives of the Belgian and French representatives to the UN Security Council that they were 'headed for a sour time, methinks' unless they changed, there were no similar comments about Count Sforza.[116] Her comments can also be compared to those she made about the British ambassador's wife: both Lady Franks and Count Sforza were described as intelligent and cultured, but less than forthcoming in conversation. Nevertheless, while Margaret van Kleffens pitied Lady Franks and applauded her efforts to talk and smile more, she made no remarks about being sorry for Count Sforza nor did she expect him to change. That he did not make an effort, at least not in order to have a conversation with the Dutch ambassador's wife, seems not to have struck her as inappropriate. Rather than blaming or pitying him, Margaret van Kleffens simply concluded that he was certainly cultured, but 'an old man and full of years'.[117] When she gave up, it was she who was ungenerous (whether she meant toward Count Sforza or toward her husband, or both).

Besides testifying to a gendered (coupled to a positional) difference in social expectations, the quote about Sforza contains a reference to trying to make people talk about themselves. As Margaret van Kleffens's comment about her husband's ability to 'make a granite rock talk' reveals, this 'last-resort stratagem' was not solely used by women but by diplomats in general. Besides the flattering aspect of showing personal interest, the personality reports discussed earlier testify to the diplomatic value of both political and personal information about others. Whether male or female, it served diplomatic actors well to be capable of interesting conversation while staying clear of controversial topics, to be accommodating but non-committal, and to make people feel at ease. Iver Neumann even talks about a 'self-effacing script' of diplomats.[118] If we are to believe the *Hartford Times* article from 1948 already mentioned, Margaret van

---

[115] MvK diary 4 April 1949, inv nr 399, 2.05.86, NL-HaNA.
[116] MvK diary 18 February 1947, inv nr 396, 2.05.86, NL-HaNA.
[117] She wrote this in Dutch and within quotation marks, 'oud en der dagen zat', a reference to the Biblical story of Job: 'En Job stierf, oud en der dagen zat.' In English: 'And so Job died, an old man and full of years.' Job 42:17; MvK diary 4 April 1949, inv nr 399, 2.05.86, NL-HaNA.
[118] Iver Neumann, 'To Be a Diplomat', *International Studies Perspectives* 6, no 1 (2005): 89.

Kleffens had that script down to a fine art. The article said that she moved 'unobtrusively from group to group', managed 'a long chat with each guest' and never forgot a name. She 'adroitly' made sure strangers were introduced so that they had someone to chat to. After a description of her hair, skin, eyes and 'pleasing accent', her diplomatic aptitude is coupled to her invisibility: 'Quiet almost to the point of self-effacement, she is one of the most gracious and popular hostesses in the diplomatic corps.'[119] I have yet to come across an equally positive description of a man as self-effacing.

Besides the stronger demand put on women to place others than themselves in the spotlight, diplomatic dinner discourse was gendered in at least two different ways. One was a concrete division of male and female spheres and topics. The other lay in gendered ways of pursuing common goals and talking to people in mixed spheres. When it comes to divided spheres, one of the advantages of diplomatic couples was that diplomats could target the men while their wives targeted the women. As with the interviews and public speeches mentioned above, the female networks that Margaret van Kleffens entertained were often arranged around matters that were perceived as feminine. Eelco van Kleffens was well aware of his wife's usefulness in appealing to women. 'More and more it proves a shame that M. is not here', he wrote during one of his wartime trips to the United States without her. '[E]veryone asks about her and she could work the ladies, and a number of gentlemen too', he added.[120] The last comment shows that Eelco van Kleffens missed his wife's help, not only in working the ladies. Though part of the gendered division of tasks between a diplomat and his wife lay in the concrete division between men's and women's networks, most of their dinner diplomacy work took place in mixed contexts.

Conversation when men and women were together was gendered too, but in other ways. While at same-sex events, the topics themselves were often man- or woman-orientated, the topics of general daily diplomatic dinner conversations were only partly divided along gendered lines. True, in the 1940s, diplomatic 'talking shop' was in principle (though not always in practice) a male prerogative, but as the above has shown, it was usually a *faux pas* to talk shop during dinner, for men as well as for women. That does not mean that there were no occasions when dinner invitations were made with the express purpose of discussing

---

[119] R Johnson, 'Tea Happy at Dutch Embassy' *Hartford Times*, 20 March 1948.
[120] EvK diary 18 February 1942, inv nr 206, 2.05.86, NL-HaNA. Also printed in van Kleffens, *Majesteit, U Kent Het Werkelijke Leven Niet : De Oorlogsdagboeken van Minister van Buitenlandse Zaken Mr. E.N. van Kleffens*. Edited by M.J. Riemens (Nijmegen: Vantilt, 2019), 48. 'Meer en meer blijkt het jammer dat M. er niet bij is; iedereen vraagt naar haar en zij zou de dames kunnen bewerken, en een aantal heren er bij.'

business. 'E. dines tonight with the American Chargé d'Affaires Schoenfeld, on business', Margaret van Kleffens wrote in June 1944 for example, 'and I with Marc and Miesje' (van Weede, a fellow Dutch diplomatic couple).[121] In this case, social dining was completely separate from business dining, the wife taking care of the former while leaving the latter to her husband.

Another manner in which the two were separated along gendered lines was the particular way in which some social dinners were combined with business when both men and women were present. An invitation to a home dinner might well be made to informally discuss state affairs, such as the Churchill dinner highlighted earlier. In those cases, however, work-related talk would generally be postponed until after dinner, when the men would retire without the ladies (save the occasional female head of state or ambassador), which signalled the boundary between business and pleasure. Even in reasonably informal settings, such as when Dutch ambassador to London Edgar Michiels van Verduynen came over to their house during the war, he first had tea with both Eelco and Margaret van Kleffens and then retreated with her husband to the study to talk shop – notwithstanding the fact that, according to her diary, she had talked shop with Michiels van Verduynen herself a couple of weeks earlier, during one of her husband's absences.[122]

Sometimes, keeping dinner and business talk apart appears more symbolical than practical, as in Margaret van Kleffens's description of French-Dutch talks at the end of the Second World War, for which Eelco van Kleffens travelled to France to meet with General Charles de Gaulle and Georges Bidault of the French provisional government:

> An amusing story was of the dinner at de Gaulle's house in the Bois de Boulogne ... Mme. De Gaulle and her daughter received them, seated at the far end of a large drawing-room, on stiff chairs. Neither of them stood up to welcome their guests, nor did Mme. De G. say a word of thanks for the flowers E. had sent her, which were (n.b.!) in the room! E. found these de Gaulle ladies very awkward and hopeless in conversation. After a very good four-course dinner, the host, Bidault the Foreign Minister (whom E. found in no way remarkable) and E. retired into a corner, and talked for over two hours, while the rest of the company sat in a stiff circle looking supremely bored.[123]

---

[121] MvK diary 27 June 1944, inv nr 393, 2.05.86, NL-HaNA.
[122] MvK diary 6 July 1943, inv nr 393; MvK diary 19/20 June 1943, inv nr 392, 2.05.86, NL-HaNA.
[123] MvK diary 23 March 1945, inv nr 394, 2.05.86, NL-HaNA. The abbreviation n.b. stands for nota bene.

The non-political sphere of the meal itself was emphasized by the presence of people not included in post-dinner talks, such as wives and daughters. In this case, the image of the men retiring into a corner to talk about state affairs while the rest of the company remained in the room and sat around being bored might seem absurd. It is probably not the setting a researcher finding and reading the official records of these talks would imagine, since those do not mention the context but only what was said on the subjects of the three men's discussions (to wit Dumbarton Oaks, the Rhine-Westphalian problem, and the French and Dutch positions on overseas territories – read: colonies). A copy of the French record of the talks can be found in the British National Archives under the heading 'Intelligence Passed to the Prime Minister', which gives these talks an allure of political significance that, to the uninitiated, might seem at odds with the image of three men talking in a corner of De Gaulle's dining room while the other dinner guests looked on.[124]

The pattern is not all that different from that of smaller, more informal dinners. 'We women sat in silent adoration........' Margaret van Kleffens noted in 1949 (the many dots are hers), describing how, at a small neighbourly dinner in Washington, DC '[t]he men' – Adolph Miller, one of the original Governors of the US Federal Reserve System, Justice Felix Frankfurter of the US Supreme Court, and Eelco van Kleffens – 'had endless heated discussions about politics, on a most impractical level, each outvying the other in knowledge of the lessons of history'.[125] A big difference, of course, is that while Eelco van Kleffens's discussions with De Gaulle and Bidault concerned concrete relations between the countries they represented and were followed by official reports, his talk with Justice Frankfurter and Mr Miller was a non-committal discussion about politics. The similarity says something, however, about how strong the norm was of structuring the culture of dinner diplomacy around the diplomatic couple. Whatever the actual deviations, the norm ruling dinner discourse was clearly gendered: while men 'talked shop', women 'sat in silent adoration'.

In practice, the dividing line lay more between mixed dinner talks and all-male or all-female talks than between male and female choices of topics. Several notes in Margaret van Kleffens's diaries show that when topics were not picked

---

[124] French Foreign Ministry circular on talks between de Gaulle and van Kleffens, 23 March 1945, Government Code and Cypher School: Signals Intelligence Passed to the Prime Minister, Messages and Correspondence 1940–1945, HW 1, UKNA.
[125] MvK diary 10 May 1949, inv nr 399, 2.05.86, NL-HaNA. Adolph Miller was retired at this point but had been one of the original Governors of the US Federal Reserve System. Felix Frankfurter served on the US Supreme Court. I have not been able to ascertain the identity of Mrs Ellis who, according to Margaret van Kleffens, was from California.

for public relations reasons, women could very well talk about the political concerns of their countries too, at least with one another. After a lunch in New York City in 1946 with the wife of the Belgian representative to the United Nations and another Finnish-Belgian lady, Margaret van Kleffens noted in her diary that 'in talking with Belgians I am glad to find a strong desire towards closer economic + political ties with us (and Luxemburg), and for unity of action between us where foreign policy is concerned'.[126]

The topics of conversation were not necessarily different for men and women. What made a person a good diplomatic conversationalist was, in several ways, similar for both men and women. Both should make an effort to learn languages, to understand foreign customs, to socialize with many people in a friendly way, to be prepared to make speeches in public and talk about interesting (but non-controversial) things. These aspects are the most visible in the sources as comments about people failing to act appropriately. For example, it was their lack of these qualities which caused Margaret van Kleffens to dismiss all wartime (male) Dutch ministers in exile except her own husband and Prime Minister Pieter Sjoerds Gerbrandy as 'quite unfit for anything but home consumption' and, after the war, to call the (female) spouses of the French and Belgian representatives to the United Nations 'absolute babes in the wood here'.[127]

The description of the De Gaulle dinner makes for an unusually graphic image of how male and female spheres were both mixed and separated. It helps spot some differences in how women and men were supposed to behave. Margaret van Kleffens noted the failure of the De Gaulle ladies to live up to expectations: they were far too stiff, did not provide a warm welcome for their guests and were awkward and hopeless in conversation. Her husband had behaved as he should: he had sent flowers to the hostess in advance. Yvonne de Gaulle, on the other hand, had failed to thank him for them. It does not matter in this context whether the account of Eelco van Kleffens was correct or unfair to Yvonne and Élisabeth de Gaulle. Even if he had deliberately depicted them in bad light, say to make his wife feel better about not having been present, it reveals how women could be depicted in a bad light.

Heterosexual flirtation was a regular feature of dinner diplomacy, complete with a gendered division of tasks, as not only the De Gaulle story but also the story about Dicky Wilson and the Dutch prince and the section on dressing for dinner have shown. By flirting in this context, I do not mean actual romantic

---

[126] MvK diary 19 February 1947, inv nr 396, 2.05.86, NL-HaNA.
[127] MvK January 1941 account, inv nr 391; MvK diary 18 February 1947, inv nr 396, 2.05.86, NL-HaNA.

involvement, but a form of heterosexually gendered interaction. Margaret van Kleffens treated successful flirtation in this sense as a virtue. The prince talked about serenading her sister. Her husband sent the female hostess flowers. Men should make grand gestures and pay women compliments. Women should graciously thank them, dress up for and listen adoringly to them and talk to them about their topic of choice.

Even when the flirting was less obvious than in the case of the Dutch prince, elements of the pattern were unmistakably present. Two days before the signing of the North Atlantic Treaty, hosting a bunch of 'tired statesmen', Margaret van Kleffens offered Dean Acheson some relief by talking to him about his hobby, for example: 'gladioli, of which he raises thirty varieties in his country garden.' The secretary of state had been in 'an unusually rosy humour'.[128] After a lunch at the Danish embassy, Margaret van Kleffens noted that to Henrik – using the ambassador's first name – 'life is a matter to be taken earnestly', so that they had talked about 'the relative desirability of character and imagination, and of manners and morals!' It seems that Danish Ambassador Henrik Kauffmann could get away with having a melancholy character and Margaret van Kleffens humoured him, noting with evident satisfaction in her diary that 'experience has made me able to be nearly all things to nearly all men, conversationally speaking'.[129]

Heterosexual relations were a crucial part of dinner diplomacy. The presence of women and the element of flirtation emphasized that dinners were occasions for apolitical socializing. It helped create a relaxed atmosphere conducive to good personal relations. This not only had consequences for the persistence of the norm of the heterosexual diplomatic couple – male diplomat with female wife – but also meant that women could be invited to dinners even if their rank or position did not match that of the male guests since they were supposed to be apolitical. Besides family members such as her sister, Eelco van Kleffens's secretaries (who were not, I should emphasize, lower-class women) were frequent guests at informal gatherings. During the war, dinner guests occasionally included Dutch women with whom Margaret van Kleffens worked at the Red Cross who did not have any diplomatic position whatever.[130] It is unlikely that

---

[128] MvK diary 2 April 1949, inv nr 399, 2.05.86, NL-HaNA.
[129] MvK diary 12 December 1949, inv nr 400, 2.05.86, NL-HaNA.
[130] See, eg, Margaret van Kleffens's account of the first night of the 1940–1941 London Blitz, MvK January 1941 account, inv nr 391, when not only Eelco van Kleffens's secretary Elly van Alphen was present, but also one of Margaret van Kleffens's Red Cross colleagues. There are also several references to his Washington secretary Pauline Schimmelpenninck coming for lunch or dinner when there were other guests, see, eg, MvK diary 6–9 August 1947, 1 March, 18 and 29 April 1948, inv nr 397, 2.05.86, NL-HaNA.

men of similar (lack of) standing would have been invited to dine with ministers and ambassadors.

The invited women were, of course, not just any women but women from the right social circle; still, it was easier for women than for men to be invited to fill any empty chairs at mixed-gender diplomatic dinners. In a time when almost all diplomats and statesmen (sic) were men, dinners were arranged for their sake, but women were added to the mix to beautify and enliven them and contribute to a relaxed atmosphere. When Margaret van Kleffens in 1946 complained about a party being dull, she added 'almost all men', as if by way of explanation.[131] 'I have come to the conclusion', she wrote on 9 March 1948, 'that the basis of a good party are attractive and talkative women, and good, imaginative food.'[132]

Women's role as attractive and accommodating, humouring men by modestly flirting with them made them diplomatically apt in a way that was not available to male diplomats among themselves. Heterosexual flirtation was probably a feature of any socializing, but in diplomatic contexts, a woman's ability to flirt made her useful for diplomatic purposes since flirting was an excellent way to make someone open up. Men flirted too, but in a world where they held the political positions while women were ostensibly apolitical one could even argue that a man who was a flirt was a bigger diplomatic risk than an asset. Margaret van Kleffens was clearly proud of her ability to charm men. About an otherwise 'ghastly party' in New York in April 1947, she noted:

> However, I was able to pursue my vague flirtation with le tendre Alexandre (Parodi). The poor wretch is about as happy in America as a fish in the Sahara. But, in this wilderness of barbarians, he has now found *me* – 'un pur esprit', bless the guileless fool's soul! – so I must needs teasingly console him, his wife being, like every right-thinking Frenchwoman, generally 'fatiguée'.[133]

The comment can be read both as manipulative and as light-hearted. Again, it is impossible to draw a line between personal and political feelings and behaviour. The flirtation with Alexandre Parodi seems to have had an element of sincere fondness – years later, when they met again in Portugal, she wrote about Parodi in her diary: 'With true French gallantry he sent me roses and we picked up the flirtation cut off when we left New York five years ago.'[134] In December 1949 she

---

[131] MvK diary 3 April 1946, inv nr 395, 2.05.86, NL-HaNA.
[132] MvK diary 9 March 1948, inv nr 397, 2.05.86, NL-HaNA.
[133] MvK diary 19/20 April 1947, inv nr 396, 2.05.86, NL-HaNA. Meaning of the words in French: *le tendre* = the tender, *un pur esprit* = a pure spirit; *fatiguée* = tired.
[134] MvK diary 18 Nov 1952, inv nr 403, 2.05.86, NL-HaNA.

referred to her post-dinner interaction with Pulitzer prize-winning Washington journalist Arthur Krock as 'a happy flirtation, involving much quoting of Shakespeare, Keates + Shelley'.[135] Other times, however, the flirtation was less genuinely cheerful and she more evidently played along purely for political purposes. 'Two of our country's worst enemies in Congress, Senators Pepper and Malone, were among our fellow guests at the Dominican Embassy tonight', she noted in April 1949. She found Senator George Malone, who sat beside her, 'a dreadful man' who had a 'chip on the shoulder re us (read: Indonesia)'. Despite her evident antipathy towards him, she 'smilingly underwent back-slapping, knee-patting, and hand-squeezing, all in the good cause!'[136]

Concluding remarks on diplomatic aptitude

Some of the things that made people diplomatically apt outside the office were fairly universal. A diplomat, as well as his spouse, should be sympathetic. They should be capable of small talk, preferably in several languages (and especially in the language of the country where they were posted). They should smile, be able to chat about things that interested others and be friendly but non-committal. However, diplomatic aptitude was not one thing in the mid-twentieth century. Not only did diplomacy demand work of a diversity of people with different professional skills, but what was considered diplomatically apt behaviour also depended on a person's position and the setting.

One of the most salient patterns, consistent with the observation that mid-twentieth century diplomacy was organized as a job for a heterosexual couple rather than a single diplomat, is the way in which diplomatic aptitude was gendered and sexualized. An apt male diplomat was casually well-dressed, talked business with other men but did not bore women with whom he should rather make interesting conversation, expressing admiration for their beauty, food and decorations. Women should make a visible effort to make themselves as well as the surroundings beautiful for men, talk intelligently to them about their topics of interest and exhibit admiration for their work and expertise. There were women who had more leeway by virtue of having more power in their own right, but even exceptions to the rule were partial: a woman with a brilliant journalistic career or a female ambassador might speak with more authority and be less

---

[135] MvK diary 20 December 1949, inv nr 400, 2.05.86, NL-HaNA.
[136] MvK diary 7 April 1949, inv nr 399, 2.05.86, NL-HaNA.

inclined to silent admiration, but she would still be expected to take a special interest in matters perceived as feminine. Her abilities and position were not judged in the same way as those of a man. While nobody would even think of blaming a man for driving his wife to drink by outshining her, for example, the opposite was implied often enough.

To a distant observer such as myself, in a hindsight determined by changed norms and influenced by the ability to collect and plough through numerous accounts, picking them apart, sorting them, and placing similar notes side by side, it seems obvious that female diplomatic actors adhered to a norm that catered to male pleasure. Yet, Margaret van Kleffens might not consciously have realized that this is what she was doing. 'Sometimes', she noted in her diary in 1947 (in almost the same words that she would use about her humouring of Henrik Kauffmann a couple of years later), 'it seems to me that for a short time, albeit under false pretences, I can in conversation be almost all things to almost all men.'[137] This gives the distinct impression not only that she catered to men, but that she did so strategically, not by natural inclination but – in her own words – under false pretences. In this particular case, her comments about an opera production had been 'apparently sufficiently to the point' to dumbfound the male conductor and make him 'stare at me across the dining room all during dinner'.[138] The quote shows that she was aware of what she was doing. However, when she talked about Madame Erkin, wife of the Turkish ambassador in Washington, she framed her colleague's behaviour as a sexualized femininity that belonged to a foreign culture:

> As I talked with, and watched, her (she must be junior to me in age), I perceived in countless subtle ways that her every gesture, inflection of voice and mannerism is designed with but one aim: that of pleasing the Male. No doubt an unconscious relic of harem-days, which she has not known, though her older relatives must have.[139]

Margaret van Kleffens apparently thought Madame Erkin as oblivious as I sometimes think her. Distance puts things in perspective. The appearances and behaviour of the Turkish ambassador's wife probably deviated in some ways from the appearances and behaviour of an average Western diplomat's wife. Margaret van Kleffens did not recognize them as similar to her own. Even though

---

[137] MvK diary 17 June 1947, inv nr 396, 2.05.86, NL-HaNA.
[138] MvK diary 17 June 1947, inv nr 396, 2.05.86, NL-HaNA.
[139] MvK diary 10 February 1949, inv nr 398, 2.05.86, NL-HaNA.

there can be little doubt that both aimed to please men, she interpreted Madame Erkin's manners as a remnant of an exotic past that was nothing to do with her own behaviour. As pointed out in Chapter 10, gendered preconceptions intersected with racialized ones.

As with the racial slurs that she used despite perceiving herself as someone who believed in equal rights for all peoples, Margaret van Kleffens seems to have been blissfully ignorant of her own sexism and misogyny. The cultural bias that becomes visible through this discrepancy reveals a dominant pattern that influenced Western views of diplomatic aptitude. It was not a matter of inherently diplomatic skills: what constituted proper diplomatic behaviour depended on your position in a partly explicit, partly implicit hierarchy. How a diplomatic actor was supposed to dress or talk to be considered diplomatically apt in the mid-twentieth century depended not only on what position he or she fulfilled, but also on skin colour, national background and gender.

Conclusion

Behind the scenes of building the postwar world

From beginning to end this book has shown how, in daily diplomatic work, the political was intrinsically interwoven with the personal. From love and marriage to homemaking and entertaining, matters that were deeply anchored in the physical bodies and emotional constitutions of the individuals who worked for the Foreign Service, whether salaried or not, were at the heart of diplomatic work done outside the office. That work was not optional but necessary for anyone charged with maintaining diplomatic relations. Moreover, it had political value not in spite of its personal character but often precisely because of it. Arenas and assets had a marked political value by virtue of being (semi-)private.

This concluding chapter is not primarily a summary of main findings from the different parts of the book. It is an attempt to add an additional step by discussing the broader political implications of the patterns of personal diplomacy uncovered. Those implications concern, first of all, how mid-twentieth century Western upper-class norms shaped postwar diplomatic culture and how that influenced who could participate in diplomatic work and on what conditions. Secondly, effects on the political alliances and decisions of the day are discussed in light of the book's final empirical part, revisiting the introduction's mention of a perceived link between political behaviour and personal relationships. Finally, diplomacy is discussed as a likeminded institution in the context of the postcolonial entry of newly independent states into the diplomatic arena.

Everyday power structures in Western diplomacy

The main theme of this book has been that the mid-twentieth century daily diplomatic work that took place outside the office presupposed a male diplomat with a female wife with a division of tasks along gendered lines. The long-lasting consequences for female diplomats have been discussed in Part I, while Parts II, III and IV showed in more detail how some fields of diplomatic expertise were firmly female-coded: housekeeping, heading domestic staff, preparing dinner parties, adding beauty and mastering the art of attentive listening, to name the most obvious. It still seems to be common among female diplomats to claim that women work in different ways than men, that they have more talent than male diplomats for fostering relationships and taking a so-called 'soft' approach.[1] To the extent that these differences in male and female diplomatic styles indeed still exist, they are likely a remnant of a very strong heterosexually gendered diplomatic norm – so strong that it is even perceived as natural.

To understand its persistence, it is vital to realize that people who did not fit the norm did not necessarily challenge it but were able to function by playing the game. Men without wives relied on other women they trusted to stand in and women who were neither diplomats themselves nor married to one could gain access to diplomatic circles by agreeing to play the part of suitable female company. The book's final empirical part pointed to how practices of male chivalry and female attentiveness testify to norms associated with heterosexual courtship. Individual homosexual men seem to have been accepted as a rather unproblematic matter of fact as long as they did not openly practice their sexuality or contest the existing norms. This means that, on an individual level, it paid off to profess a norm that denied the rights of one's own group. Even the success of lesbian hostess Elsa Maxwell depended on her ability to make fun of herself because of her deviation from the norm of female beauty and grace. In a way, she confirmed the norm by building her fame on her presentation of herself as a hopeless rule-breaker: loud, ugly, straightforward and demanding – and consequently, no wonder, unmarried. That would not have been possible other than in light of a strong norm for women to be quiet, beautiful, non-committal, responsive and eager to marry. Maxwell never openly acknowledged her homosexuality but publicly vehemently condemned same-sex love.[2] And although several male diplomats were widely known or believed to be homosexual, they were tolerated as diplomats only as long as they remained firmly closeted. The casual use of the derogative term 'pansies' for these men, together with the idea that homosexual men could be recognized by their typically feminine abilities also confirmed the male–female division of tasks.

---

[1] Ann Towns '"Diplomacy Is a Feminine Art": Feminised Figurations of the Diplomat'. *Review of International Studies* 46, no 5 (2020): 573–93; B Niklasson, 'The Gendered Networking of Diplomats'. *The Hague Journal of Diplomacy* 15, no 1–2 (2020): 13–42.

[2] S Staggs, *Inventing Elsa Maxwell: How an Irrepressible Nobody Conquered High Society, Hollywood, the Press, and the World*. New York: St Martin's Press, 2013, 110–12, 273–75, 363–66.

Mid-twentieth century expectations reflected the idea that building personal relationships was more natural for women than men, as Barbara Bodine claimed much later.[3] Margaret van Kleffens was more forgiving towards Carlo Sforza, Dean Acheson and Henri Spaak than towards herself or Gladys Rose Vandenberg when it came to appropriate social conduct. The higher demands on women's social skills were nothing to do with some inherently female ability, as the initial difficulties of, for example, Barbara Franks or Margaret van Kleffens herself (when it came to speaking in public) show. They were simply so important in the given context that a woman had to master those skills to be successful. Building relationships was a way for women to exercise power in a system where their gender made access to certain positions unlikely, if not impossible. Conversely, typically female positions, such as that of hostess, excluded men. In fact, it was more unthinkable for a man to fill the female-coded role of diplomatic spouse than it was for women to take on the male-coded role as diplomat. There are no indications that Margaret van Kleffens perceived the women she met and entertained who did have positions of their own – royalty such as Queen Wilhelmina, political women such as Viyaja Lakshmi Pandit, Eleanor Roosevelt, Utah Congresswoman Judge Reva Beck Bosone, or newspaper people such as Molly Thayer and Helen Reid – as less competent than men, out of order or unnatural. Assumptions followed the numbers though: men present at diplomatic dinners were always there by virtue of something else – their political work or economic position for example – while most women were present by virtue of their relationship to a man.

In mixed company, this often meant that the focus of any political discussions or 'talking shop' centred on men. It did not mean that men (as a group or category) had more power in off-the-record diplomatic contexts than women, if power is taken to mean access to the diplomatic dinner table and potential influence on personal diplomatic relations. On the contrary: for an upper-class woman to be invited to join a diplomatic dinner, it could be enough to be pleasant and beautiful. A man was only invited if he was perceived as already having political influence. For all the male dominance of the diplomatic profession, the daily diplomacy described in this book was, in many ways, a woman's world in the mid-twentieth century. Women's presumed lack of power in diplomatic relations rests on an assumption that female spheres were outside the structures of power. However, as this book has shown, women's work and female spheres were essential to everyday diplomatic work. Indeed, women's

---

[3] Towns, '"Diplomacy Is a Feminine Art"', 592.

ability to depoliticize and personalize important relations was a crucial diplomatic asset. It seems to me that to place that work outside the realm of power is a mistake. As the British classicist Mary Beard has put it, 'if women are not perceived to be fully within the structures of power, surely it is power that we need to redefine rather than women?'[4]

As the (informal) power structures of diplomacy take on new meaning in light of the cooperation between couples, nuances of other mechanisms of inclusion and exclusion call for attention. Even though the gendering of everyday diplomatic work has been the primary focus of this book, it has also shown how daily diplomacy was steeped not only in gendered but also in classed and racialized perceptions. Chapter 10 showed that beauty and extravagance were diplomatic assets only if they had the correct gender, race and class connotations, for example. Chapter 3 mentioned how perceptions of trustworthiness were tied to ethnicity, nationality, gender and marital status. Throughout, the book has shown how classed, gendered and racialized perceptions co-created power relations that were complex and shifted depending on context. How gendered, racialized and class hierarchies intersected and were normalized at the everyday micro level and how that influenced the diplomatic macro level are questions that deserve research and thought beyond the reach of this book. It would be key to include a non-Western perspective as well as to study the roles in diplomatic hierarchies of people who were not from an upper-class background to better understand how international political power and the transnational cultural norms that ruled personal interaction intersected.

It is clearly worthwhile not only to look beyond the official and formal levels of diplomacy, but to recognize the complexity of the relationships between formal and official and informal and non-official levels. Those relationships can provide a more nuanced view of how international relations functioned in practice and help explain the (lack of) change. When it comes to formal recruitment processes, for example, many diplomatic services broadened and aimed to democratize their recruitment system after the Second World War. However, as Nevra Biltekin has argued in the case of Swedish diplomatic professionalization, the very process of establishing a meritocracy often, in practice, meant formalizing ideals that benefitted men from an upper-class background. The process may have been depersonalized, but to fulfil the (now institutionalized) diplomatic suitability requirements candidates still needed the

---

[4] Mary Beard, *Women & Power: A Manifesto* (London: Profile Books, 2017), 83.

kind of economic and cultural (personal) capital that was primarily accessible to married elite men.[5]

The findings of this book add another layer by showing how informal diplomatic circles were more readily available to upper-class women than just any upper-class man, as mentioned above. Gender and class intersected differently in informal and in formal situations in ways that complicate the notion of male dominance. Change the context to diplomatic hostess and diplomatic suitability was unmistakably coded female. Power relations are complex and their mechanisms do not yield unambiguous hierarchies or straightforward explanations. That does not make them less important for understanding the history of international relations. Based on the study at hand, I shall offer some preliminary thoughts on the question of how micro-level, lived hierarchies and habits influenced diplomatic relations at the macro level.

Political impact of personal relationships

One of the most important observations of this book is that personal relationships were often considered to be diplomatically advantageous. That gave the cooperation and gendered division of tasks between a mid-twentieth century diplomat and his wife advantages that seriously improved their aggregated diplomatic aptitude. This explains much of the persistent reluctance of Diplomatic Services to give up a system of male diplomats with female spouses. Keeping the profession male and heterosexual was about so much more than believing men to be better suited for the job, or even getting 'two for the price of one'. If they were to become more than a marginal phenomenon, female diplomats threatened to change a politically useful perception of (most) women as apolitical. Wives were crucial for representation, helped build networks, could prevent 'shop-talk' and enhance the informal atmosphere and sense of goodwill at a party. In terms of who was trusted to do what, it is relevant, in this context, to note not only what wives were trusted to do, but also what they could not. Wives were not trusted to make official commitments or requests on behalf of their countries. Remember the wartime visit of Margaret van Kleffens to

---

[5] N Biltekin, *Servants of Diplomacy: The Making of Swedish Diplomats, 1905-1995*. Stockholm: Department of History, Stockholm University, 2016, 192–96; see also Elin Bjarnegård and Meryl Kenny, 'Comparing Candidate Selection: A Feminist Institutionalist Approach', *Government and Opposition* 51, no 3 (2016): 370–92 on the 'stickiness' of informal institutional frameworks.

Clementine Churchill mentioned in Chapter 8? She went to great length to disguise her political errand as small talk, inconspicuously bringing the matter up in conversation as a personal opinion. Openly asking for British postwar support for the Netherlands would have undermined her credibility, since wives did not have the power to negotiate on behalf of their countries.

Now consider the other side of that coin. Wives were not perceived as responsible for their countries' policies and that gave them a different kind of power. They could be used to depoliticize an issue, making it less sensitive by moving it from the political to a personal sphere. Signalling that something was (merely) a women's issue might make it less politically charged and offer the opponent an opportunity to give in without losing face. This seems to have been the reasoning behind the British Foreign Office's request that Clementine Churchill take up the issue of Soviet war brides of British subjects with Polina Molotov, the example this book started with. The presumed apolitical character of women also made them invaluable public relations assets, as they could make media appearances to create goodwill even when their countries were under heavy international criticism for their policies. When the Netherlands militarily intervened in Indonesia and her husband constantly had to defend the Dutch government's actions, Margaret van Kleffens could work on Dutch popularity by providing a 'woman's eye-view of Holland' on the radio, appear on television with Jansen the dog, or sponsor a series of lectures on gardening – all without having to answer a single critical question about the former Dutch colony.[6]

The political advantages of wives' ability to personalize and depoliticize relationships are unmistakable. However, for the sake of those who still consider the real diplomatic work that which took place in the institutions dominated by men, let me at least discuss how women's personal relationships with officials off the record might actually have affected specific on-the-record political decisions. Not long after Margaret van Kleffens's 1947 comment about pursuing her flirtation with Alexandre Parodi, Dutch military action in Indonesia caused the United Nations Security Council to turn up the heat on the Netherlands. In that light, her encouragement of the infatuation of the French representative to the UN Security Council appears as a politically sound strategy as the goodwill of Parodi was suddenly crucial in very concrete political terms. As mentioned in

---

[6] Margaret van Kleffens's radio talk 'Woman's Eye View on Holland' (that she wrote herself and co-presented with a Mrs Luther) is described in a newspaper clipping and in the entries of MvK diary 13 and 14 January 1948, inv nr 397; her sponsoring of gardening talks in an undated, unnamed newspaper clipping in MvK diary 6 February 1948, inv nr 397: a newspaper notice mentioning the appearance of the wife of the Netherlands Ambassador and the poodle Jansen on the 'Meet Mrs. Markel' programme is glued in MvK diary 11 July 1948, inv nr 398, 2.05.86, NL-HaNA.

the book's introduction, Margaret van Kleffens apparently saw their personal relationship as relevant to his political behaviour. But was it? It is worth the effort to take a closer look at the circumstances. The aim is not to prove her right or wrong but rather to discuss in broader terms whether she was justified to associate French goodwill with her modest flirting with a French representative. Conclusively demonstrating clear-cut links of cause and effect in this mini case study would require a close scrutiny and accurate assessment of French personal papers to which I have not had access, if they even exist. Nevertheless, this incident offers a good opportunity to address the larger issue of how diplomatic social encounters and a sense of cultural affinity could influence political decision-making.

On 25 August 1947, the United Nations Security Council adopted resolution 30, an Australian-Chinese resolution on the Indonesian question. The resolution noted 'with satisfaction' that the parties had taken steps to cease hostilities (in accordance with UNSC resolution 27 of 1 August 1947) and that the Netherlands Government had declared its intention to organize a 'sovereign, democratic United States of Indonesia'. It also noted that the Netherlands Government intended to ask the career consuls already stationed in Batavia – from Australia, Belgium, China, France, and the United States – to report on the situation there, while the Republic of Indonesia had 'requested appointment by the Security Council of a commission of observers'. In line with the Dutch wish, the resolution requested 'members of the Council which have career consular representatives in Batavia to instruct them to prepare jointly for the information and guidance of the Security Council reports on the situation in the Republic of Indonesia'. It also requested both the Dutch and the Indonesian governments to grant the consuls access to 'all facilities necessary for the fulfilment of their mission' and resolved 'to consider the matter further should the situation require'.[7]

Eelco van Kleffens was no longer a representative to the Security Council (the Netherlands only had a one-year term) but defended the Netherlands in the Indonesian question as the recently appointed Dutch ambassador to Washington. Eagerly assisted by the Belgian UNSC representative Fernand van Langenhove, he had tried but failed to keep the issue off the Security Council agenda altogether by claiming that it was an internal affair falling under what Article 7, § 2 of the UN Charter referred to as 'domestic jurisdiction'. Still, for the Netherlands, matters could have been much worse. There had been a lot of criticism of the

---

[7] UN Security Council, 'Security Council Resolution 30 [The Indonesian Question]', S/RES/30 § (1947). Available at: www.refworld.org/docid/3b00f1ae0.html (accessed 29 June 2021).

resolution, among other things because the consuls already stationed in Batavia might be pro-Dutch and because they did not represent all the countries of the Security Council. Before the resolution was accepted on 25 August, the Soviet representative to the UNSC Andrei Gromyko suggested an amendment, which would have meant imposed arbitration by a commission representing all eleven nations of the Security Council (Australia, Belgium, Brazil, China, Columbia, France, Poland, the Soviet Union, Syria, the United Kingdom, and the United States) rather than the non-committal good offices of the consuls. Moreover, the Soviet amendment included the resolve to keep the Indonesian question on the agenda of the Security Council, rather than only vowing to take it up again 'should the situation require'.

Considering what this book has shown about the importance of personal interaction, it is reasonable to assume that the consuls who lived their daily lives in Batavia, with their wives and families, presumably interacting socially with Dutch officials, would be inclined to be more pro-Dutch than those who lived elsewhere. That, and the importance of getting the issue off the Security Council agenda, made the vote on Gromyko's amendment politically critical to the Netherlands. A substantial majority of the members of the Security Council (seven) voted in favour of the amendment. Two countries abstained (China and the United Kingdom). Only two members voted against the amendment: the Belgian representative, who had unsuccessfully tried to argue that the whole issue was inadmissible, and the French representative, Alexandre Parodi.[8]

One person's vote decided the fate of the Netherlands. Despite an overwhelming majority in favour of Gromyko's amendment, Parodi's vote meant that it was rejected since France was a permanent member of the Security Council and therefore had a right to veto. In her diary, Margaret van Kleffens noted that the Netherlands got off lightly 'thanks to a veto by my French friend Parodi'.[9] It is not possible to conduct experiments in history so that the impact of the French representative's flirt with Margaret van Kleffens on the French decision can never be determined with certainty, but it is tempting to consider counterfactual history as a thought experiment. What if Parodi had personally disliked the Dutch ambassador and his wife? Would he still have voted in favour of the Netherlands? Perhaps. Parodi was, after all, representing France. Presumably, he had instructions and could not make decisions based on his own

---

[8] Ministerie van Buitenlandse Zaken, *Indonesië in de Veiligheidsraad van de Verenigde Naties (Januari 1946-September 1947)*, Publicaties van Het Ministerie van Buitenlandse Zaken ('s Gravenhage: Staatsdrukkerij- en Uitgeverijbedrijf, 1947), 55–57.
[9] MvK diary 25 August 1947, inv nr 397, 2.05.86, NL-HaNA.

personal preferences. However, his personal feelings of goodwill, at least to some degree, would have coloured the reports he sent back to France about the issue which, in turn, would have coloured his instructions, increasing, at the very least, his ability to support the Dutch in public, on behalf of his country.

A different but related example shows that personal proximity influenced diplomatic reporting, which, in turn, had an impact on national attitudes. In Sweden, a country of professed anti-colonialism, there was a public tendency to interpret UNSC resolution 27 (calling for a laying down of arms in Indonesia) as two superpowers ganging up on a small state rather than focusing on the Dutch colonial role or condemning the military intervention. The attitude is in line with a July 1947 memo sent to the Swedish Foreign Office on the Indonesian question by the Swedish envoy to the Netherlands, Joen Lagerberg. That memo in turn is an almost literal reproduction of pro-Dutch arguments of an ill-concealed propagandistic nature, complete with conspiracy theories, emotional lashing out about malicious individuals betraying the benevolent Netherlands, and casting doubt on the sudden ability of the United States and the Soviet Union to agree on anything. The report implied that the superpowers had simply used the Netherlands for a win in the Security Council that was in their own interests.[10] Lagerberg had clearly been talking to his Dutch colleagues and evidently trusted or liked them enough to convey their version of the story without even an attempt at a critical note.

Other supporting evidence pertains to Eelco van Kleffens himself and the leeway he had to act in the Security Council. To be sure, he could not personally determine the policy of the Netherlands. 'These are hard days for E', Margaret van Kleffens even wrote in her diary on the eve of the second military intervention of the Netherlands in Indonesia. 'He does not agree with our Govt's line of action ... yet he has to defend their standpoint here with conviction, alas unfelt.'[11] Ten days later, they got word hostilities were imminent. 'So here is,' she wrote, 'at long last, that which E. and so many others have tried to prevent ever since the last "police action" ended 1 ½ years ago.' She called it a 'sad, sad shame' and lamented the 'awful position' of her husband, whose task it was as an ambassador to 'defend our cause here with outward conviction' regardless of his attempts to change the current policy. 'He says that, were he still a member of our Govt., he would lose no time in resigning.'[12]

---

[10] The matter is described in more detail in Erlandsson, *Window of Opportunity: Dutch and Swedish Security Ideas and Strategies 1942–1948*, 192–93 The memo itself (Lagerberg to Undén 7 July 1947) can be found in HP01Cn, UD 1920 års dossiersystem, National Archives of Sweden in Stockholm (SE-RA).
[11] MvK diary 8 December 1948, inv nr 398, 2.05.86, NL-HaNA.
[12] MvK diary 18 December 1948, inv nr 398, 2.05.86, NL-HaNA.

Still, Eelco van Kleffens did have considerable influence on Dutch foreign policy. One of the reasons the Indonesian question was so frustrating for him personally might be that he was used to having more power. According to Dutch historian Albert Kersten, Eelco van Kleffens almost singlehandedly determined the Dutch foreign policy during the war, as foreign minister-in-exile.[13] And even though the government decided to intervene militarily in Indonesia against his advice, it subsequently left the defence of the Dutch in the Security Council up to him. Margaret van Kleffens complained in her diary how, upon their arrival in Washington, DC, her husband had to go to defend his country in the Security Council right away with hardly any time to prepare, 'nor did E. receive any instructions from The Hague but was told to do "as he thought best".'[14]

What Eelco van Kleffens thought best was no doubt influenced by his background as a doctor of international law, his own position in the international community and by the people he trusted and spoke to on a daily basis. He, in turn, had considerable influence on his two immediate successors as foreign ministers, Herman van Roijen (who became instrumental in eventually bringing the Indonesian question to a peaceful resolution) and Pim van Boetzelaer van Oosterhout. Both used Van Kleffens as a mentor and asked his advice, including on Indonesia, as shown by personal correspondence between the men.[15] To the latter, Eelco van Kleffens in December 1946 complained about the provincialism of his own government and lamented the ministers' lack of insight into 'what is for sale in the world'.[16] Although the government decided to militarily intervene in Indonesia in July 1947, Pim van Boetzelaer van Oosterhout in August 1947 as minister voted against expansion of military actions in the Dutch East Indies, in line with the advice of his predecessor.

Even though UNSC representatives did not determine their countries' policies, they were not without personal influence. In her recent article on Indonesian diplomacy in the UNSC, Jennifer Foray talks of how informal alliances and positions developed in 1946 and 1947.[17] Those informal alliances

---

[13] A. E. Kersten, *Buitenlandse zaken in ballingschap: groei en verandering van een ministerie, 1940–1945* (Alphen aan den Rijn: Sijthoff, 1981), 284–93.
[14] MvK diary 28 July–5 August 1947, inv nr 397, 2.05.86,
[15] Correspondence between Eelco van Kleffens and Pim van Boetzeler van Oosterhout, inv nrs 298 and 302 and between EvK and Herman van Roijen, inv nr 305, 2.05.86, NL-HaNA.
[16] Personal letter from Eelco van Kleffens to Pim (real name Carel Godfried Willem Hendrik) van Boetzelaer van Oosterhout (Dutch Minister of Foreign Affairs 3 July 1946 to 7 August 1948), 12 December 1946, inv nr 298, 2.05.86, NL-HaNA. My translation.
[17] Jennifer L Foray, 'The Republic at the Table, with Decolonisation on the Agenda: The United Nations Security Council and the Question of Indonesian Representation, 1946–1947'. *Itinerario* 45, no 1 (2021): 124–51 at 141.

are perfectly mirrored in the diplomatic socializing visible in the materials I have studied. While it is empirically nearly impossible to prove any direct links between specific personal interactions and particular political decisions, the patterns of personal interaction highlighted in this book are strikingly similar to the patterns of political support.

The story of personal political patterns of the treatment of the Netherlands in the Security Council, does not end with how Parodi helped the Netherlands out of the woods with his veto. The next day, 26 August 1947, Parodi also supported a resolution brought forward by the Belgian, Van Langenhove, to ask the International Court of Justice to give 'an advisory opinion concerning the competence of the Security Council to deal with the [Indonesian] question'. The British representative Alexander Cadogan also voted in favour, as did the United States representative Herschel V Johnson. Since nobody else voted for the resolution, there was no majority and it was rejected, even though only Poland voted against it (the rest abstained).[18]

Looking for a common denominator between the four representatives who supported the Netherlands as defended by Eelco van Kleffens, it is possible to emphasize rational national interests, à la Hans Morgenthau. An international relations realist might note that the United Kingdom, France and Belgium all had colonies and therefore would be reluctant to create a precedent that could potentially be turned against them. The support of the United States was in line with a policy of support for the Netherlands as their 'staunch ally', a policy that only gradually changed between mid-1947 and August 1948.[19]

Fernand and Nancy van Langenhove, Alexander and Theodosia Cadogan, Alexandre Parodi, and Herschel Johnson were also among the people with whom Eelco and Margaret van Kleffens had close personal relationships. Margaret van Kleffens met frequently with Nancy van Langenhove and Theo Cadogan (with as well as without their husbands), flirted with Alexandre Parodi and, in 1946 and 1947, found herself so often seated next to Herschel Johnson at New York parties that she started to call him 'my eternal neighbour'.[20] She was also on friendly terms with Nicholas Lawford (a.k.a. Valentine Lawford), the alternate British delegate to the United Nations Security Council. She called him 'gifted and

---

[18] Ministerie van Buitenlandse Zaken, *Indonesië in de Veiligheidsraad van de Verenigde Naties (Januari 1946–September 1947)*, 58–59.

[19] For an overview of this change, see Frances Gouda and Thijs Brocades Zaalberg, *American Visions of the Netherlands East Indies/Indonesia: US Foreign Policy and Indonesian Nationalism, 1920–1949* (Amsterdam: Amsterdam University Press, 2002), 25–43.

[20] MvK diary 6 January 1947. Other mentions of sitting next to Johnson on 27 June, 26 July, August 31, 8 November and 16 December 1946, 4 March 1947, inv nr 396, 2.05.86, NL-HaNA.

energizing' and clearly enjoyed his company. 'Much fun and late to bed' she noted after another couple had taken her and Lawford out to dinner and dancing in her husband's absence. A bad dinner party became more bearable because he sat near her at the table, 'so some sport'.[21] Meantime, a few days before the described UNSC vote, her husband mentioned in a letter to Foreign Minister Van Boetzelaer van Oosterhout that the Belgian alternate delegate Joseph Nisot discussed his Security Council actions in advance with him, when filling in for Fernand van Langenhove.[22] A lot of the diplomatic consultations and relation-building significant to on-the-record behaviour took place outside the official arenas.

Of course, Margaret van Kleffens also sometimes sat next to Andrei Gromyko or other statesmen from countries with which the Netherlands did not develop friendly relations. However, these dinner companions did not become personal friends and are never mentioned in situations of more casual socializing, like Lawford. The description of her first personal conversation with Andrei Gromyko, at the time Soviet ambassador to the United Nations, is interesting for what it implies about the connection between political and personal interaction. During her husband's presidency of the United Nations Security Council, they gave a dinner for the other Security Council members, their wives, and the Netherlands delegation and she was seated between the Brazilian Veloso and the Russian Gromyko. 'This closer acquaintance with the boeman [Dutch for bogeyman] I had rather dreaded,' she wrote about Gromyko in her diary, 'being unable to think up any non-banal subject on heaven or earth that did not seem to hold some seed of controversy.' It turned out better than she expected though.

> Gromyko's English is quite good and he even cracked a few earthy jokes. Methinks he is coarse, shy, intelligent and unhappy; one imagines that his government has a stranglehold on him through some relative(s) held in Russia as potential 'hostages' should comrade Gr. get it into his head to be naughty.[23]

The comment testifies not only to her appreciation of language skills and the ability to keep things light, but to the connection that Margaret van Kleffens apparently made between personal and political likability. A discrepancy between the perceived characteristics of a country (the aggressive, hostile, uncivilized Soviet Union) and of the person who represented that country (shy, intelligent, English-speaking Gromyko) seems to have caused some cognitive

---

[21] MvK diary 16 October 1946, 18 February and 16 April 1947, inv nr 396, 2.05.86, NL-HaNA.
[22] Personal letter from Eelco van Kleffens to Dutch Foreign Minister Pim van Boetzelaer van Oosterhout 16 August 1947, inv nr 302, 2.05.86, NL-HaNA.
[23] MvK diary 2 August 1946, inv nr 396, 2.05.86, NL-HaNA.

dissonance, solved by imagining that Gromyko was not representing that country of his own free will.

Despite Gromyko making a reasonable impression on her, and despite her finding his wife unsophisticated but not unpleasant – 'a rather sweet and pathetic little paysanne' – the Gromyko's never became part of the inner circle with whom the Van Kleffenses frequently dined. After a dinner party a few months after that described above, Margaret van Kleffens noted in her diary that she had once again been seated next to Herschel Johnson and that she sat between him 'and to my disgust, Gromyko'.[24] Her staunch hostility towards the Soviet Union seems not to have allowed any personal goodwill towards that country's representative.

While, in this case, the friendliness of Gromyko was not enough to change her perception of the Soviet Union, it is possible to imagine that in a less clear-cut case, a favourable impression of the personality of an individual diplomat might favourably influence the impression of the country he (or she) represented. However, one should probably not exaggerate the capacity of personal dinner diplomacy as such to change overarching political relations between states. Even where political relations were claimed to be good, as between the Netherlands and the states of East Indonesia and West Kalimantan, the intimate dining of Eelco and Margaret van Kleffens with President Soekawati and Prime Minister Nadjamoeddin of East Indonesia and the Sultan and Sultana Hamid II of West Kalimantan did not include any attempt to build a personal friendship. It seems rather that close personal relationships could only influence diplomatic on-the-record decisions where there was a pre-existing sense of being likeminded. Margaret van Kleffens's flirt with Alexandre Parodi might just have saved the day. Flirting with Andrei Gromyko would probably have been useless.

Claiming that there was an interplay between personal and political relationships is not the same as claiming that personalized behind-the-scenes work always led to (or even aimed at) better personal relationships. In fact, I have not found any example of a good personal relationship with any person who represented a country perceived as hostile. Diplomatic couples invested huge amounts of time and energy in dinner diplomacy, but there was a big difference between meeting and socializing at dinners and becoming friends. There were other reasons to talk to as many people as possible on as relaxed terms as possible, not in the least information exchange, or, as Eelco van Kleffens might have put it, getting a sense of what was for sale in the world. The point I am trying to make, however, is that good political relationships and good

[24] MvK diary 6 January 1947, inv nr 396, 2.05.86, NL-HaNA.

personal relationships overlapped. Many relationships were never deliberately personalized, such as those with people perceived as inferior or politically unimportant. East Indonesia and West Kalimantan serve as a case in point because of their importance in one specific context only. That led to an invitation to an intimate dinner, but a lack of political respect permeated the personal descriptions of that dinner, marking distance.

Even the ambivalence of the American position towards the Netherlands regarding Indonesia corresponds to an ambivalence in the personal Dutch–American relations. While the Netherlands played the loyal ally-card and United States representatives were treated to all the most generous and personalized shapes of dinner diplomacy imaginable, there are quite a few negative personal comments about Americans in general, often placing them in contrast to Europeans. 'An extremely pleasant, quiet *civilized* dinner party tonight given by Simon Bland', Margaret van Kleffens wrote in May 1948 for example. 'The company was entirely English, except for ourselves and one American Admiral; and it is remarkable how much more at home we Dutch feel in this milieu than in the American.'[25] Where there was a mutual admiration, such as between Eelco and Margaret van Kleffens and United States Under Secretary of State Robert and Adele Lovett, that seems to have tangibly improved the states' relations. For one, it was reflected in the ability to work together efficiently. The successful cooperation between Eelco van Kleffens and Robert Lovett was at least partly responsible for securing Dutch participation in the North Atlantic Treaty. When it came to Indonesia, Eelco van Kleffens told his successor as Dutch foreign minister that he had spent so much time talking to Lovett about it that Lovett had come to adopt the Dutch point of view. 'Indeed,' he told Van Boetzelaer van Oosterhout, 'Mr. Lovett has now reached the point where his terminology is even orthodox Dutch: he speaks neatly of "police action" and uses similar terms from our vocabulary.'[26] The Dutch–American relationship remained more ambivalent than relations with the Europeans. 'One feels in a different, less raw, more congenial climate with these Europeans,' Margaret van Kleffens wrote after a dinner at the British minister plenipotentiary and his wife in Washington, 'even though the women are so strikingly less friendly and forthcoming than American

---

[25] MvK diary 17 May 1948, inv nr 398, 2.05.86, NL-HaNA. Simon Bland was the son of Nevile and Portia Bland. See also her letter to Portia Bland about the dinner among the latter's papers, from Margaret van Kleffens to Portia Bland, dated 21 May 1948, BLND 6/22, UK-CAC.
[26] Personal letter from Eelco van Kleffens to Pim van Boetzelaer van Oosterhout, 10 September 1947, inv nr 302, 2.05.86, NL-HaNA. My translation.

women.'²⁷ As the last comment shows, Margaret van Kleffens did make at least a few female American friends.

Regardless of the exact influence of individual personal relations on political cooperation, it is clear that people who liked each other saw more of each other and introduced each other to their friends, so that the networks of the likeminded were extended and inevitably strengthened. Adele Lovett, for example, 'out of kindhearted sympathy with my predicament of meeting so few contemporaries' introduced Margaret van Kleffens to the wife of Chip Bohlen and the sister of Averell Harriman, among others.²⁸ One friendship not only opened up for others in the same circle, but also increased the likelihood of revaluating people who might otherwise never have made it into the 'inner circle' because the first impression had not been entirely favourable. After a 1948 dinner, Margaret van Kleffens expressed her hope that the Walter Lippmann's would eventually become part of their 'inner circle' because she liked them so much. 'But my discovery of the evening', she added, 'was the fact that Harald J. Coolidge (whom I had hitherto regarded as a rather silly, callow and pimply appendage of his socially ambitious wife), is a most interesting zoologist.'²⁹ After one dinner at the Belgian embassy, she said they had dined in 'pleasant company of 24, I could almost say "24 of the gang"' and after another she named some of the guests (among whom were Bob and Adele Lovett) before concluding: 'Washington is no different from all other cities, small and large, in that you always, on a certain level, find yourself among the same group of people.'³⁰ Her comments are reminiscent of those of her young sister around 1930 talking about meeting the usual crowd at The Hague parties. A third time, in 1949, she made the implication explicit: 'Dined at Silvercruys's, in familiar company.... Type gravitates towards type as inevitably as water streams downhill.'³¹

Diplomacy as a likeminded institution

Taking into account that type gravitated towards type in diplomatic socializing, and that personal socializing tended to coincide with diplomatic patterns of political support, a final question deserves consideration: how were postwar

---

²⁷ MvK diary 12 February 1949, inv nr 398, 2.05.86, NL-HaNA.
²⁸ MvK 9 February 1948, inv nr 398, 2.05.86, NL-HaNA.
²⁹ MvK diary 9 February 1948, inv nr 398, 2.05.86, NL-HaNA.
³⁰ MvK diary 5 February 1948, inv nr 397, and 13 September 1948, inv nr 398, 2.05.86, NL-HaNA.
³¹ MvK diary 14 February 1949, inv nr 398, 2.05.86, NL-HaNA.

diplomatic relations influenced by the fact that diplomats built stronger personal relationships with those who were considered 'likeminded' based on a cultural affinity that was classed and racialized? In their introduction to *Diplomatic Cultures and International Politics*, Fiona McConnell and Jason Dittmer write that diplomatic culture 'enables the mediation of difference, the process of connection "across alien boundaries"' (citing Der Derian). As they go on to point out, however, the process of overcoming alienation or separateness also reproduces its conditions.[32] Ostensibly, dinner diplomacy brought diplomats together across cultural divides, but it also highlighted cultural differences, as became evident, for example, in the chapter on diplomatic food. As the previous section highlighted, treating someone with courtesy during obligatory dinners was very different from inviting them to take part in more informal, personal dinner diplomacy.

In the mid-twentieth century, Western Washington embassy dinners without American or Western European guests was a rare event. Although Eelco and Margaret van Kleffens occasionally expressed their appreciation of individual non-Westerners in a primarily Western context, they generally showed little desire to strengthen their personal ties with non-Westerners. A description of a 1948 reception hosted by the Ecuador embassy is exemplary of a diplomatic culture which widened rather than bridged the divide between the West and the rest as it were. 'To a quite literally stinking reception at Ecuador this afternoon', Margaret van Kleffens wrote.

> The unknown and unseen diplomats (such as these), when found with the necessity of giving a reception, appear to proceed quite simply by hiring a hotel ballroom and then inviting the whole 'social list' of W'ton, regardless of whether the invited are known to them or not. The result is a raucous and undignified mixture of stink, germs, and champagne-guzzlers.[33]

Aside from the denigrating remark about smell, the quote reconfirms the value of personalized, semi-private relations highlighted throughout this book and the devaluing of events perceived as impersonal. This put countries without the means to host at an impressive embassy building of their own at a disadvantage. It also shows how hard it was for those who did not already have the right connections and manners to make it into the inner circles of diplomatic

---

[32] Jason Dittmer and Fiona McConnell, 'Introduction: Conceptualising Diplomatic Cultures', in *Diplomatic Cultures and International Politics: Translations, Spaces and Alternatives*, ed. Jason Dittmer and Fiona McConnell (Abingdon: Routledge, 2015), 4–5.
[33] MvK diary 6 January 1948, inv nr 397, 2.05.86, NL-HaNA.

Washington. If it was *faux pas* to invite people you did not already know, how would you break the vicious circle?

Of course, not everyone might have been as judgmental as Margaret van Kleffens. Occasionally, a happenstance personal liking of someone who did not belong to the regular 'us' could potentially broaden the view. Still, as the above has shown, diplomatic socializing was much more likely to strengthen existing patterns of friendships than lead to the creation of new alliances. Dinner diplomacy in cases where goodwill did not already exist often did little to improve relations. As Chapters 8 and 10 have shown, it did not help Eelco and Margaret van Kleffens build good relations with the non-Republic parts of the Dutch former colony even though, from a purely rational political perspective, the Netherlands would have done well to build better relations with East Indonesia and West Kalimantan, or with the non-Western members of the UN Security Council for that matter.

The former colonial subjects were clearly not perceived as equals, let alone likeminded and the ambassadorial couple did not attempt to personalize their relationships with them, as they did with others. Though political circumstances forced them to put on a show of goodwill, the diaries of Margaret van Kleffens reveal that it was, indeed, just a show. A personal letter from her husband to the Dutch foreign minister nine days before Parodi's veto similarly shows less concern with actually gaining the sincere goodwill of the leaders of East Indonesia and West Kalimantan than with convincing others that they had it. Even though the Security Council had refused to hear them, Eelco van Kleffens wrote, the arrival of the non-Republic Indonesian leaders was useful. They could be brought in touch with the press and, he added, 'we can bring these people in contact with a few members of the Security Council, like Nisot, Parodi, Cadogan, Johnson and perhaps a few more.'[34] With the caveat that Nisot was at the time filling in for Van Langenhove who was on vacation, the delegates named as suitable for these personal approaches are precisely the people who ended up supporting the Netherlands.

The pattern becomes even clearer in light of the story of Pangeran Adipati Soejono, a moderate proponent for Indonesian independence who served as a minister without portfolio in the Netherlands government-in-exile during the Second World War. Surprisingly little has been written about this first Muslim

---

[34] Personal letter from Eelco van Kleffens to Dutch Foreign Minister Pim van Boetzelaer van Oosterhout, 16 August 1947, inv nr 302, 2.05.86, NL-HaNA. My translation from Dutch.

and only Indonesian ever to join a Netherlands government.[35] In short, Soejono was the top adviser of Dutch Minister of Colonies Hubertus van Mook and was added to the exile-government in June 1942 after the members of the cabinet (though some reluctantly) agreed that it would be opportune to include an Indonesian minister.[36] On 10 June 1942, the 'historic moment' of welcoming a 'son of the Indonesian people' was celebrated with applause by the ministers, hailing Soejono's personality, knowledge and experience, as well as his prestige among the population of the Netherlands East Indies.[37]

In practice, however, the ministers turned out to attach less value to his advice as an expert on Indonesia than to his symbolic value in the face of international public opinion. When Soejono argued for a recognition in principle of Indonesia's right to independence, warning that Indonesians were not as pro-Dutch as the cabinet believed and would not accept a return to colonial rule after the Japanese occupation, he was met by barely contained indignation. His fellow ministers seemed shocked that he expressed opinions that were not in line with the Dutch self-image. One after the other spoke to refute him. Some questioned Soejono's ability to speak for all Indonesians or to know their minds at all (which did not keep, for example Eelco van Kleffens, from expressing his own belief that most Indonesians would 'want cooperation with the Netherlands'); several others emphasized that perhaps Indonesia was not entirely free, but nor was the Netherlands, since it had 'obligations to fulfil towards the Indies'.[38] Only seven months after becoming minister, Soejono suddenly died. He was not replaced.[39]

At the time, Margaret van Kleffens lamented in her diary that 'our "bruine hoeder"' (Dutch for 'brown keeper') had died of heart failure and described his Islamic funeral as an exotic and strange event.[40] For all his skills and sophistication, an alien element like Soejono was acceptable only in as far as he could be

---

[35] A number of news outlets in February 2007 wrongly presented Moroccan-born Ahmed Aboutaleb, who was then named Dutch deputy minister for social affairs, and Turkish-born Nebahat Albayrak, installed as state secretary (junior minister) for Justice, as the first Muslim members of a Dutch cabinet. Soejono seems to have been forgotten. See, eg, Arthur Max, 'Netherlands Gets Its First Muslim Ministers', *Indian Express*, 21 February 2007. Available at: http://archive.indianexpress.com/news/netherlands-gets-its-first-muslim-ministers/23862/ (accessed 28 June 2021); Fred Ernst, 'Dutch Cabinet Gets Its First Muslim Member', *NBC News*, 22 February 2007. Available at: www.nbcnews.com/id/wbna17264627 (accessed 28 June 2021).

[36] Louis de Jong, *Het Koninkrijk Der Nederlanden in de Tweede Wereldoorlog*, vol. IX:1 ('s Gravenhage: Staatsuitgeverij, 1979), 352–55.

[37] Typed copy of the Dutch cabinet protocol of 10 June 1942, inv nr 246, 2.02.05.02, NL-HaNA.

[38] Typed copy of the Dutch cabinet protocol of 13 October 1942, inv nr 246, 2.02.05.02, NL-HaNA.

[39] As far as I can tell, the matter of including an Indonesian minister was never discussed again after Soejono's demise, at least not as recorded in the minutes of the cabinet.

[40] MvK diary 5 and 8 January 1943, inv nr 392, 2.05.86, NL-HaNA. She had not attended the funeral herself but described what her husband had told her.

perceived as a 'brown keeper' of Dutch interests. The few times Margaret van Kleffens spoke appreciatively of Indonesians was when they had managed to adopt Western ways and showed undivided loyalty to the Netherlands. Even then, it is quite clear that their ethnicity made any true integration impossible. This was the case with Soejono's wife and daughter. A 1948 diary note reveals that Margaret van Kleffens kept in touch with them after the war and that his daughter, by then worked for the Dutch embassy in the United States. 'Raden Ajoe Soejono came to say goodbye,' she wrote in her diary on 12 December 1948, 'as she is going back to the Indies, leaving her completely Westernized daughter Loes behind (she has a job in the embassy).'[41]

The Javanese Soejonos can be viewed as a textbook example of doing what the Dutch claimed Indonesians should do if they wanted more freedom for Indonesia: adapt to, cooperate with and treat the Dutch as benevolent. Not only had her husband been a Dutch politician, but Raden Ajoe Soejono's son, the brother of Loes (or Soepianti, her birth name), Irawan Soejono, was also a Dutch resistance hero. Like his father, he was in favour of Indonesian independence, but believed that the Nazi's had to be beaten and the Netherlands liberated first. He fought in the underground movement in the Netherlands, where he studied, under the thoroughly Dutch-sounding *nom de guerre* 'Henk' and was shot dead by a German soldier during a raid in January 1945.[42] Margaret van Kleffens's continued description of mother and daughter Soejono paint them as fully adapted to the Dutch ways of life, but also as an aberration:

> With these two Javanese ladies one has no feeling of 'never the twain shall meet.' They talk and feel as we do and are violently anti-'Republiek'. In a way Loes' westernization is a tragedy: she is and thinks as we, but nothing can change the colour of hair and skin – She is neither wholly one thing nor the other. How will she ever get a satisfactory husband?[43]

The reference to them not only behaving according to Western norms but talking, feeling and thinking 'as we do' reveals a perception that normally, differences between people of Western and non-Western customs and appearances were not only skin-deep but fundamental. What made the situation tragic was that people assumed external differences to signify internal ones, so

---

[41] MvK diary 12 December 1948, inv nr 398, 2.05.86, NL-HaNA.
[42] Lodewijk Kallenberg, 'Irawan Soejono (1920–1945) Zandgraf 522, Vak D: Verzetsheld van Indonesische Afkomst', in *Nader Belichte Personen* (Leiden, The Netherlands: Stichting tot instandhouding van de begraafplaats Groenesteeg, August 2016). Available at: www.begraafplaatsgroenesteeg.nl/N_B_personen/Irawan%20Soejono%20-%20versie%20website.pdf (accessed 28 June 2021).
[43] MvK diary 12 December 1948, inv nr 398, 2.05.86, NL-HaNA.

that true integration was impossible. Soepianti could change her name to the Dutch-sounding Loes and she could change how she was and thought, but she could never change the way others would perceive her as non-Western because of the colour of her skin and hair. While that made marriage to a Westerner difficult, the comment also paints her westernization as an obstacle to a marriage to a Javanese man, revealing Margaret van Kleffens's belief that cross-cultural marriages were bound to fail.

In the broader context of daily diplomatic work, these perceptions and convictions are significant. Even after the Dutch recognition of the Republic of Indonesia, they functioned as invisible barriers behind the apparent equalities of diplomatic protocol. Her judgement of their new Indonesian colleagues, after the Republic of Indonesia finally had been recognized by the Netherlands, goes to the heart of the matter. 'We dined with our Indonesian colleagues the Sastroamidjojo's' Margaret van Kleffens wrote in her diary in April 1950. 'It was a very sticky evening, as they just don't (yet) know how to behave according to Western ideas.'[44] The inserted 'yet' indicates that she did not rule out pleasant socializing with people of other cultures and ethnicities *per se*, but that it was entirely natural to her to assume that it could only be achieved if they learned the correct – Western – ways. On the one hand then, there was a tendency to absolutize cultural differences. On the other hand, Western norms were treated as self-evidently superior or even universal and a *sine qua non* for acceptance into the transnational community of diplomats. Considering this in combination with the insight that the personal politics of daily diplomacy tended to reinforce existing alliances rather than help build new ones, the practices and norms of everyday diplomatic work seem central rather than peripheral to understanding the development of postwar diplomatic relations.

Western diplomacy was not only a gendered but a likeminded institution. Normative elements based on perceptions of class and race were neither conducive to good postwar relations between East and West nor between the so-called western world and formerly colonized territories. As Naoko Shimazu has convincingly argued, the 1955 Asia-Africa conference – popularly known as the Bandung conference after the Indonesian city it was held in – was staged as a symbolic demonstration of solidarity that also points to normatively defined elements of diplomacy. Bandung, Shimazu says, 'was an act of confident assertion vis-à-vis the ruling elite of international society, and not a passive act of seeking acceptance.'[45]

---

[44] MvK diary 18 April 1950, inv nr 401, 2.05.86, NL-HaNA.
[45] Naoko Shimazu, 'Diplomacy as Theatre: Staging the Bandung Conference of 1955', *Modern Asian Studies* 48, no 1 (2014): 233.

Just like Loes Soepianti Soejono, non-Western diplomats would always be viewed as exceptions in a diplomatic community moulded after upper-class Western traditions, even if they tried to adapt. Bandung showed a different way. Anti-colonialism and anti-racialism became a way to unite the nations gathered in Bandung, as Vijay Prashad has pointed out.[46] Additionally, there were domestic motives: Shimazu shows how the diplomatic performance at Bandung was aimed at the populations at home as well as at international society.[47]

Strikingly, though, the participants at Bandung relied on many practices that were essentially similar to those of Western diplomacy to achieve their goals of bonding and to turn the mechanisms of exclusion against the (uninvited) Western powers. As Shimazu has shown, these practices displayed a clearly gendered division of tasks, the dress and food were used both symbolically and for lavish entertaining, while social interaction included both larger gatherings and intimate, personalized dinners where politics were deliberately not discussed.[48] Just as among Western diplomats, it would seem, the higher political status, the higher the honour of being treated as a personal friend rather than a mere political contact.

Despite the apparent common *esprit de corps* of the diplomatic profession, separate circles of cultural affinity made up the social fora that ultimately defined diplomatic relations behind the scenes. The studied sources show that prejudicial judgements influenced the way that diplomatic social encounters operated. They also show that personal relationships were politically relevant and that they were underpinned by a gendered division of tasks. This book goes some way towards explaining the persistence of diplomacy as a transnational institution that has long been organized around – and has even flaunted – racial, gender and class difference and hierarchies. It has shown that the way Western diplomatic culture was organized in the mid-twentieth century not only tended to cement gender norms, but also created a serious systemic social diplomatic handicap for non-Western countries. Furthermore, the example of Bandung shows that at least some of the strategies employed in Western daily diplomacy were also used to mark distance to Western influence reinforcing, rather than fundamentally contesting, normative elements based on a gendered, racialized and classed division of tasks.

---

[46] Vijay Prashad, *The Darker Nations: A People's History of the Third World* (New York: The New Press, 2007), 49.
[47] Naoko Shimazu, 'Performing "Freedom": The Bandung Conference as Symbolic Postcolonial Diplomacy', in *Diplomatic Cultures and International Politics*, ed. Jason Dittmer and Fiona McConnell (Abingdon: Routledge, 2015), 71–88.
[48] Shimazu, 'What is Sociability in Diplomacy?'

While the diplomatic practices of the postwar world contributed to strengthening some political ties by making them personal, they ruled out the personalization of other political relations. Only if we presumed that personal relationships did not matter politically would this be irrelevant to so-called 'big' politics. But the evidence shows they did, not only in exceptional and famous cases, but on an everyday basis. This book has brought some crucial practices out of the shadows, but there is still much work to be done. For all its detailed descriptions, it shows only a fraction of the diplomatic work done by people who may not have made their way into the history books but who, in practice, created the conditions for postwar diplomatic relations. It is high time we gave more of them their political due.

Bibliography

Archives

The National Archives of the United Kingdom, Kew (UKNA)
FO – Records created or inherited by the Foreign Office

> 181 Foreign Office and Foreign and Commonwealth Office: Embassy and Consulates, Union of Soviet Socialist Republics (formerly Russian Empire): General Correspondence
> 366 Foreign Office and Diplomatic Service Administration Office: Chief Clerk's Department and successors: Records
> 371 Foreign Office: Political Departments: General Correspondence from 1906–1966

HW – Records created or inherited by Government Communications Headquarters (GCHQ)

> 1 Government Code and Cypher School: Signals Intelligence Passed to the Prime Minister, Messages and Correspondence 1940–1945

The National Archives of the Netherlands (Nationaal Archief), The Hague (NL-HaNA)

2.02.05.02 Archive of the Cabinet (Ministerraad)
2.05.51 Foreign Service Directorate (1940) 1945–1954 (1955)
2.05.86 Archive of E.N. van Kleffens 1919–1983
2.05.117 Ministry of Foreign Affairs Code-Archive 1945–1954
2.05.317 Archive of the Ministry of Foreign Affairs, Board of Examiners for investigation into the suitability and competence for the Foreign Service
2.21.183.70 Archive of J.H. van Roijen 1940–1989

The National Archives of Sweden (Riksarkivet), Stockholm (SE-RA)

Ministry for Foreign Affairs Archive, dossier system of 1920 (UD 1920 års dossiersystem)

> HP01Cn The Netherlands

Churchill Archives Centre, Cambridge (UK-CAC)

ACAD – The Papers of Sir Alexander George Montagu Cadogan

  8 Lady Theodosia Cadogan

BLND – The Papers of Sir (George) Nevile (Maltby) Bland

  6 Personal Papers: Minister/Ambassador to the Netherlands 1939–1948

CSCT – The Papers of Clementine Ogilvy Spencer-Churchill, Baroness Spencer-Churchill of Chartwell

  9 Household and Domestic

Cadbury Research Library, Birmingham (UK-CRL)

Avon Papers – Personal and political papers of Anthony Eden, 1st Earl of Avon, MP and papers of the Eden family, 1760–1980 (predominantly 1904–1977)

AP 3 Papers and correspondence relating to official appointments and awards and to various functions, hosted or attended by Lord and Lady Avon

Netherlands Institute of War Documentation, Amsterdam (NL-NIOD)

233b Collection Netherlands government in London 233b

  98 Diary of Eelco van Kleffens, kept during three work trips (10 January–7 March 1942, 17 June–16 August 1942, 24 May–5 July 1943)

Private archive of Clive Wilson, London (UK-Wilson)

Correspondence of Aileen Emilie Wilson née Horstmann. The letters have since been donated to NL-HaNA.

Other references

'Acecarbromal'. In *DBpedia*. Available at: https://dbpedia.org/page/Acecarbromal (accessed 28 June 2021).

Aggestam, Karin and Ann Towns. 'The Gender Turn in Diplomacy: A New Research Agenda'. *International Feminist Journal of Politics* 21, no 1 (2019): 9–28.

Akkerman, Nadine. *Invisible Agents: Women and Espionage in Seventeenth-Century Britain*. Oxford: Oxford University Press, 2018.

Amerian, Stephanie M. 'Buying European: The Marshall Plan and American Department Stores'. *Diplomatic History* 39, no 1 (2015): 45–69.

Ardener, Shirley and Hilary Callan. *The Incorporated Wife*. London: Croom Helm, 1984.

Ashcroft, Bill. *On Post-Colonial Futures: Transformations of Colonial Culture*. London and New York: Continuum, 2001.

Baalen, C C van. 'De Politiek en de Rechtsgelijkheid van Vrouwen op het Gebied van Arbeid (1955)'. *Politiek(E) Opstellen* 18 (1998): 99–115.

Bastian, Corina, Eva Kathrin Dade, Hillard von Thiessen and Christian Windler, eds. *Das Geschlecht der Diplomatie: Geschlechterrollen in den Außenbeziehungen vom Spätmittelalter bis zum 20. Jahrhundert*. Köln/Weimar/Wien: Böhlau, 2014.

Beard, Mary. *Women & Power: A Manifesto*. London: Profile Books, 2017.

Biltekin, Nevra. *Servants of Diplomacy: The Making of Swedish Diplomats, 1905–1995*. Stockholm: Department of History, Stockholm University, 2016.

Biltekin, Nevra. 'The Diplomatic Partnership: Gender, Materiality and Performance in the Case of Sweden c. 1960s–1980s'. *Genesis* XI, no 1–2 (2012): 253–65.

Biltekin, Nevra. 'The Performance of Diplomacy: The Residence, Gender, and Diplomatic Wives in Late Twentieth-Century Sweden'. In *Women, Diplomacy and International Politics since 1500*, edited by Glenda Sluga and Carolyn James, 254–68. Abingdon and New York: Routledge, 2015.

Biltekin, Nevra. 'Unofficial Ambassadors: Swedish Women in the United States and the Making of Non-State Cultural Diplomacy'. *International Journal of Cultural Policy: CP* 26, no 7 (2020): 959–72.

Bjarnegård, Elin and Meryl Kenny. 'Comparing Candidate Selection: A Feminist Institutionalist Approach'. *Government and Opposition* 51, no 3 (2016): 370–92.

Bloch, Maurice. 'Commensality and Poisoning'. *Social Research* 66, no 1 (1999): 133–49.

Bloemendal, Albertine. *Reframing the Diplomat: Ernst van Der Beugel and the Cold War Atlantic Community*. Brill, 2018.

Boué, Séverine. 'Les Réceptions à la Résidence de France à Washington: Vitrine Gastronomique de la France et Outil Diplomatique des Ambassadeurs (de 1893 à Aujourd'hui)'. *Bulletin de l'Institut Pierre Renouvin* 50, no 2 (2019): 33–45.

Buma, Dé. *Donderdag Komt de Koerier. De Kleurrijke Levensreis van een Diplomatenvrouw*. Amsterdam: Van Soeren & Co, 2000.

Callan, Hilary. 'The Premiss of Dedication'. In *Perceiving Women*, edited by Shirley Ardener, 87–104. London; New York: Dent, 1975.

Canby, Margaret Hart. 'Dutch Hostess Serves Tea; Brilliant Party at Union'. *Washington Evening Star*, 14 November 1947.

Cassidy, Jennifer A and Sara Althari. 'Introduction. Analysing the Dynamics of Modern Diplomacy through a Gender Lens'. In *Gender and Diplomacy*, edited by Jennifer A. Cassidy, 1–31. Abingdon and New York: Routledge, 2017.

Chapple-Sokol, Sam. 'Culinary Diplomacy: Breaking Bread to Win Hearts and Minds'. *The Hague Journal of Diplomacy* 8, no 2 (2013): 161–83.

Conway, Martin and José Gotovitch. *Europe in Exile: European Exile Communities in Britain, 1940-1945*. 1st edn, New York: Berghahn Books, 2001.

Cook, Karen S, Russell Hardin and Margaret Levi. *Cooperation without Trust?* Vol 10. New York: Russell Sage Foundation, 2005.

Cook, Karen S, Margaret Levi and Russell Hardin. *Whom Can We Trust? How Groups, Networks, and Institutions Make Trust Possible*. New York: Russell Sage Foundation, 2009.

Costigliola, Frank. 'Pamela Churchill, Wartime London, and the Making of the Special Relationship'. *Diplomatic History* 36, no 4 (2012): 753–62.

Costigliola, Frank. *Roosevelt's Lost Alliances: How Personal Politics Helped Start the Cold War*. Princeton, NJ: Princeton University Press, 2012.

Dittmer, Jason and Fiona McConnell. 'Introduction: Conceptualising Diplomatic Cultures'. In *Diplomatic Cultures and International Politics: Translations, Spaces and Alternatives*, edited by Jason Dittmer and Fiona McConnell, 1–20. Abingdon: Routledge, 2015.

Eichenberg, Julia. 'Informal Encounters and Transnational Networks. European Diplomacy in British Exile during the Second World War'. New Diplomatic History Conference: Diplomacy between Crisis and Cooperation. Aarhus, Denmark, 2021.

Eichenberg, Julia. 'Legal Legwork: How Exiled Jurists Negotiated Recognition and Legitimacy in Wartime London'. In *Crafting the International Order. Practitioners and Practices of International Law since c. 1800*, edited by Marcus M Payk and Kim Christian Priemel (Oxford: Oxford University Press, 2021) 162–90.

Eichenberg, Julia. 'London Calling. Adressbücher des britischen Exils im Zweiten Weltkrieg'. In *Zeithistorische Forschungen* 16, no 2 (2019): 363–74.

Eichenberg, Julia. 'Macht Auf Der Flucht. Europäische Regierungen in London (1940–1944)'. *Zeithistorische Forschungen/Studies in Contemporary History* 15 (2018): 452–73.

Eijl, Corrie van and Marlou Schrover. 'Inleiding'. In *Bronnen Betreffende de Registratie van Vreemdelingen in Nederland in de Negentiende en Twintigste Eeuw*. Broncommentaren 5. The Hague: Instituut voor Nederlandse Geschiedenis, 2002.

Ellender, Lulah. *Elisabeth's Lists. A Life between the Lines*. London: Granta Books, 2019.

Enloe, Cynthia. *Bananas, Beaches and Bases: Making Feminist Sense of International Politics*. 2nd, completely revis and updat edn Berkeley, CA: University of California Press, 2014.

Enquêtecommissie Regeringsbeleid 1940–1945. 2C, Verhoren. Gravenhage: Staatsdrukkerij, 1949.

Erlandsson, Susanna. 'Kvinnor och Genusperspektiv i ett Splittrat Forskningsfält: Modern Diplomatihistoria'. *Historisk Tidskrift* 141, no 3 (2021): 553–63.

Erlandsson, Susanna. 'Off the Record: Margaret van Kleffens and the Gendered History of Dutch World War II Diplomacy'. *International Feminist Journal of Politics* 21, no 1 (2019): 29–46.

Erlandsson, Susanna. *Window of Opportunity: Dutch and Swedish Security Ideas and Strategies 1942–1948*. Uppsala: Acta Universitatis Upsaliensis, 2015.

Erlandsson, Susanna and Rimko van der Maar. 'Trouw aan Buitenlandse Zaken. Margaret van Kleffens, Anne van Roijen, de ambassade in Washington en de betekenis van het diplomatiek partnerschap voor de naoorlogse Nederlandse buitenlandse betrekkingen'. *Tijdschrift voor Geschiedenis* 134, no 3 (2021).

Erlandsson, Susanna and Sari Nauman. 'Tillit och Diplomati. Ett Forskningsuppslag'. In *Tillit och Diplomati: En Diskussionsbok om Personliga Relationer och Diplomatiska Processer 1670–1990*, edited by Susanna Erlandsson and Sari Nauman. Uppsala: Opuscula Historica Upsaliensia, 2019.

Erlandsson, Susanna and Sari Nauman. 'Tillit som Verktyg för Diakrona Jämförelser av Diplomati. Repliker, Slutsatser och Nya Frågor'. In *Tillit och Diplomati: En Diskussionsbok om Personliga Relationer och Diplomatiska Processer 1670–1990*, edited by Susanna Erlandsson and Sari Nauman, 129–42. Uppsala: Opuscula Historica Upsaliensia, 2019.

Ernst, Fred. 'Dutch Cabinet Gets Its First Muslim Member'. *NBC News*, 22 February 2007. Available at: www.nbcnews.com/id/wbna17264627 (accessed 28 June 2021).

Farias, Rogério de Souza. '"Do You Wish Her to Marry?" Brazilian Women and Professional Diplomacy, 1918–1938'. *Diplomacy & Statecraft* 28, no 1 (2 January 2017): 39–56.

Fasseur, Cees. *Eigen Meester, Niemands Knecht: Het Leven van Pieter Sjoerds Gerbrandy Minister-President van Nederland in de Tweede Wereldoorlog*. Amsterdam: Uitgeverij Balans, 2014.

Fischler, Claude. 'Commensality, Society and Culture'. *Social Science Information* 50, no 3–4 (2011): 528–48.

Foray, Jennifer L. 'The Republic at the Table, with Decolonisation on the Agenda: The United Nations Security Council and the Question of Indonesian Representation, 1946–1947'. *Itinerario* 45, no 1 (2021): 124–51.

Giudici, Giacomo. 'From New Diplomatic History to New Political History: The Rise of the Holistic Approach'. *European History Quarterly* 48, no 2 (2018): 314–24.

Glissenaar, Frans. *Indië Verloren, Rampspoed Geboren*. Hilversum: Verloren verleden, 2003.

Goldberg, Eve. 'Elsa Was Best Known for Her Parties'. *The Gay & Lesbian Review Worldwide* 20, no 5 (2013).

Gordon, Evelyn Peyton. 'Mme. van Kleffens'. *Washington Daily News*, 18 November 1947.

Gordon-Lazareff, Hélène, ed. 'Mme Bonnet a Emporté Paris Dans Sa Valise-Avion'. *Elle – L'hebdomadaire de La Femme* 1946 (23 July 1946): 4.

Gouda, Frances and Thijs Brocades Zaalberg. *American Visions of the Netherlands East Indies/Indonesia: US Foreign Policy and Indonesian Nationalism, 1920–1949*. Amsterdam: Amsterdam University Press, 2002.

Gram-Skjoldager, Karen. 'Never Talk to Strangers? On Historians, Political Scientists and the Study of Diplomacy in the European Community/European Union'. *Diplomacy & Statecraft* 22, no 4 (2011): 696–714.

Gruffydd Jones, Branwen. '"Good Governance" and "State Failure": Genealogies of Imperial Discourse'. *Cambridge Review of International Affairs* 26, no 1 (2013): 49–70.

Gullace, Nicoletta F. 'Sexual Violence and Family Honor: British Propaganda and International Law during the First World War'. *The American Historical Review* 102, no 3 (1997): 714–47.

Hardin, Russell. *Trust and Trustworthiness*. New York: Russell Sage Foundation, 2002.

Harris Rimmer, Susan. 'Women as Makers of International Law: Towards Feminist Diplomacy'. In *Research Handbook on Feminist Engagement with International Law*, edited by Kate Ogg and Susan Harris Rimmer, 26–43. Cheltenham, UK: Edward Elgar Publishing, 2019.

Harris, Ruth. 'The "Child of the Barbarian": Rape, Race and Nationalism in France during the First World War'. *Past and Present*, no 141 (1993): 170–206.

Hellman, Lisa. 'När Tilliten inte är ett Val. Kinesisk-Ryska Relationer i Slutet av 1600-talet'. In *Tillit och Diplomati. En Diskussionsbok om Personliga Relationer och Diplomatiska Processer 1670–1990*, edited by Susanna Erlandsson and Sari Nauman, 37–50. Uppsala: Opuscula Historica Upsaliensia, 2019.

Hellsing, My. 'Tillit inom Hovpolitiken. Exempel från den Franska Beskickningen i Stockholm 1783–1789'. In *Tillit och Diplomati. En Diskussionsbok om Personliga Relationer och Diplomatiska Processer 1670–1990*, edited by Susanna Erlandsson and Sari Nauman. Opuscula Historica Upsaliensia 56. Uppsala: Opuscula Historica Upsaliensia, 2019.

Herzl, Tova. *Madame Ambassador: Behind the Scenes with a Candid Israeli Diplomat*. Lanham: Rowman & Littlefield, 2015.

Hjorthén, Adam. *Cross-Border Commemorations: Celebrating Swedish Settlement in America*. Amherst: University of Massachusetts Press, 2018.

Hochschild, Arlie. 'The Role of the Ambassador's Wife: An Exploratory Study'. *Journal of Marriage and Family* 31, no 1 (1969): 73–87.

Holmes, Marcus. *Face-to-Face Diplomacy: Social Neuroscience and International Relations*. Cambridge University Press, 2018.

Hopkins, Michael F. 'Focus of a Changing Relationship: The Washington Embassy and Britain's World Role since 1945'. *Contemporary British History* 12, no 3 (1998): 103–14.

Hunt, Michael H. *Ideology and U.S. Foreign Policy*. New Haven, CT: Yale University Press, 2009.

Ikonomou, Haakon. 'Hellé Bonnet, the Washington Scene and Cold War Couture'. New Diplomatic History Conference: Diplomacy between Crisis and Cooperation. Aarhus, Denmark, 2021.

Jakubec, Pavol. 'Together and Alone in Allied London: Czechoslovak, Norwegian and Polish Governments-in-Exile, 1940–1945'. *International History Review* 42, no 3 (2020): 465–84.

Johnson, Robbie. 'Tea Happy at Dutch Embassy'. *Hartford Times*, 20 March 1948.

Jong, Louis de. *Het Koninkrijk Der Nederlanden in de Tweede Wereldoorlog*. Vol IX:1. XII vols s-Gravenhage: Staatsuitgeverij, 1979.

Kallenberg, Lodewijk. 'Irawan Soejono (1920–1945) Zandgraf 522, Vak D: Verzetsheld van Indonesische Afkomst'. In *Nader Belichte Personen*. Leiden, The Netherlands:

Stichting tot instandhouding van de begraafplaats Groenesteeg, August 2016. Available at: www.begraafplaatsgroenesteeg.nl/N_B_personen/Irawan%20 Soejono%20-%20versie%20website.pdf (accessed 28 June 2021).

Kent, Lonore. *First Lady of the Embassy*. Washington, DC: Netherlands Embassy, 1952.

Keohane, Robert. 'International Relations Theory: Contributions of a Feminist Standpoint'. In *Gender and International Relations*, edited by Rebecca Grant and Kathleen Newland, 41-50. Milton Keynes: Open University Press, 1991.

Kersten, A E *Buitenlandse zaken in ballingschap: groei en verandering van een ministerie, 1940-1945*. Alphen aan den Rijn: Sijthoff, 1981.

Keys, Barbara. 'Henry Kissinger: The Emotional Statesman'. *Diplomatic History* 35, no 4 (2011): 587-609.

Keys, Barbara. 'The Diplomat's Two Minds: Deconstructing a Foreign Policy Myth'. *Diplomatic History* 44, no 1 (January 2020): 1-21.

Keys, Barbara and Claire Yorke. 'Personal and Political Emotions in the Mind of the Diplomat'. *Political Psychology* 40, no 6 (2019): 1235-49.

Kleffens, Eelco Nicolaas van. *The Rape of the Netherlands*. London: Hodder and Stoughton, 1940.

Kleffens, EN van. *Belevenissen I, 1894-1940*. Alphen aan de Rijn: AW Sijthoff, 1980.

Kleffens, EN van. *Belevenissen II, 1940-1958*. Alphen aan de Rijn: AW Sijthoff, 1983.

Kleffens, EN van. *Majesteit, U Kent Het Werkelijke Leven Niet : De Oorlogsdagboeken van Minister van Buitenlandse Zaken Mr. E.N. van Kleffens*. Edited by MJ Riemens. Nijmegen: Vantilt, 2019.

Kloek, Els. *Vrouw Des Huizes : Een Cultuurgeschiedenis van de Hollandse Huisvrouw*. Amsterdam: Balans, 2009.

Koprowski, Elizabeth, 'Four Steps to Becoming a Diplomat', 14 July 2016 on the Keystone Masterstudies website. Available at: www.masterstudies.com/article/ Four-Steps-to-Becoming-a-Diplomat/ (accessed 29 June 2021).

Lerner, Thomas. '"Mina chefer visste att jag var gay"'. *Dagens Nyheter*, 24 January 2006.

Lindström, Peter and Svante Norrhem. 'Diplomats and Kin Networks: Diplomatic Strategy and Gender in Sweden, 1648-1740'. In *Gender and Political Culture in Early Modern Europe, 1400-1800*, edited by James Daybell and Svante Norrhem 68-86. Abingdon and New York: Routledge, 2017.

Maar, Rimko van der and Hans Meijer. *Herman van Roijen 1905-1991: Een Diplomaat van Klasse*. Amsterdam: Boom, 2013.

Macomber, William. *The Angels' Game: A Handbook of Modern Diplomacy*. New York: Stein and Day, 1975.

'Magician Entertains Tiny Tots at Netherlands Embassy Fete'. [paper name unreadable], 26 December 1948. Clipping in MvK diary inv nr 398, 2.05.86. NL-HaNA.

Maguire, Elizabeth. 'Dutch Embassy's New Chatelaine is Charming Mme. van Kleffens'. *Washington Post*, 27 August 1947.

Maguire, Elizabeth. 'Mme. van Kleffens Assists Santa: Dutch Get Yule Treat at Embassy Party'. *Washington Post*, 25 December 1949.

Maguire, Elizabeth. 'Mme. van Kleffens Entertains for Children'. *Washington Post*, 28 December 1947.

Manne, Kate. *Down Girl: The Logic of Misogyny*. New York, NY: Oxford University Press, 2018.

Max, Arthur. 'Netherlands Gets Its First Muslim Ministers'. *Indian Express*, 21 February 2007. Available at: http://archive.indianexpress.com/news/netherlands-gets-its-first-muslim-ministers/23862/ (accessed 28 June 2021).

McCarthy, Helen. *Women of the World: The Rise of the Female Diplomat*. London: Bloomsbury, 2014.

Melchior, Marie Riegels. 'Catwalking the Nation: Challenges and Possibilities in the Case of the Danish Fashion Industry'. *Culture Unbound* 3 (2011): 55–70.

Mercer, Jonathan. 'Emotional Beliefs'. *International Organization* 64, no 1 (2010): 1–31.

Mercer, Jonathan. 'The Illusion of International Prestige'. *International Security* 41, no 4 (2017): 133–68.

Milner, Helen. 'International Theories of Cooperation Among Nations: Strengths and Weaknesses'. *World Politics* 44, no 3 (1992): 466–96.

Ministerie van Buitenlandse Zaken. *Indonesië in de Veiligheidsraad van de Verenigde Naties (Januari 1946–September 1947)*. Publicaties van Het Ministerie van Buitenlandse Zaken. Gravenhage: Staatsdrukkerij- en Uitgeverijbedrijf, 1947.

Morgenthau, Hans. *Politics Among Nations: The Struggle for Power and Peace*. New York, NY: AA Knopf, 1948.

Morrow, Elise and Mary van Rensselaer Thayer. 'We Toured the Embassy Kitchens'. *Saturday Evening Post* 1949 (29 October 1949): 32–33, 126, 128, 130.

Mösslang, Markus and Torsten Riotte, eds. *The Diplomats' World: A Cultural History of Diplomacy, 1815–1914*. New York; Oxford: Oxford University Press, 2008.

Nair, Deepak. 'Sociability in International Politics: Golf and ASEAN's Cold War Diplomacy'. *International Political Sociology*, no Generic (2019).

Nash, Philip. 'American Women at the UN: From Breakthrough to Dumping Ground?' Op eds by prominent historians. *History News Network* (blog), 19 April 2020. Available at: https://historynewsnetwork.org/article/175049 (accessed 29 June 2021).

Nash, Philip. *'Breaking Protocol: America's First Female Ambassadors, 1933–1964*. Lexington: The University Press of Kentucky, 2019.

Nauman, Sari. 'Ordens Kraft: Politiska Eder i Sverige 1520-1718'. Nordic Academic Press, 2017.

Nauman, Sari and Helle Vogt. 'The Private in the Public: Scandinavia in the Eighteenth Century'. In *Private/Public in 18th-Century Scandinavia*, edited by Sari Nauman and Helle Vogt, 1–16. London: Bloomsbury Academic, 2021.

Neumann, Iver B. *At Home with the Diplomats: Inside a European Foreign Ministry*. Ithaca: Cornell University Press, 2012.

Neumann, Iver B. "Sited Diplomacy". In *Diplomatic Cultures and International Politics: Translations, Spaces and Alternatives*, edited by Jason Dittmer and Fiona McConnell, 79–92. London: Routledge, 2015.

Neumann, Iver B. 'The Body of the Diplomat'. *European Journal of International Relations* 14, no 4 (2008): 671–95.
Neumann, Iver B. 'To Be a Diplomat'. *International Studies Perspectives* 6, no 1 (2005): 72–93.
Neumann, Iver B and Halvard Leira. *Aktiv Og Avventende. Utenrikstjenestens Liv 1905–2005*. Oslo: Pax Forlag, 2005.
Newsinger, John. 'A Forgotten War: British Intervention in Indonesia 1945-46'. *Race & Class* 30, no 4 (1989): 51–66.
Niklasson, Birgitta. 'The Gendered Networking of Diplomats'. *The Hague Journal of Diplomacy* 15, no 1–2 (2020): 13–42.
Papanek, Hanna. 'Men, Women, and Work: Reflections on the Two-Person Career'. *American Journal of Sociology* 78, no 1 (1973): 852.
Pernot, Annemie. 'Vrouwen in de Diplomatie'. In *Grenzen, Geweld En Gender. Internationale Betrekkingen Feministisch Bekeken*, edited by Joke Wiericx and Machteld de Metsenare, 111–25. Brussels: VUB-press, 2009.
Petersen, Nikolaj. 'Danish and Norwegian Alliance Policies 1948–49: A Comparative Analysis'. *Cooperation and Conflict* 14, no 3 (1979): 193–210.
Prashad, Vijay. *The Darker Nations: A People's History of the Third World*. New York: The New Press, 2007.
Satow, Ernest and Nevile Bland. *A Guide to Diplomatic Practice*. 4. London: Longman, 1957.
Scott, Joan W. 'The Evidence of Experience'. *Critical Inquiry* 17, no 4 (1991): 773–97.
Scott-Smith, Giles and Kenneth Weisbrode. 'Editorial'. *Diplomatica* 1, no 1 (2019): 1–4.
Shimazu, Naoko. 'Diplomacy as Theatre: Staging the Bandung Conference of 1955'. *Modern Asian Studies* 48, no 1 (2014): 225–52.
Shimazu, Naoko. 'Performing "Freedom": The Bandung Conference as Symbolic Postcolonial Diplomacy'. In *Diplomatic Cultures and International Politics*, edited by Jason Dittmer and Fiona McConnell, 71–88. Abingdon: Routledge, 2015.
Shimazu, Naoko. 'What is Sociability in Diplomacy?' *Diplomatica* 1, no 1 (2019): 56–72.
Sluga, Glenda and Carolyn James, eds. *Women, Diplomacy and International Politics since 1500*. Abingdon and New York: Routledge, 2016.
Sluyser, Meyer. *-, daar zaten wij: impressies over 'Londen '40–'45'*. Kosmos, 1965.
Smedley, Beryl. *Partners in Diplomacy*. Ferring: The Harley Press, 1990.
Smith, Sidonie and Julia Watson. *Reading Autobiography: A Guide for Interpreting Life Narratives*. 2nd edn Minneapolis: University of Minnesota Press, 2010.
Smyth, Denis, ed. *Part III, From 1940 through 1945. Series F, Europe*. British Documents on Foreign Affairs: Reports and Papers from the Foreign Office Confidential Print, Vol 19. Bethesda, Md.: University Publications of America, 1997.
Smyth, Denis, ed. *Part IV From 1946 through 1950, Series F, Europe 1950*. British Documents on Foreign Affairs: Reports and Papers from the Foreign Office Confidential Print, Vol 23. Bethesda, MD: University Publications of America, 2003.
Staggs, Sam. *Inventing Elsa Maxwell: How an Irrepressible Nobody Conquered High Society, Hollywood, the Press, and the World*. New York: St Martin's Press, 2013.

Stephenson, Elise. 'Domestic Challenges and International Leadership: A Case Study of Women in Australian International Affairs'. *Australian Journal of International Affairs* 73, no 3 (2019): 234–53.

Stephenson, Elise. 'The Most Successful Female Diplomats? Women with Wives'. *BroadAgenda* (blog), 10 August 2020. Available at: www.broadagenda.com.au/home/the-most-successful-female-diplomats-women-with-wives/?fbclid=IwAR34ipfaFLmFB32pIL7GOMPFRsUVlMHpIwesp4vLEmJFgZHNTconSFUbb7E. (Accessed 29 June 2021).

Thayer, Charles Wheeler. *Diplomat*. United States, 1959.

Thayer, Mary van Rensselaer. '. . . And President's Smile Flashed, The Marine Band Played, And Chandeliers Sparkled As the "Dips" Lined Up'. *Washington Post*, 3 December 1947.

Thayer, Mary van Rensselaer. 'Gifts to Green Thumbers'. *Washington Post*, 26 November 1947.

Thayer, Mary van Rensselaer. 'Tom Clarks Entertain – Hush Hush Party Honors President; Needed – A Class for Dancing Diplomats'. *Washington Post*, 12 May 1948.

'The Netherlands Ambassador's Wife Visits Patients'. *Washington Post*, October 1947.

The Vienna Convention on Diplomatic Relations (1961). Available at: https://treaties.un.org/pages/ViewDetails.aspx?src=TREATY&mtdsg_no=III-3&chapter=3&clang=_en (accessed 29 June 2021).

Tickner, J. Ann. 'Hans Morgenthau's Principles of Political Realism: A Feminist Reformulation'. In *Gender and International Relations*, edited by Rebecca Grant and Kathleen Newland, 27–40. Milton Keynes: Open University Press, 1991.

Towns, Ann. 'Gendered Appearance as Diplomatic Labor'. Paper presented to the GenDip-Diploface Workshop, 19 November 2020.

Towns, Ann E. '"Diplomacy Is a Feminine Art": Feminised Figurations of the Diplomat'. *Review of International Studies* 46, no 5 (2020): 573–93.

UN Security Council. Security Council Resolution 30 [The Indonesian Question], S/RES/30 § (1947). Available at: www.refworld.org/docid/3b00f1ae0.html (accessed 29 June 2021).

Undén, Östen and Karl Molin. *Anteckningar: 1918–1952*. Vol 24. Uppsala: Stockholm; Kungl. Samf. för utgivande av handskrifter rörande Skandinaviens historia, 2002.

United States. Congress. Senate. Committee on Agriculture and Forestry. 'Administration of Federal Food and Drugs Act: Hearings before the Committee on Agriculture and Forestry, United States Senate, Seventy-First Congress, Second Session, on Administration of Federal Food and Drugs Act. February 12 to June 30, 1930'. Washington, District of Columbia: US Govt. Print. Off, 1930.

Updike, John. 'Smoke Signals'. *The Guardian*, 10 January 2004. Available at: www.theguardian.com/books/2004/jan/10/biography.fiction (accessed 29 June 2021).

'Van Alkemadelaan 350, Ruychrocklaan 171'. In *Monumentenzorg Den Haag*, 19 December 1993. Available at: www.monumentenzorgdenhaag.nl/monumenten/van-alkemadelaan-350-ruychrocklaan-171 (accessed 29 June 2021).

Watton, Cherish. 'Women's Scrapbooks of Political and Diplomatic Activity, c.1890–1939'. MPhil dissertation in Modern British History, University of Cambridge, Faculty of History, 2018.
Weisbrode, Kenneth. 'Vangie Bruce's Diplomatic Salon. A Mid-Twentieth-Century Portrait'. In *Women, Diplomacy and International Politics since 1500*, edited by Glenda Sluga and Carolyn James, 240–53. Abingdon and New York: Routledge, 2015.
Wheeler, Nicholas J. *Trusting Enemies: Interpersonal Relationships in International Conflict*. Oxford,: Oxford University Press, 2018.
Wood, Molly M. 'A Diplomat's Wife in Mexico'. *Frontiers* 25, no 3 (2004): 104–33.
Wood, Molly M. '"Commanding Beauty" and "Gentle Charm": American Women and Gender in the Early Twentieth-Century Foreign Service'. *Diplomatic History* 31, no 3 (2007): 505–30.
Wood, Molly M. "Diplomatic Wives: The Politics of Domesticity and the "Social Game" in the U.S. Foreign Service, 1905-1941'. *Journal of Women's History* 17, no 2 (2005): 142–65.
Wood, Molly M. 'Wives, Clerks, and "Lady Diplomats": The Gendered Politics of Diplomacy and Representation in the U.S. Foreign Service, 1900–1940'. *European Journal of American Studies*, Vol 10, no 1 (2015).
Woolf, Virginia. *A Room of One's Own*. London: Penguin Books, 2004.
Young, John. *David Bruce and Diplomatic Practice: An American Ambassador in London, 1961–9*. New York: Bloomsbury Publishing Inc, 2014.
Zeeman, Bert. 'Jurist of Diplomaat? Eelco Nicolaas van Kleffens (1939–1946)'. In *De Nederlandse Ministers van Buitenlandse Zaken in de Twintigste Eeuw*, edited by Duco Hellema, Bert Zeeman and Bert van der Zwan, 139–51. Den Haag: SDU Uitgevers, 1999.

Index

Acheson, Dean 81, 106, 121, 152–53, 169
Afifi Pasha, Hafez 120
Aghnides, Hellé *see* Bonnet, Hellé, née Zervoudaki
Aghnides, Thanassis 45, 60, 85, 87, 100
Aldrich, Harriet 83
Aldrich, Winthrop 83
Ali, Asaf 137
Alphen, Elly van 71, 169 n.130
Anderson, Eugenie 18, 48
Anderson, John Pierce 17, 18
aristocracy *see under* class background
Asia-Africa conference *see* Bandung conference
Åström, Sverker 48
Attlee, Clement 93

Bandung conference *see under* Indonesia
Beale, Marie Oge (widow of Truxtun Beale) 141
Bech, Joseph 8
Beck Bosone, Reva *see* Bosone, Reva Beck
Benediktsson, Bjarni 155
Berle, Adolf 145
Bernhard of the Netherlands, Prince 62, 86, 87, 105, 148, 168–69
Bidault, Georges 166
Bland, Nevile 17, 18, 77, 85, 148
Bland, Portia 85
Bloom, Sol 106
Boetzelaer van Oosterhout, Pim van 184, 186, 188
Bogomolov, Alexander 133
Bonnet, Hellé, née Zervoudaki 46, 110, 117, 135–37, 147, 155
Bonnet, Henri 117
Bosch van Rosenthal, Johan Jeronimus Balthazar 97
Bosch van Rosenthal, Titia Margaretha 97
Bosone, Reva Beck 177
Brewster, Owen 40

Broek, Johannes van den 86
Bruce, Evangeline 107
Buma, Dé 62–63, 77–78, 81, 105–6
Buma, Han 62–63, 77
Butler, Mrs Harold (Olive?) 159
butlers 45, 67, 69, 71, 129
    see also Caponetti, Vladimiro; domestic staff; Vergeer, butler
Bylandt, Emilia Maria Nilla van, née Corradi 71
Bylandt, Willem van 34, 71

Cadogan, Alexander 41, 44, 151, 185, 191
Cadogan, Theodosia 41, 120, 151, 153, 185, 186
Caponetti, Vladimiro 66, 71, 73
Capper, Arthur 137
Cayzer, Harold Stanley 138
Chamberlain, Neville 6, 41
Charles of Belgium, Prince-Regent 152
chauffeurs *see* Mac, chauffeur; Popham, chauffeur; Redwing, James
    see also domestic staff
chefs *see* cooks
children
    care of 26, 36, 57, 77
    colonial subjects compared to 144; *see also* colonialist tropes
    female presumed interest in 160
    part of diplomatic image 79–80, 82, 85
Churchill, Clementine 1–2, 6, 79–80, 112, 126, 180
Churchill, Mary 80
Churchill, Winston 6, 81, 126
class background
    attitudes towards lower classes 69, 71, 143; *see also* domestic staff
    consciously used as diplomatic tool 133–37, 140
    intersecting with gender 38, 46, 51, 54, 143–45, 169–70, 177–79

intersecting with ethnicity 38, 142–45; *see also* racialized perceptions
intersecting with Western norms *see* cultural bias
overlap upper-class/nobility and diplomats 27–28, 51, 58, 98–99, 127, 178–79
Cold War perceptions, *see under* Soviet Union
colonialist tropes 143–44, 191–94
see also racialized perceptions
Connally, Tom 106
cooks 59–60, 62, 69–71, 73, 120–22
see also domestic staff; Ducluzeau, Henri; Maria, cook; Wiltshire, Mrs, cook; Zepeda, Rosa de
Coolidge, Harold Jefferson Jr 141, 189
Coolidge, Helen Carpenter 141
Cott, Catherine Pearl van *see* Horstmann, Catherine Pearl
Crown Princess Juliana *see* Juliana of the Netherlands
cultural bias 116, 125, 142–45, 172–73, 188–96
see also racialized perceptions

Daubanton, Mr ChJH and Mrs 141
de Gaulle *see* Gaulle, Charles de
de Geer *see* Geer, Dirk Jan de
de Zepeda *see* Zepeda, Rosa de
decolonization, *see* Bandung conference; colonialist tropes; Indonesia; Indonesian question
Delden, Didie van (Sultana Hamid II) 142–43, 145
Dendramis, Mme (wife of Vasileios Dendramis) 118, 136
Dijxhoorn, Adriaan 43
diplomats' husbands *see* male spouses of diplomats
Dirksen, Everett (misspelled Derksen by MvK) 85
dogs *see* Jansen the Poodle; Vicky the Cairn terrier
domestic staff 6, 28, 45, 57–62, 65–74
Ducluzeau, Henri 117, 121
Dutch decolonisation *see* Indonesian question

Dutch East Indies *see* Indonesia; Indonesian question
Dutch-Indonesian relations 126, 142–47, 191–94
see also under Indonesia; Indonesian question

Eden, Anthony 2, 39, 41, 89, 137–38, 161
Eden, Clarissa 89, 161
Eisenhower, Dwight D 141
Eisenhower, Mamie 141
elite culture *see* class background
Erkin, Mme (wife of Feridun Cemal Erkin) 172
Erlander, Tage 48
Esmarch, August 17
ethnicity *see* colonialist tropes; cultural bias; racialized perceptions
see also under class
Ethridge, Willie Snow 156
Eysinga, Willem van 27

Farley, Jim 156
female diplomats 3, 131, 134, 176
consequences of diplomatic couple norm for 18–26, 47–48, 139, 179
spouses of 25–26; *see also* male spouses of diplomats
see also Anderson, Eugenie; homosociality; marriage bar; Pandit, Vijaya Lakshmi
financial means *see* wealth
Folchi-Vici, Anna *see* Hägglöf, Anna
footmen *see* domestic staff; Gerard, footman; Piet, footman
Frankfurter, Felix 167
Franks, Barbara 85, 151, 157–58, 161, 164
Franks, Oliver 85, 151
Fulbright, Betty 111

Gaulle, Charles de 166
Gaulle, Élisabeth de 166–68
Gaulle, Yvonne de 166–68
Geer, Dirk Jan de 61
gender and class *see under* class background
gender and ethnicity/race *see under* racialized perceptions
Gerard, footman 71

Gerbrandy, Pieter Sjoerds 168
Gladys, maid 67
Glover, Charles Carroll Jr 141
Glover, Marion Everett Wise 141
Gonzalez, laundress 66
Gore-Booth, Patricia 1–2, 6
Gore-Booth, Paul 1–2, 6
Graeff, Andries Cornelis Dirk de 60
Gromyko, Andrei 152, 182, 186–87
Gromyko, Lydia Dmitrievna 187

Haersma de With, Hendrik Maurits van 86
Haersma de With, Sophie Louise van, née van den Broek d'Obrenan 86
Hägglöf, Anna, née Folchi-Vici, 144–45
Hägglöf, Gunnar 144
Hammarskjöld, Dag 49
Hardy, Oliver 103
Harinxma thoe Slooten, Binnie Ph 102
Harriman, Florence 155
health issues 63–64, 124–25, 149, 157–59, 161
heterosexuality *see under* female diplomats; homosexuality
Hewes, Clarence Bussey 141, 148
Hitchcock, Jessie, née Crounse 140
Hitler, Adolf 6
homosexuality 26, 48–50, 176
    heterosexuality as cornerstone of diplomatic practices 5, 15, 18–26, 168–72
homosociality 109, 137, 140, 160, 167–68
Horstmann, Aileen Emilie 'Dicky' *see* Wilson, Aileen Emilie 'Dicky', née Horstmann
Horstmann, August Carl Herbert 28–29, 70
Horstmann, Catherine Pearl, née van Cott 28, 70
household staff *see* domestic staff
husbands of diplomats *see* male spouses of diplomats

Ibarra García, Oscar 147
Indonesia
    Bandung conference (1955) 116, 194–95
    decolonisation of *see* Indonesian question

Dutch attitudes towards Indonesians 142–48, 191–94
Dutch military intervention in 64–65, 113, 180, 184; *see also* Indonesian question
non-Republic states of 112–13, 146, 187–88, 191
Indonesian question 8, 93–94
    and American treatment of Dutch 107, 171, 188
    and Dutch diplomatic strategies 105, 112–14, 126, 171, 180–88, 191–92
    and media 74, 114
    in the United Nations Security Council 113, 180–88

Jackson, Justice Robert H 155
Jansen the Poodle 9, 65–66, 82, 161, 180
Johnson, Herschel V 185, 187, 191
Johnson, Robbie 109–10, 136
journalists *see* Johnson, Robbie; Luce, Henry; McCormick, Anne; Morrow, Elise; Reid, Helen Rogers; Thayer, Mary Van Rensselaer 'Molly'
Juliana of the Netherlands, Crown Princess (Queen 1948–1980) 43, 62, 86

Kaeckenbeeck, Georges 100, 151
Kaeckenbeeck, Josephine 100, 151
Kauffman, Charlotte 141
Kauffmann, Henrik 137–38, 141, 169
Kindler, Hans 146
Kleffens, Adrianus van 27
Knatchbull-Hugessen, Elisabeth 41
Knatchbull-Hugessen, Hughe Montgomery 102
Kolff, Cornelis 141
Koo, Wellington 146–47
Koo, Hui-Lan *see* Oei Hui-Lan
Krock, Arthur 171

Lagerberg, Joen 183
Lawford, Nicholas (aka Valentine) 185
Leão Veloso, Pedro 152, 186
Leão Veloso, Virgínia de Castro 152
Lee, Elinor 159
Limburg Stirum, Catharina Maria van 33
Lippman, Helen 189
Lippman, Walter 189

Lostar, Basri 102
Loudon, Alexander 61
Loudon, Betty 61
Lovett, Adele 123, 188–89
Lovett, Robert 123, 188–89
Luce, Henry 114
Luther, Mrs 159

Mabel, house-parlourmaid 69
Mac, chauffeur 66, 73
McCormick, Anne O'Hare 155
McCormick, Francis J 156
Macmillan, Dorothy 89
Macmillan, Harold 89
Macomber, William 23–24
maids *see* domestic staff; Gladys, maid; Mabel, house-parlourmaid; Nelly, maid
male spouses of diplomats 22–26, 47–48
  see also Anderson, John Pierce
Malone, George 171
Margriet of the Netherlands, Princess 119
Maria, cook 67
marriage bar 18, 21, 24–26, 36, 47
Massigli, Odette Isabelle, née Boissier 135
Maxwell, Elsa 135, 163, 176
Michiels van Verduynen, Edgar 43, 119, 166
Michiels van Verduynen, Henriëtte 53, 119
Miller, Adolph 167
Milliken, Eugene 85
Molotov, Polina 1, 6, 180
Molotov, Vyacheslav 1–2
money *see* wealth
Mook, Hubertus van 152, 192
Morrow, Elise 117, 120–21

Nadjamoeddin Daeng Malewa 145–46
nationality and marriage 38–39, 46–47
Nehru, Jawaharlal 50
Neighbors Club 111
Nelly, maid 66
Netherlands East Indies *see* Indonesia; Indonesian question
Nisot, Joseph 186, 191
Nixon, Miss 97
nobility *see* class background

Oei Hui-Lan 146–47
overlap nobility–diplomats *see under* class background

Pallandt, Floris van 115
Palme, Olof 48
Pandit, Vijaya Lakshmi 50–51, 110, 139, 177
Parodi, Alexandre 1–2, 6, 170, 180–82, 185, 187, 191
Pepper, Claude 171
Pereira, Pedro Theotonio 141
Philips, Frits 146, 156
Piet, footman 73
Popham, chauffeur 69
President of East Indonesia (1946–1950) *see* Soekawati, Tjokorda Gde Raka
President of West Kalimantan (1946–1950) *see* Syarif Hamid II, Sultan
Prince Bernhard *see* Bernhard of the Netherlands, Prince
Prince-Regent Charles *see* Charles of Belgium, Prince-Regent
Princess Margriet *see* Margriet of the Netherlands, Princess

Queen Juliana *see* Juliana of the Netherlands, Crown Princess (Queen 1948–1980)
Queen Wilhelmina *see* Wilhelmina of the Netherlands (Queen 1890–1948)

racialized perceptions 38, 72, 142–49, 190–94
  intersecting with gender 38, 142–45, 193
  see also cultural bias
Raeder, Cecilie 98
Raeder, Jack 98
Rape of the Netherlands, see The Rape of the Netherlands
Red Cross 52, 53, 101–2, 169
Redwing, James 72
Regis de Oliveira, Sylvia 163
Reid, Helen Rogers 110, 156, 177
Reid, Ogden 110, 156
Reston, James B 141
Reston, Sally 141
Reuchlin, Aimée 40, 47, 104

Reuchlin, Otto 40
Ries, Leopold Abraham 50
Robert, cleaner 147
Roijen, Herman van 34–35, 42, 71–72, 82, 122, 129, 184
Roijen-Snouck Hurgronje, Anne van 29, 34–35, 42, 71, 82, 111, 122, 129, 158
Roosevelt, Eleanor 50–51, 110, 177
Roosevelt, Franklin Delano 6, 38, 133
Russell, Lady 52

Salisbury, Elizabeth 89
Salisbury, Robert 89
Satow, Ernest 17, 18, 77
Scheltus, GA 97
Schermerhorn, Wim 93
Schimmelpenninck, Pauline 169 n.130
Schoenfeld, Rudolf 166
secretaries 29, 42, 71, 98 n.15, 102, 107, 129, 169
Servatius, BWN 21–22
Sforza, Carlo 163–64
Silvercruys, Robert 49, 152–53, 189
Simopoulos, Mme (wife of Charalambos Simopoulos) 45
Sjöborg, Erik 86, 119
Smedley, Beryl 75, 134, 136
Snouck Hurgronje, Aarnout Marinus 29, 60
Snouck Hurgronje, Anne *see* Roijen-Snouck Hurgronje, Anne van
Soejono, Irawan 193
Soejono, Loes Soepianti 193, 195
Soejono, Pangeran Adipati 191–93
Soejono, Raden Ajoe 193
Soekawati, Tjokorda Gde Raka 112–13, 145–46
Soenario Wiranata Kusuma, Maria 47
Soviet Union
    attitudes towards 80, 116, 132–33, 183, 187
    depictions of 73, 79, 118–19, 152, 186–87
    political relations with 1–2, 80, 182–83
Spaak, Paul-Henri 8, 152–53, 155
Spaatz, General Carl 155
Stalin, Joseph 6
Steel, Catherine 98
Steel, Christopher 98
Stirling, Alfred 141

Stirling, Dorothy 141
Stoutz, Maxime de 102
Strauss, Lewis 89
Sultana Maharatu Mas Makhota *see* Delden, Didie van
Sultan Syarif Hamid II *see* Syarif Hamid II, Sultan
Sunario Wiranata Kusuma, Raden Ajoe Malia *see* Soenario Wiranata Kusuma, Maria
Syarif Hamid II, Sultan 112–13, 142, 145–46

Taft, Robert 85
Tarchiani, Teresa 118
Teixeira de Mattos, Betty 77–78, 87 n.85, 138
Thayer, Mary Van Rensselaer 'Molly' 114, 117, 120–21, 136–37, 160, 177
The Rape of the Netherlands 42, 68
Thomen, Luis Francisco 113, 124, 149
Tjarda van Starkenborgh Stachouwer, Alidius 43
Truman, Bess 155, 162
Truman, Harry S 6, 155

Undén, Östen 48, 139

Valkova, Mme (wife of Vasily Valkov) 79
van Alphen *see* Alphen, Elly van
van Boetzelaer van Oosterhout *see* Boetzelaer van Oosterhout, Pim van
van Bylandt *see* Bylandt, Willem van
van Cott *see* Horstmann, Catherine Pearl, née van Cott
van Delden *see* Delden, Didie van (Sultana Hamid II)
van den Broek *see* Broek, Johannes van den
van Eysinga *see* Eysinga, Willem van
van Haersma de With *see* Haersma de With, Hendrik Maurits van
van Kleffens *see* Kleffens, Adrianus van
Van Langenhoeve, Fernand 181, 185, 191
Van Langenhove, Nancy 185
van Limburg Stirum *see* Limburg Stirum, Catharina Maria van
van Mook *see* Mook, Hubertus van

van Pallandt *see* Pallandt, Floris van
Van Rensselaer Thayer *see* Thayer, Mary Van Rensselaer 'Molly'
van Weede *see* Weede, Marc van; Weede, Miesje van, née van Lynden van Sandenburg
Vandenberg, Arthur 83–85
Vandenberg, Gladys Rose 141, 152–53
Vandenberg, Hazel 83–84
Vandenberg, Hoyt 141
Vanlangenhove *see* Van Langenhoeve, Fernand; Van Langenhoeve, Nancy
Vergeer, butler 71
Vicky the Cairn terrier 69, 84
voluntary work 22, 52–53, 101

wealth, diplomatic need of 27–28, 34, 60, 127, 136, 190,
 see also class background
Weede, Marc van 166
Weede, Miesje van, née van Lynden van Sandenburg 166
Wellington Koo, Mme *see* Oei Hui-Lan
Welter, Charles 61
Whitney, Cornelius Vanderbilt 156
Widdemer, Margaret 156
Wilhelmina of the Netherlands (Queen 1890–1948) 81, 104, 123, 135, 146
Willy, maid 66
Wilson, Aileen Emilie 'Dicky', née Horstmann 28, 47, 62, 67, 82, 87–88, 98–99, 140, 168–69
Wilson, Clive 83
Wilson, Edith 141
Wilson, Raymond 62, 67
Wiltshire, Mr, fire fighter/gardener 69, 70
Wiltshire, Mrs, cook 69, 70, 122
Windsor, Duke and Duchess of 83

Young, George Peregrine 41

Zepeda, Rosa de 65–66, 73, 117, 121–23
Zervoudaki, Hellé *see* Bonnet, Hellé, née Zervoudaki
Zorab, Helen 53

www.ingramcontent.com/pod-product-compliance
Lightning Source LLC
Chambersburg PA
CBHW052108300426
44116CB00010B/1582